The PLEASURE WAS MINE

70 Years in Education

The PLEASURE WAS MINE

70 Years in Education

Finis E. Engleman

The Interstate
Printers & Publishers, Inc.
Danville, Illinois

Library of Congress
catalog card number: 71-143328

THE PLEASURE WAS MINE. Copyright © 1971 by The Interstate Printers & Publishers, Inc. All rights reserved. Printed in the United States of America.

To

R. L. E.

FOREWORD

Few Americans who travel can resist the temptation to purchase souvenirs that will remind them of the memorable events and places they have been, and offer indisputable evidence that they have been there. A life-long friend of mine has the walls of his living room covered with pictures he has collected, each one from a different country. Their artistic merit may be debatable but the conversational advantages they offer make all his efforts worthwhile. The trouble, however, with most of the items people accumulate is that they continue to consume space long after one's enthusiasm dampens.

A more lasting satisfaction can come from collecting intangible keepsakes—mental pictures that occupy no space—recollections of interesting people, places, and events that can be conjured up at will for our pleasure and enjoyment. Keepsakes of this kind enable us to save something besides money for our old age, something which, at that late date, money cannot provide.

Finis E. Engleman has completed his intangible collection. *The Pleasure Was Mine* is a highly perceptive and personal account of 70 years of education—often hilarious, always insightful, frequently prophetic. Many of the horizons he envisions are yet untouched frontiers of educational practice. The author is mindful that while he is a descendant of the past, he is a parent of the future and, as Herbert Spencer wrote, "his thoughts are as children born to him, which he may not carelessly let die."

Edward Caird—one of Scotland's wisest philosophers—once said, "Everyone carries with him a certain moral atmosphere which to a great extent determines the relations into which he comes with his fellow men. Thus, men are continually shedding off, as it were, some part of their personality in the society around them." I have been the grateful beneficiary of Dr. Engleman's shedding process.

To Finis E. Engleman I owe a considerable debt. For many years I was the recipient of the gentle, sensitive Engleman-type friendship and leadership. He guided me through three years as an officer of the American Association of School Administrators when he served as its executive secretary and in 1961 he undertook the not inconsiderable task of preparing me to serve as president of the organization. He taught me most of what I know about being an executive secretary—but not all that he knew.

Since the days when Finis taught a small rural school in Missouri, American life has quickened and changed. A new urgency dominates the educational scene in America. But the basic human values, the love and regard for our fellows, for human dignity, and the compassion that Finis taught through example, wit, and challenge have not changed. Their threads are woven throughout this book.

The Pleasure Was Mine provides an unexcelled opportunity for the reader to relive some of the author's most cherished moments, the hours of loneliness that only school administrators know, the pain of a switching by the schoolmaster, and the joys of teaching and learning. The story concludes with a penetrating analysis of some of the issues, problems, and opportunities confronting the school administrator in the 70's. This is in keeping with his philosophy of life, a philosophy he expressed eloquently when in 1967 he wrote: "It is to the future that I would turn your attention. The past, at best, gives only temporary footing. Only as we stretch our reach for tomorrow will we express the faith our obligations and responsibilities as administrators demand."

I urge you to reserve an evening or two for *The Pleasure Was Mine* and prepare to relive your memories.

        Forrest E. Conner

        Executive Secretary
        American Association of School Administrators

TABLE OF CONTENTS

Part One

Chapter I 3

Chapter II 23

Chapter III 45

Chapter IV 53

Chapter V 67

Part Two

Chapter VI 77

Chapter VII 85

Chapter VIII 93

Part Three

Chapter IX 107

Chapter X 139

Chapter XI 165

Part Four

Chapter XII 185

Chapter XIII 197

Chapter XIV 207

Part One

CHAPTER I

My introduction to public education occurred in the year 1901. The place was Red Hill School—a one-room school in Cedar County, Missouri. The teacher was a stern but kindly man named Horace Middlebrook. I remember that first day. It was warm; the door was wide open and so were the windows. House flies buzzed about sometimes and lit on worried, sweaty brows. I had accompanied my two older brothers, the elder carrying the dinner bucket stuffed with baked sweet potatoes, cold biscuits, smoked "side meat" rashers, and a jar of molasses mixed with butter.

The double seats were in rows tightly screwed to the battered floor. There were four rows. On the far side were the largest, in the middle were two rows for the nine- to twelve-year-olds, and on the side next to the stove and door were the smallest. A "recitation" bench which would seat ten or a dozen pupils graced the front facing the teacher's desk and the blackboard which stretched the width of the front wall.

Guarded by the teacher's desk was the built-in bookcase holding as many as twenty books, mostly for the older pupils. Stretched across the top of the blackboard stood in bold relief the letters of the alphabet. The top line was in block letters; the bottom line in Spencerian script.

The two dozen pupils were classified in four groups: the A class, the B class, the C class, and the primary. My oldest brother took a desk at the rear of the A class, my next older brother was in the middle—in the C class row—and I found a seat in the primary group.

Up until the morning recess the teacher occupied himself with the older children. I sat and made marks on my slate. So did a long-haired lad somewhat older than I who sat directly in front of me. His restlessness and foot shuffling finally irritated Mr. Middlebrook, so as a form of embarrassment and punishment he was ordered to stand beside his desk. I had his full height to observe. His long uncombed hair finally got the better of me and I reached up and gave it a pull. As if pierced by a poisoned arrow, he let out a whoop and turned on me. The teacher quickly recognized my guilt and ordered me to stand too. I was petrified and seized the desk and refused to budge, though the teacher tugged halfheartedly at my arm. Then he leaned down and said, "You stay in at noon."

Finally the lunch hour came, and as my brothers and lunch bucket went out the door, so did my security. I headed out after them. The teacher didn't seem to observe my action. Once outside all the pupils gathered around to warn me of the dire consequences of my disobedience. As the hour wore on my apprehension rose. My brothers gave me no solace.

When we were seated for the afternoon the teacher solemnly marched down the aisle with a hickory branch in his right hand. He told me to come to the front of the room with him for a switching. Again I seized the desk and started to cry. Again he was unable to budge me. So he started striking me across the shoulders. I glanced toward the door. It was open.

Quick as a flash I slid across the double seat and dashed for the door. On I went to the road, and over Red Hill I dashed for home and security. I didn't look back. Half way home I began to slow my crying and my brain began to contemplate. What would happen when I got home? Would my father thrash me and send me back? He was a kind but stern man. My fears of my father grew stronger than my dread of the teacher. But I just didn't have the courage to go back. So I crawled under the barbed wire fence into a newly plowed wheat field and played in the shade of a huge walnut tree waiting for my brothers to pass by and spread the dire news at home.

Shortly after 4:00 P.M.—dismissal time—I saw coming over the hill, not my brothers, but the schoolmaster. I hid behind the tree and watched him hurriedly pass, obviously headed for my home. Now, thought I, I will really get punished when my father joins forces with Mr. Middlebrook. When I finally got home the teacher was gone. My father never mentioned my behavior. Neither did the teacher.

Strangely, I quickly learned to love the teacher. Strangely, too, I mastered the complex skill of reading. No competence has ever brought so many hours of pleasure.

I loved going to this one-room school with its barren walls and rugged furniture and muddy playing field. In the early years I learned much by listening to the older children "recite" and by watching them cipher at the blackboard. We eagerly looked forward to the coming of Friday afternoon. Then, two teams were organized, using the youngest to the eldest. We alternated between ciphering and spelling. I was never a very good speller, but by the time I was eleven or twelve I became very fast and accurate in mathematical calculations. I also learned that if I was finally pitted against one more rapid in addition, subtraction, multiplication, and division, and I had a choice, I would take division of decimals, which often tripped an opponent.

My favorite subject was history. The American history books were exciting to me, even though filled with dates, battles, and names. There were a few books on our European cultural background. It was there that I learned a bit of Greece, Rome, and Western Europe. Such names as Socrates, Alexander the Great, Cleopatra, Hannibal, Julius Caesar, and Henry the VIII became part of my vocabulary. I learned of Runnymede, the Crusades, and Martin Luther. Of all the books available my favorite was *Fifty Famous Stories Retold*.

With the help of the textbook readers, I sensed the beauty of poetry and good prose. In those days the children's readers were largely made up of literary gems from the English language, together with many stories emphasizing sound puritan morals. Since declamation was highly respected, the textbook readers that included oratorical specimens, such as Address to the Slaves, Mark Anthony's Funeral Address, Webster's Bunker Hill Monument oration, and the Gettysburg Address were read and reread and memorized.

Good use of such materials was made when the school had "Entertainments"—usually in celebration of Thanksgiving, Christmas, Washington's Birthday, and school closing. Simple dramatic skits, too, were part of the ritual, and many a modest, frightened pupil stammered his lines or forgot them. Of course, the parent visitors liked what their children did. Naming the bones of the body and reciting the states and capitals also demonstrated to parents that the teaching was thorough and the learning of high quality. The test of a good rural school was skill in oral reading, handwriting, and arithmetic. Much importance was placed on grammar, punctuation, and spelling. He who could make a blackboard diagram of a long complex sentence was considered to be a top-notch scholar.

The progress of pupils in the rural one-room schools of that day was almost entirely on an individual basis. In fact the nongraded school was a common pattern. Children in mathematics, for instance, seldom were kept at the same pace, nor was the same degree of competency or scholarship sought. The interested and able children only raced against themselves. Too, the structure of the operation and program encouraged much independence of work. The better students took great pride in being able to do complex percentage operations and to solve problems in square and cube root and compound interest. But the crowning achievement was to be told by the teacher to attack the one hundred "demon" problems at the back of the advanced arithmetic text. Of course, the lack of supervision led to some bad habits, such as pecking with pencil or chalk while adding.

During the eight years I attended the rural school there were only three schools that ran for so long as six months. The others closed after five. The school year was short because the tax funds were meager and the farm work seasons were long. Plowing for oats began when the frost was only partly out of the ground, and preparing the soil for corn planting began in early March. September was busy with wheat sowing and corn cutting. The corn husking went well into the cold weather. Children, particularly those over ten, were needed for the many tasks of farming.

During the school year my responsibilities at home brought insights into living and gave me stature. No greater pride did I have than when my mother commended me for my help by saying, "You are a little man."

During my last year at the one-room school the teacher encouraged me to have a try at algebra and rhetoric. He also permitted me to "hear" the primary class read and recite. Possibly he had heard of the Lancastrian method. At any rate, I became a "teacher's aide" before leaving the elementary school.

The playground was a three-acre field. On one side was the rough outline of a baseball field with healthy sized flint rocks for bases. There we played "town" ball and three-cornered catch. On the other side was the field where we played "old sow." Andy over, back man, dare base, and fox and geese were popular also.

Discipline was not rigid, as I recall, but the whole community respected the teacher and followed his directions. When there was infraction of the rules, switchings resulted for serious cases; standing in the corner, sitting on the recitation bench under the direct eye of the teacher, and staying in during recess were the punishments for lesser offenses.

Since all rural schools were under the general supervision of the county superintendent of schools, he alone could examine pupils who sought an elementary school diploma. When I was fourteen I decided to try the county examinations since I wanted to attend high school. With the teacher's approval two of us rode horseback six miles to an examination center. How proud my parents and I were when the notice of my satisfactory marks arrived, together with a signed diploma.

Since much of my early education was enhanced by home and farm, possibly a few words about my family and home relationships are in order.

My parents were hard working, proud, and respected. The 265-acre farm was too large for my father and four sons to cultivate and manage. Forty acres were leased to a farmer who owned limited acres.

The family was almost a self-contained and self-sustained unit. Corn and wheat provided the meal and flour for bread. Livestock, chickens, vegetables, berries, and fruit were all raised on the farm. Fish from the river that ran through the farm and squirrel, rabbit, and quail offered a change of diet. Of course, milk, butter, and eggs were in good supply. I must say, however, that my mother sometimes gave meager servings of eggs and butter when she needed cash; their sale would provide for staples such as sugar, salt, pepper, and coffee, as well as for yarn, calico, overalls, shoes, kerosene, and the like. Tea was unknown to us except for the spring tonic—a tea made from dried sassafras roots, but a coffee-pot simmered on the back of the stove at almost all hours.

Since a general purpose farm requires a vast complex of activities, each member of the family had regular and special work responsibilities. Water had to be carried from the spring or tugged from a 100-foot well, wood had to be chopped, kerosene lamps and lanterns cleaned and filled, ashes carried out, floors swept, and all livestock and poultry fed and their living quarters cleaned. The cows had to be milked and the milk strained and placed in the springhouses. Always it fell to me to milk the cows, but I was careful to see that the calves got their share.

All these and more were the late afternoon and early morning chores. The *hard* work, except during the months when school was in session, took place between 7 A.M. and 6 P.M. This was the time for plowing, harrowing, planting, hoeing, thinning, cultivating, and harvesting.

As I think of my early childhood, I remember the satisfaction I had in being part of a working team. Knowing that my efforts, my work, my assumption of responsibilities helped sustain the family gave me personal stature. Surely any growing child is deprived if he doesn't have a chance to share in the family responsibilities. Yet parents today find it difficult to share these responsibilities with their children.

Of course, not all my tasks were enjoyable. Thinning, hoeing, and cutting corn, pulling cockleburs where the copperhead snakes made their home, and shocking bearded wheat I found distasteful, particularly when the heat was stifling and the chigger bugs abundant.

All the Englemans read in the evenings. Our lamps burned long after the lights were out in neighboring farm houses.

Two of my friends, living about two miles away in opposite directions, also liked to read, so we exchanged our very meager reading material. The Horatio Algier books were available, as were paperback series of such titles as *Young Wild West, Pluck and Luck,* and *The Liberty Boys of '76.* I managed to find funds for a subscription to the *Youth's Companion,* a monthly publication. It could be used for barter to get other materials.

Taking grain to the grist mill, selling produce, and shopping were done Saturday afternoon at the tiny village four miles away. All the family made the trip except me. I preferred to hunt in the woods and fields or to fish in the streams. From age eight to fourteen, my constant companion was a mongrel dog named Fred. I believed him to have superior intelligence and a truly humanitarian spirit. He could dive after stones in the creek, he could climb ladders into the haymow, he could find rabbits where other dogs would overlook them. What a friend and constant companion he proved to be! Either of us would have given up his life for the other.

My life has been joyful because I learned the significance of being physically tired and then the joy of rest. The kindness of solitude likewise was recognized early.

Recently I discovered Lewis Wilde's little verse, *To Be*. Because it echoes so much of my experience, my feelings, my philosophy, I quote it here:

>Today must die,
>>Because it was begun that it might end.
>
>There could be no togetherness,
>>If we were never alone.
>
>It would mean nothing to laugh,
>>If there were never any tears.
>
>We could not rest,
>>If we were never tired.
>
>There is no end,
>>Without a beginning.
>
>A smile could not brighten a face,
>>That never knew a frown.
>
>To be sad,
>>Is to have the ability to enjoy happiness.

On the farm a schedule of work to be finished at a given time seemed imperative. If I were plowing a field, for example, I would note a weed, a stump, or a stone and establish the estimated time to reach it. There seemed to be a personal satisfaction in accomplishing a set goal in a given time span.

Often in later years, as my family traveled across the eastern United States by automobile, I irritated my wife by checking the road map, estimating the time it would take to reach specific towns along the way, and then driving like mad to reach each point on time. I had a compulsion to keep these senseless schedules, and conflict arose when my wife insisted on seeing some monument or stopping to linger in an antique shop. Even on vacation, I seem to demand a time schedule and a set of accomplishments for each hour or each day. My retirement years have changed this obsession only a little.

The nearest high school was about ten miles away—in Humansville—a long 2 1/2-hour drive or ride over muddy, rocky roads. I could not commute that long distance, so I roomed and boarded with a widowed aunt.

While at high school I learned a new game called basketball. There was no gymnasium, but an outside court was laid out and backboards and hoops affixed. On this court I learned the skill that later won me a place on the college varsity.

During my freshman year I took five "solid" subjects—English, ancient history, Latin, physical geography, and algebra. No modern languages were offered. I did not distinguish myself in any area that I recall but I learned to study methodically. Two weeks before the term ended my father permitted me to stop and return to the farm, where I was badly needed. Fortunately, the high school authorities understood my problem and recorded my grades as complete.

The curriculum pattern of the high school was rigidly academic. No art, music, homemaking, industrial arts, commercial, or vocational subjects were available. Science was limited to physical geography and physics. Even though most students had been admitted because of superior records in elementary school, the dropout rate was excessive.

The teachers, though subject matter oriented, seemed to show interest in the students. Little or no attention was given to the social needs of pupils nor to their special academic or musical or dramatic interests. There were no extracurricular activities except basketball and track for both boys and girls. Even so, I saw no evidence of student militancy. Because of competing high schools twenty miles away the spirit ran high, and those who made the teams stood out as heroes. The competitive games were played on Saturday afternoons. To go to and from schools in one day was quite an ordeal for surreys or carriages rented from the local livery barns. The journey began in the early morning and ended well after dark in the evening. These long trips were usually made with the boys and girls in separate vehicles, but sometimes there were switchings which permitted a girl to ride beside her boyfriend.

When the spring plowing was finished, I decided to go with my brother to the county seat for a try at the teachers' examinations. The local school board had offered me the teaching position if I could secure a county teacher's examination certificate. So we packed the wagon with grain and hay for the mules, together with quilts and food enough for three days for the two of us. We also included the wagon bows and canvas cover. These afforded us protection from the elements as we slept cozily inside the wagon at night, at the camp spot near where the examinations were given. No lodging or board bills were incurred, thanks to our frugal arrangements.

The examinations were extensive, but they covered the areas I would teach—mathematics, spelling, physiology, geography, history, grammar—as well as diacritical marking, schedule making for a one-room school, and principles of school discipline. Three days were consumed in taking all the examinations required for the third class certificate. My brother, more scholastically advanced, took the examinations for the second class certificate, which included additional academic subjects such as algebra, Latin, and science.

In due time my marks on the examinations arrived and I was certified as an elementary school teacher—and with only one year of high school! But I accepted the board's invitation to teach the local school and could hardly wait for September to arrive to begin my first full-time employment, at $35 per month, for six months. I might proudly interject here that the board was sufficiently pleased at the end of the six months that they added a seventh. Thus history was made, since Red Hill had never before afforded a term of seven months.

My first worry as I prepared for the opening day of school was how to schedule classes for all groups and all subjects. My brother, a teacher with two years' experience, came to the rescue and showed me how to plot the day into fifteen and twenty minute periods, allotting time somewhat as follows:

>   9:00- 9:10—Opening Exercises
>   9:10- 9:25—Class A History
>   9:25- 9:40—Class B Spelling
>   9:40- 9:50—Class C Arithmetic
>   9:50-10:15—Primary Reading
>   10:15-10:30—Class A Arithmetic
>   10:30-10:45—Recess
>   10:45-11:00—Class B Arithmetic
>   11:00-11:15—Class C Arithmetic
>   11:15-11:30—Primary Numbers
>   11:30-11:45—Class A Geography
>   11:45-12:00—Writing—all groups
>   12:00- 1:00—Lunch Hour

The afternoon followed the same time allotment scheme, so that each child in his group got the teacher's attention every day in each subject. Before the year was finished, I hit upon a plan of having some subjects on alternate days, thus leaving more time for study and recitation periods. Furthermore, I grouped children with a wider age differential and staggered the years allotted for advanced subjects.

Unlike many schools of that period our opening exercises were not of a devotional character. Possibly I was too much of a dissenter; possibly I was too modest to admit publicly that there was a God. Furthermore, the community, though Christian in character, had never demanded prayer or Bible reading. My opening exercises usually consisted of reading from a book. I owned a few books from which I read a few pages to begin the day. My *Youth's Companion* was a regular standby.

Though it was difficult for me to "carry a tune," I did sing with the pupils. My music education had consisted of taking music lessons on the family parlor organ. To achieve this, at the age of twelve I rode horseback four miles to get to the teacher. My education in music was further enriched by going to "singings." Traveling singing masters usually appeared annually and provided classes in singing. The lessons were for adults at night and were usually held in the country church, which sometimes contained an organ; the school house also was used. The songs were mostly religious hymns, sung in parts. In fact, commendable harmony and good tone effects were achieved. There was a tuition charge of $1 for the ten lessons. The singing teacher often was boarded free. At the close of the short term a singing recital served as a cultural and social event for the whole community. Such was the organized adult education program of the community. The county farm agent had not as yet penetrated Cedar County, Missouri.

I played with the children at noon and during recess and, in fact, was very much one of them.

I created quite an interest in the community by laying out a basketball court in one corner of the school yard. The older boys and I cut strong oak poles from the woods nearby owned by my father. We nailed backboards of regulation size to them and at the proper height attached the unnetted metal hoops for baskets. It was with pride that I had ridden to town and given the dimensions and specifications for the basket hoops to the blacksmith.

Getting and paying for a ball was a problem, but not insurmountable. A Saturday night pie supper at the school was announced for the purpose of getting the ball that would initiate competitive athletics in the local school. Such affairs were popular. The women brought pies with names concealed on the bottom of the pan or pie plate. They were sold at auction and immediately eaten by the man who purchased and the woman who baked his pie. Bidding sometimes was vigorous, especially when a young man had "inside dope" that his best girlfriend had baked the pie being sold at a given time. Of course, other bidders, noting the young man's interest, would try to outbid him. All this added to the cash receipts.

Next came the task of coaching the teams. It was difficult in the small school of twenty-eight children to find enough big ones as players. However, other schools had heard of our new venture and had started teams too. In due time the rural schools of the area had challenged each other and interschool competition was in full flower.

Another problem was uniforms. The boys could play in shirts and overalls, but the girls must have better protection. So the mothers gathered together in a sewing bee to produce middy blouses and baggy black cotton or sateen bloomers for the girls. The parents and young ones made up the cheering sections as they patiently stood on the sidelines. Naturally some elders in the neighborhood raised eyebrows when they heard that girls were cavorting in public wearing bloomers.

Basketball competition led to rivalry in other fields, and with my school and my brothers leading the new excitement, contests were arranged in declamation, debating, ciphering, spelling, voice, and writing.

As I think of my first efforts at teaching I know they were poor indeed. All I had had in the way of preparation was the chance to watch my own teachers perform. But the educational program was simple and the opportunities for personal initiative and self-education great. The young ones were neglected most and I wonder how they ever learned to read. The method was to first learn the names of the letters of the alphabet, then the sounds of letters and combinations of vowels and consonants. But somehow the printed pages were mastered—at least the bright ones, strongly motivated by parents, did so.

But the science of pedagogy was emerging. American leaders were translating the writings of Herbart, Rousseau, and Pestalozzi. The great voices of John Dewey and Meriam were heard across the land. Books on teaching and learning were distributed at county institutes, and state teachers associations were formed to promote better teaching and discover new materials of instruction. Reading circles conducted by the county superintendent emerged. The new high school teacher education curriculum that appeared gave modern professional techniques of teaching. Even the psychology of learning and new information on child development were transmitted to high school students who planned to teach in the rural schools. I bought my first book, *Teaching the Common Branches*, and read it carefully.

All the pupils were from farms and all were poor. Money was scarce even though some farms were as large as the family could possibly manage. Even though poverty was almost universal, people were proud and did not feel deprived. During my attendance at Red Hill School and during my teaching experience there, never did I ever hear of a theft.

Not once did the county superintendent appear to guide and advise me. Luckily, I had no school board member who appeared to give directions as was the case in nearby schools. So my first year's teaching went unsupervised.

It seems appropriate that I pause to summarize some of the special qualities and characteristics of this period in history as I noted them. Although the first decade of the twentieth century was the period when the flying machine and the automobile turned the tide of history and new sources of energy—gasoline and electricity—hurried the industrial and technological revolution, public education moved slowly. The one-room school still played a major role. Hard surfaced roads hardly existed, and most people lived on farms. Even in the cities schools often were not consolidated, and the public high school was highly selective where available at all. Its curriculum was generally classical and designed only as a preparation for college. The large centers sometimes included manual training in the curriculum, but these offerings were not considered respectable by the academic world. However, the Kalamazoo Decision, declaring it to be legal to use public taxation for the education of secondary school pupils, was being accepted. The public high school now stood as a threat to the private academy, and the magnificent dream of those who believed universal education should extend through grade twelve was in reach.

For the rural areas, however, mud roads and poor transportation seemed to doom the growth of the public high school. But the educational expectations of more and more people were growing. Normal Schools were growing in number and providing low tuition secondary education and two years of college to young people in many regions. America was still a farming nation, but thanks to the land grant colleges and the system of adult education provided by the county farm agent, animal husbandry and grain production methods began to release manpower from the farm and into the industrial centers now emerging. For the first time in America's history enough food, shelter and clothing could be produced by a declining population of farm laborers. This was the first step toward an industrial society. But the more complex society required a more diversified type of education, as the next several decades proved. There were occasional voices raised to question the limited opportunities for education and the restrictive academic character of the high school curriculum, but secondary education for all was only a dream for most of the rural areas prior to the First World War. Resistance to taxation for any purpose, particularly for educating some other person's child, was a strong deterrent to the spread of public education.

With the support of state teachers associations, the state departments of education, and the county superintendents, legislatures in most states began to set certification standards for teachers. They were low but, nonetheless, a beginning. In many of the states the most common teaching certificate was issued by the county superintendent who gave the examinations. Often no scholastic credentials, not even high school graduation, were demanded. The lowest certificate was granted on passing of county examinations on the "common branches." There was another certificate granted on demonstrated proficiency in such subjects as algebra and ancient history. As I have mentioned, near the end of this decade state superintendents issued certificates to those completing a planned teacher education program in the approved high schools. This program was taken in the junior and senior year and included rigid reviews and the proving of one's competence in arithmetic, American history, geography, grammar, writing, and spelling. Elementary school methods, school management, and discipline, as well as the findings of psychologists who were beginning to learn about teaching and learning, were also part of the teacher education program.

In addition, the Normal Schools strengthened their programs, and standard college grade offerings for two years or more appeared. Of course, a one-year program beyond high school still qualified one for a certification to teach, which was issued by the Normal School. This highly prized credential was called the Regents Certificate in some states.

This decade and the next saw the beginnings of inservice education for teachers. Reading circles sponsored by the state and county superintendents together with the cooperation of state teachers associations proved to be popular and effective in acquainting teachers with the literature on new methods and materials. A young teacher's purchase of the reading circle professional book often proved to be his initial step in building a personal professional library.

The rural one-room schools generally were the center of community social affairs. Spelling bees, ciphering matches, and amateur dramatic productions served as amusement for all in the community. Candy breakings, pie suppers, and box suppers were popular with the adults, as were debates on such provocative subjects as "Resolved, that the railroads have contributed more to America than have the steamboats." But transportation was slow, and the difficulty of travel tended to isolate people from anyone more than four miles away and, in turn, to force education into very limited proportions. Furthermore, the agrarian life was so economically limited that children from an early age joined the adults in the struggle to produce the basic necessities of life. So there was little time for education in school. Freedom from work for children or adults was yet a long way in the distance.

But the decade of 1910-1920 brought advances in curriculum concept and methods, as well as substantial increases in educational opportunities at all levels from kindergarten to graduate school.

Greatly affecting educational philosophy and curriculum design was the National Education Association's special report, the "Seven Cardinal Principles of Secondary Education." These seven objectives called for an almost complete revamping of the high school curriculum. Never before had there been such an onslaught on the academic and classical curriculum. It seemed rank heresy to many scholars for a national committee of respectable professionals to insist that the public high schools should set as curriculum goals: (1) command of the fundamental processes, (2) citizenship, (3) ethical character, (4) vocational training, (5) worthy use of leisure, (6) health, and (7) worthy home membership.

These broadened purposes were particularly helpful as the yearning for universal education grew. Indeed, with these broadened goals for education, the curriculum of the common school was ready for the most significant alteration since the tuition-free public high school had begun. These objectives were the forerunners of the curriculum revision revolution that swept both the elementary and the high school in the twenties.

Compulsory school attendance now appeared on the statutes, and enforcement would have been even more difficult had not the new objectives brought a greatly extended and humane curriculum.

Furthermore, between 1910 and 1920, the scientific and measurement age in education really began. The work of Simon and Binet in France caught the attention of men like Otis, Thorndyke, and Terman. Soon the individual mental test called "The Terman Revision of Simon-Binet" became the first relatively successful effort to give the teaching profession a standardized tool to assess mental power to learn. Soon Otis, Thorndyke, and others invented and standardized mental tests for group testing. These had their basic tryouts with the young men entering World War I.

Mental tests were followed by achievement tests in the various academic fields. Some were designed to help determine grade levels and to aid in classification; others had the primary purpose of giving diagnostic information to the educator.

All this, for the first time, threw into bold relief the fact that children differed. It became clear that a program and method needed to be devised for the individual learner. Few authorities on mental testing realized that deficiencies revealed by mental tests were not necessarily due to inheritances, but often to meager home and community environments.

As previously stated, most people in America during this decade completed their education on or before graduation from the common school. In fact, there were few who graduated and those who did were given examinations by the county superintendent in a central location, usually at the county seat of government. I was the first pupil from my rural school to take and pass these examinations. The ordeal was fraught with nervous tension and the ride of several miles on horseback was an adventure for a fourteen-year-old boy. Of course, girls were seldom expected to complete the common branches.

There was much drill, memory work, together with frequent repetition of what had previously been learned. Proficiency in handwriting was considered of great importance. Copy books and slates for practice were tools needed by every child. The valid evidence of an education was skill in handwriting. A "good hand" distinguished an adult as a scholar and gentleman. Mastery of spelling and arithmetic constituted an even greater objective than mastery of reading.

On the closing day of school the parents came for a basket dinner and stayed for the program given by the school children. Every child had a part to play. Some spoke poetry they had memorized; others gave declamations and performed in spelling and arithmetic; still others participated in what was called a dialogue—simply dramatic acts. A chorus sang a church hymn. I remember another competitive activity: Four of the older pupils, with chalk in hand, stood at the blackboard. On the word "go" of the teacher each sketched a map of the United States with each state outlined and named, and then located and named the state capitals. If no mistakes were observed by the teacher, who was the referee, the first one finished was declared the winner.

Since I lived at home and continued to do farm chores I saved my entire salary of $245. It would be many years before I again ended a year of teaching with that much savings.

The school board urged me to teach the following year, but I had my mind set on further education.

Since the state Normal School in Springfield, Missouri, offered a secondary school program as well as three years of college and since the school operated year round on a quarter plan, I decided that going there would permit me to accelerate. So I did not return to high school but took the railroad train to the "big city."

Since my cash outlay was my teaching salary of $245, together with the small sum resulting from the sale of some hogs, it was my intent to study for four quarters and then return to teaching to replenish the exchequer. But my expectations were to mount as conditions developed during the year which made it possible for me to continue my academic career until interrupted by the beginning of the First World War and my enlistment in the U.S. Navy.

The Southwest Missouri State Teachers College, even at its beginning as a four-year accredited college, could boast of a strong faculty, mostly drawn from colleges in the East. Not only were there strong scholars among the staff, but there were excellent teachers too, committed to helping students and to building a strong institution of higher learning. The second year I was there the college attained full four-year accredited rank.

I enjoyed my scholastic experiences. My strongest and best-liked professors were in the fields of history, literature, economics, sociology, and physics. My marks were not of summa cum laude rank, but at graduation time they were high enough to permit my selection by the faculty as commencement orator. Almost from the first I plunged into extracurricular activities such as being on the staff of school publications and participating in debates, oratorical contests, and athletics. I took little work in physical education, but I was a two-letter varsity man every year and, in addition, earned a track letter twice. Also, although the college did not compete intercollegiately in tennis, I was the college runner-up during my sophomore and junior years.

Football and basketball took much time but were personally rewarding. I was never captain of the football team but I was named all-conference tackle in 1916. Basketball was my favorite sport, and I was rewarded by my teammates who named me captain in 1917 and by the sportswriters who selected me as all-conference center. That year, too, competing in a conference of thirteen colleges, Southwest Missouri State Teachers College won the championship.

My social life in college was largely limited to the various social and forensic activities on Friday nights at the debating clubs. There were five of these organizations, coeducational in membership, and they served, in many ways, the functions ordinarily performed by fraternities and sororities. Competition between them rested largely in debates and oratorical contests. Naturally, they held dances on occasion. Dancing was generally an all-college affair with the long halls of the administration building serving as dancing space, while the college orchestra or a section of it provided the music. There were other all-college entertainments such as plays, concerts, and Chautauqua speeches. During the summer a traveling troupe of players provided theater, including Shakespeare, Molière, and Sheridan. Many of these I attended if I could find the cash for my date and me. Incidentally, I dated a reasonable number of girls at college but didn't ever fall in love.

Soon after I went out for football practice the coach took a liking to me. He also was the basketball coach. He did all he could to make it possible for me to stay in college. It was he who first mentioned my name to the president and business manager as a possible candidate for student manager of the college-owned book store. The book store stocked texts and reference books, as well as art supplies, gym suits, notebooks, stationery, tablets, pencils, ink, etc. (Fountain pens had not yet been invented.) It was operated by two students who ordered all textbooks requested by professors and all other materials to be sold. These two young men bought and sold, kept accounts, and reported inventories and cash at intervals.

The store was kept open from 7:30 to 9 A.M., 12:30 to 1 P.M. 4 to 6 P.M. on weekdays, and all morning on Saturday. Other than on opening and closing days of each term when business was brisk, one man could handle the purchasers. Consequently, we staggered our time schedule. Since I was on the varsity during fall and winter terms my partner always took the late afternoon shift while I went out for practice.

During the debating season I was particularly busy and without doubt spent too little time on study and laboratory work and too much time earning a living, debating, and playing basketball and football. Incidentally, we debated such topics as free trade, workmen's compensation, compulsory school attendance, state aid to schools, the right to picket, and the right to organize and strike. Of course, the European war was a vital topic in the winter of 1917. Although many students opposed our entering the war, once war was declared I heard little opposition expressed.

During the spring and summer months I put in my strongest academic efforts, although I supplemented my book store salary by spading professors' gardens and baby-sitting with their children. These jobs paid 15¢ per hour. I made $20 per month plus tuition for labors in the book store. Incidentally, the tuition at the state teachers colleges was $15 per quarter or $45 for a full academic year.

After the first year, the book store employees were given a room with cots in the basement of the main building. For these lodging accommodations we were responsible as custodians. In addition to being watchmen (while we slept or studied), we opened the auditorium, gymnasium, and social club rooms and served as caretakers. Likewise, we turned off all lights and locked all outside doors once the audience and participants had left.

With lodging and a minimum of $20 monthly, I was a capitalist with adequate income to be assured of housing, food, and incidentals such as laundry. Board at cooperative clubs cost from $10 to $15 per month so I had at least $7 for laundry and social activities. What I made baby-sitting, mowing lawns, and gardening at 15¢ per hour during the summers, I set aside for winter clothes.

But war was brewing, and I met another obligation during that senior year. As editor of the *Annual* and as an officer in my class, further distractions appeared to consume my time. But nothing could overshadow the war clouds blowing in from Europe.

So when war finally was declared several of the men, I among them, applied for the first officers' training camp. But the papers of each of us somehow went astray. The call to officers' school came quickly, but none to those whose papers had gone from Teachers College. In a few days apologies for the mixup came from the military and we were placed on call for the second officers' training group. By then the nation was in fever heat. "The world must be saved for democracy," and fast.

So I told the coach I was going to enlist in the Navy as an apprentice seaman. He asked to go with me to the recruiting office. As we sat on the trolley just off the campus waiting for the motorman to check his fares, we saw four other athletes running and waving their hats. They had somehow learned my Navy intent and had decided to enlist also. So there went the basketball team. Luckily the season had just closed.

To my dismay, the recruiting officer discovered that I had a growth on a large blood vessel. I could be admitted only after an operation. From the recruiting station I called a surgeon. He agreed to operate the next day, so to the hospital I went, determined to get in the Navy. Soon I was well and duly sworn in. I was sent to Newport, Rhode Island, boot camp.

When the boot training was over, there were anxious moments as we watched all draft bulletins with names and designated ships. One evening, as I read the bulletin board, I saw a request for college-trained men to go into a new branch of the Navy called the Naval Air Reserve Flying Corps. Enlisted men who could pass certain tests, particularly concerning gasoline engines, would be sent to school in Bay Shore, Long Island, and at the conclusion of the course would be rated as second-class quartermasters for aviation. That meant a fast promotion from apprentice seaman to second-class petty officer.

I was interested, although I didn't know anything about a gasoline engine. I had never driven a car. However, in due time I passed the tests and was given orders to report to the air station at Bay Shore.

Next day I found myself on a brand new naval air station and in school learning airplane nomenclature and the mysteries of how to assemble a plane and care for its many wires, struts, and pontoons. The engine had many mysteries, some of which we were able to investigate firsthand. Again examination time came, and again I passed. Now I could sew on my two petty-officer stripes and my pay went up three steps, to $44 per month, as I remember.

I was immediately assigned the responsibility, along with another second-class petty officer for aviation, of keeping two planes flying during daylight hours. We alternated each week between night and day work. Soon instructors and cadets alike who used my planes became friendly, and when a student began his solo work he often would invite me for a hop. Thus I was introduced to flying with inexperienced and sometimes quite inept and unskilled pilots. But I liked it, and these experiences prepared me for my next opportunity.

Once again, reading the bulletin board and other naval publications paid off for me. Two months after assuming my duties as petty officer, a naval bulletin urged enlisted men with college degrees to apply for flying duty. Although I had enlisted a few months before graduation and, therefore, had no bachelor's degree, I did have a picture taken in cap and gown to be used in the college annual. This, with a copy of my scholastic record and a completed application form, was hurriedly mailed to the Navy Department in Washington. Within a short time I received orders to report for ground school training at the Massachusetts Institute of Technology. Upon arriving in Cambridge, I was told my status would be Air Cadet with the rank of Chief Petty Officer and a salary of $60 per month. Furthermore, I could now remove my sailor's suit and purchase the forest green, tailored uniform of the Naval Reserve flying officer. Again I was forced to borrow money for uniforms.

The program and achievement requirements of MIT were rigid, and the workday was long. The threat of rule infractions and scholastic failure made the twelve weeks' indoctrination on the banks of the Charles a time of tenseness and worry. The major goals of all instructors seem to be to instill fear on the one hand and much data and military discipline on the other. The subjects included naval history, navy regulations, navy courts and boards, aerodynamics, theory of flight, communications, aerial navigation, and seamanship. There was also much military drill and handling of small firearms. The only recreation available was an occasional assembly with civilian entertainers.

On graduation day each cadet received orders to report for flying duty at Bay Shore or Key West. My orders assigned me to Key West.

I was delighted to get back to the realm of flying. The rigid discipline and adherence to regulation in dress at all times gave way to informality and to interesting work. The day after reporting in Key West I was issued my long-hoped-for goggles and hard helmet. No other part of the uniform made much difference there, but these two, like the white jacket and stethoscope of the medical intern, were marks of distinction. They would be ever present on the hard road to achievement of gold wings.

After about seven hours of instruction over a period of about two weeks, I passed my solo test. During the following weeks I practiced such maneuvers as intentional spins and pullouts, Immelmann turns, and steep tight turns. The most difficult was to climb slowly to ten thousand feet and kill the engine and then make figure-eight turns all the way down and land within one hundred feet of the designated buoy.

The day came far too soon for me to leave primary flight training and go for the second step which included flying with new Liberty engines and taking long navigation hops. So off a small group of us went for the Naval Air Training Station in Miami.

My next tour of duty was in Pensacola, Florida. In 1918 the air station of Pensacola was devoted to advanced training of pilots. Here, after meeting the many requirements demanded of an officer, the cadet received his cherished gold stripe and gold wings.

Finally, when I had proved competence in many types of maneuvers, had demonstrated ability to navigate accurately by utilizing time, speed, wind velocity, and direction, and had also reached rather rigid standards in bomb dropping and aerial gunnery, I was presented with the wings and ensign stripes. Now I could remove the midshipman's anchor from my cap and put on the embroidered eagle. And now the gold Navy wings adorned my left chest.

I spent only a short time flying patrols off the Gulf before the armistice was signed and I found myself released to inactive duty.

When I arrived home I learned that my mother, who had fully expected me to die in one of those "fool airplanes," had given my civilian clothes to the "Poor Farm." So it was necessary for me to continue to wear my Navy uniforms until I could earn some money. Needless to say, the glamor of the gold braided cap, gold wings, cordovan puttees, and a swagger stick caused me to be deliberate in the purchase of new clothes.

CHAPTER II

A few days after reaching home, I received a telephone call from the superintendent in Bolivar, Missouri, asking me to accept a position teaching English and physics in the high school. For several days I continued to refuse. I was not sure that teaching was my calling. Furthermore, I had a yearning to join the revolutionaries in Mexico and fly for them. The stories of Lord Byron had stimulated me. Finally, after a third plea from the superintendent, I accepted the teaching position and reported for teaching duty. I was welcomed by the boys since I was the only male member of the staff, except for the superintendent.

Spring was in the air, and I was restless for physical activity. It seemed wise to me to try to develop a track team. There were no hurdles, no jumping pits, no vaulting pole, no standards, but with the help of a lumberman, standards and hurdles were constructed. Mr. Capps, the superintendent, found money from the student funds for shot and discus. So a new extracurricular activity for the boys came into being. The season was relatively unproductive in medals won, but the school spirit rose and the boys worked hard and the girls cheered.

On the closing day of school, a little less than three months after I reported, the superintendent called me to his office and said, "Mr. Engleman, I was elected superintendent at Monett last night. I want you to go with me as high school principal." I replied, "Mr. Capps, I don't know anything about being a high school principal." "Never mind that, if you will go down and win the confidence and cooperation of those big high school boys, I will teach you to be a high school principal. You see," he continued, "the outgoing superintendent and principal were at cross purposes and the school spirit is all antagonistic. The student leaders must be understood and properly dealt with." The generation gap was a threat to harmony in 1919, and Mr. Capps recognized it.

"It's a deal," I replied. So I became one of the first administrative "interns" in the history of American education. The salary was $150 per month for nine months.

The superintendent and I arrived in Monett two weeks before the opening of school. Since he was a widower, he invited me to share an apartment in a private home where we could take our meals. During those two weeks Mr. Capps began his tutelage of the would-be high school principal. He showed me how to make class schedules and assign teaching duties. He advised me about how to work with the staff. He helped me make an inventory of instructional materials and check the status of the textbooks. Of very great importance, he checked student personnel forms with me and showed me how to keep such records current.

In addition to being principal, I was to teach physics, senior English, and sophomore plane geometry. Consequently, I had course outlines to prepare as well as a program of teaching to master. I was disappointed at the meagerness of the physics laboratory. When I looked for a dressing room and showers, there were none. However, a basement room with some benches was available so I put up hooks on which uniforms could be hung. But there were no uniforms or footballs.

Without thinking of how they would be paid for, I hurriedly got off a rush order to a Kansas City sporting goods house for twenty-five uniforms. I hoped there would be enough boys reporting for a varsity and scrub team. Incidentally, I ordered a suit to fit myself, and two footballs.

There was no football field, but adjacent to one corner of the campus was a grass pasture. It was not very level and had many flint rocks but it would have to do—if I could get possession. A school board member who had great interest in youth activities and favored a football team interceded, and soon the field was leased at a nominal fee. But there were no field markers or goalposts. These, too, were attained and when registration day came, the big boys became aware that they might have harmony with the new administration. Upon discovering that there were new uniforms and a newly laid out field, they went to the superintendent and inquired, "Who will coach us?" The reply was, "The high school principal."

During the first few days I worked harder than they. I passed, I ran, I tackled. They knew no fundamentals but they were willing to learn, and they were amazed and happy that a principal would play with them and show them some skills.

We lost the first three games. But for the remainder of that season and throughout the next two, there was not a single loss. The wins stretched to twenty-seven as I closed my last year.

Meanwhile, I quietly broke up dice games in the boiler room, as well as other prankish behavior. No one was suspended or expelled.

With the football season over I turned my attention to other extracurricular activities in which I could stir up an interest. There was no gymnasium, so basketball was eliminated. I organized and taught debate teams, school orators, and with the help of the local YMCA executives, organized a Hi-Y Club. Other teachers became interested and sponsored special interest clubs that met after school. Soon many extracurricular activities were in full swing.

My many responsibilities practically excluded attempts at professional improvement activities with my teaching staff, and from the beginning, I feared direct attempts to supervise. After all, each teacher knew that she knew more than I did about teaching. However, probably more to discover better methods for myself than to encourage growth in others, I systematically sat down with teachers in their rooms and asked such questions as, "What instructional problems worry you most?" "What kinds of methods and what materials seem best suited with your pupils and in your special teaching field?" "What do you need?" Is there anything the principal or others can do to cooperate with you?" "If you were in charge of the next faculty meeting, what would the agenda be?" "What techniques do you find useful with the slow or uninterested student?"

Gradually we built a mutual confidence in each other. I learned that some of the older teachers were the most tolerant, considerate, imaginative, devoted, helpful, and creative. For the next fifty years this conclusion was verified over and over.

With the coming of spring the big boys requested me to coach the track team. I was never a good track athlete but I had run on the mile relay team, put the shot, and tossed the discus with enough competence to win a letter—barely.

Again track and field equipment had to be constructed and bought. Monett was not a county seat, so there was no horse race track that could be used. But the football field and the streets nearby were used as a practice field.

Again, it developed that Monett high school had athletic talent. The proof was evident when we returned as winners with the big first place silver cup from the southwest Missouri meet held on the campus of the State Teachers College. The feat was repeated each of the next two years. By the end of the school year not only were the students enthusiastic and proud, but so was the whole community. School spirit and community pride in the high school were evident on every hand. The class rivalry and dangerous practice of competition between seniors and juniors to plant their colors on the dome of the school gave way to a united school spirit and pride in teams and in scholastic achievement.

At the end of my second year, Mr. Capps resigned to do graduate study. I am sure that it was his influence that caused the school board to elect me to succeed him as superintendent. (Incidentally, I had returned to the teachers college for two ten-week summer sessions and now possessed the Bachelor of Science degree. I had been chosen class speaker by the faculty, and my talk, "Ethics for Teachers," had been published in the *Missouri School Journal*.) Mr. Capps had kept his word and had consistently and assiduously monitored and instructed me in the theory and practice of high school administration. I firmly believe that it was his strong commitment to public education, his deep consideration for mankind, and his personnel management techniques that gave me reasonable success those first years and continued creditable performance over the many years ahead.

It was Mr. Capps, too, who led me into the big event of my life. One day shortly after we arrived in Monett, I was accompanying him to discuss a matter with the chairman of the board. As we walked down Fifth Street, we passed a group of young women sitting on a porch. One of them called to the superintendent and came running out to speak to him. I walked on a little way but could get a good view of the girl. She was the most striking and lovely person I had ever seen. One of Wordsworth's poems which I had just read came to mind. It began, "She was a vision of delight/When first she burst upon my sight." I could hardly wait to exclaim to my boss, "Who is that person?"

"Ruby Lane, the second and third grade teacher at Forest Park School," he replied.

"Well, will you introduce me to her?"

He did at the next faculty meeting. But that was only the beginning. I was determined to have a date with her. She refused my request every week for four months. Then on a snowy, blustery winter Saturday afternoon I called her from my office at the high school with the oft-repeated request. There was a hesitation at the other end, then the simple answer, "Yes, about eight o'clock."

Years later, she explained why she had answered in the affirmative. She somehow had believed men teachers to be sissies. But when my request to go to the movie came on such a terrible, stormy day, she had concluded, "Maybe he isn't a sissy after all." Since I had been refused so many times, it came as a surprise that the evening seemed to reveal compatability. A year later we were engaged, and on November 17, 1921, we were married.

As a superintendent, I was responsible for three elementary schools as well as the high school. The part of the job Mr. Capps had neglected was how to work with the school board. But the secretary of the board, Logan McKee, was an early bird flyer—even before me he gave demonstration flights at public picnics. He was my savior. He had the most catholic interests of any man I ever knew, and his knowledge, generosity, and kindness were prodigious.

With his guidance and help, I produced reasonable board agendas and kept the school accounts in order. It was Mr. McKee, too, who encouraged me to propose a junior high school in a 6-3-3 organizational structure. We also developed a school building program which was accepted by the board and community. I believed that my greatest educational accomplishments were the organizational and curricular restructuring, together with a new high school and two new elementary schools, but the townspeople, parents, and students seemed to think my athletic coaching was most important.

In the early spring of my third year in Monett I made an emergency trip to the Mayo Clinic in Rochester, Minnesota, with my father-in-law, who was suffering from a goiter. A telegram from the secretary of the Nevada, Missouri, school board was forwarded to me there. It requested that I go for a consultation with the board about the vacancy in their superintendency. Several days had elapsed, so I just wrote a note in reply and stated that on the following Wednesday I would have a train layover in Nevada of twenty minutes. If the board was interested in me, I suggested that they meet my train and interview me at the station.

Upon my arrival, the president of Cottey College, located in the town, was there to meet me. He urged that I stay over for a later train in the afternoon. He agreed to drive me to the offices of the various board members for interviews. I agreed and we saw all six—a lawyer, a banker, a lumberman, two doctors, and a florist. I visited each man for a maximum of thirty minutes, but gave the secretary information about my personal and professional background and asked many questions about board policy expectations. I then hurried on home to my bride of four months, who had just discovered she was pregnant.

Scarcely had a week passed when a superintendent from midstate called to ask if the board at Monett had selected a superintendent. My reply was that I had assumed they would continue me as superintendent. He asked, "Aren't you going to the job at Nevada? You were elected superintendent there several days ago."

The following day the contract came with a $400 raise in salary. I signed the contract and told my wife that we would be moving to a city with trolley cars and an annual salary of $2,800.

We traveled to Nevada in early May to locate a home. After a fruitless search for a house to rent we went to Mrs. Virginia Stockard, founder of Cottey College. She and her sister occupied the downstairs section of a college duplex; the upper apartment was occupied by the district superintendent of the Methodist Church. He was due to leave in September, so Mrs. Stockard took pity on us and said we could have it. In the meantime, she rented us a big room into which we crowded all our furniture and ourselves. There we lived through June, July, and August, taking our meals at a boarding house.

During that summer I pried into all the data available about the school system. A fine bookkeeping system had been introduced including a systematic budgeting and programming complex. I gave serious study to this and mastered the plan. I also studied the staff and salaries. I discovered that by taking advantage of a new state aid law on teacher compensation, we could raise the salary of twelve teachers by $100 per person without increasing the district output a single dollar. The interiors of the buildings needed paint, and I helped the janitors put new paint on twenty rooms in the elementary schools. I suppose by any known professional standards, painting classrooms by the superintendent would be considered a poor use of energy and time but, after all, I had few administrative skills and I did so want to do something for the teachers I had not yet met. Their joy at finding their rooms in new pastel colors gave me a 4.0 rating!

I discovered something else: the town had one section into which everybody tried to move if he wanted to "keep up with the Joneses." Many people thought the Franklin school that served this section was superior to the other four elementary schools. Consequently, I found that this form of *de facto* segregation was causing one school to be overpopulated while two adjoining schools had half-empty rooms.

The answer seemed obvious and simple to me. So I moved the boundary lines and announced the changes in the daily newspaper. All hell broke loose and I was harassed by objectors, many on the phone. My wife felt the full fury of "injured" parents. The newspapers, however, stayed neutral and I held my ground. When the monthly meeting of the school board came due, protesters appeared. But the school board firmly supported me unanimously, much to my surprise.

During the harassment I learned that the two doctors on the board were affected. Dr. Yater's twin daughters had been shifted to Bryant and Dr. Hornback's son and daughter to Blair. What staunch supporters they were, even though they doubted the quality of education in the schools to which their children were transferred! But by the end of the year, they and others who had violently protested would come to me requesting that their children be allowed to remain in Bryant and Blair.

When school opened, the older boys came to ask that we start a football team. Somehow they had heard of my coaching at Monett. Since I wished to accept every reasonable suggestion from the students, I wanted to follow theirs. But there was no teacher who could coach. Finally, after discussing the matter with the board secretary, who had two high school boys, and with the elderly board president, who wanted to present the district with a fine tract of land in the heart of town to be used as an athletic field, I agreed to quickly order uniforms and then coach the team.

So, I was soon neglecting some routine responsibilities of the superintendency but building strong support from the student body. And the town became excited when the team won the tricounty championship.

In the spring I again took an inexperienced group of boys and started track. In southwest Missouri there were three track meets each spring. These early meet results could generally be used to predict the final outcome of the official state regional meet held on the campus of the State College in Springfield. Since we had started late and the team was still in the formative stage, I decided not to attend the first meet, at Mt. Vernon, but to wait a week and go to the second one, at Carthage.

When I got to Carthage with the green, untried team, we went to the YMCA gym which was to be used as dressing headquarters. When the Monett team and coach arrived, they surrounded me and queried, "Mr. Engleman, do you have a man that can take third place in the 100 and 220? If you can thus take two points away from Springfield, we can win this meet." The meet at Mt. Vernon the previous week had ended with Springfield ahead by two points, believed by the Monett statisticians to be due to the fact that Springfield had won both second and third in the two dash events. I replied that we had a pretty fast man and he just might take third.

To the surprise of everybody, including me, the meet ended with Nevada far in the lead. We had won gold medals for first place in eleven of the thirteen events. The next week at State College the feat was repeated.

Next came the tri-state meet at Pittsburg, Kansas. Again Nevada won the big cup. It was during this track meet that I faced and coped with racism. In the trial heat of the 100 yard dash, our captain and best point winner discovered that a Negro lad from Fort Scott was to be a competitor. He refused to engage in sports with a black. Never before had I assembled in my own mind the reasons for racial justice and equality. After placing these arguments before our captain, he changed his mind and accepted a Negro as a competitor and added a new dimension to his own value system. At the end of that season I would decide that a superintendent in a town of ten thousand had more important duties than athletic coaching, and a new coach would be employed.

In mid-October, on a beautiful Friday, my wife awoke with labor pains. Since an important game was to be played that afternoon, she gave no hint of her pains to me. When I arrived home after winning the game, I learned she was in the hospital. I hurried there and found her waiting it out. Her patience was rewarded the next afternoon when Virginia Lee was born. We named her in honor of Mrs. Virginia Stockard, president and founder of Cottey College. Later she was christened by a bishop with Mrs. Stockard standing by as godmother.

In February of that year I strained the family budget and attended the annual meeting of the Department of Superintendence of the NEA, held in Chicago. The excitement of change, of expansion in education, of new research findings, and of the demand for a new curriculum charged the convention atmosphere. I became enthusiastic about new ideas and determined to bring revolution to the Nevada schools. The term *innovation* had not yet become popular, but change in program and method was imperative. For the first time I realized that I must set for myself a long and rigid program of advanced study. I was aware of the specter of obsolescence.

My detailed notes on talks and reports were translated to the faculty upon my return. My enthusiasm for what might be done was shared by some of the faculty and school board members. We talked about and tried out the project method which Collings, Meriam, and Kilpatrick supported in books and articles. Mrs. Parkhurst's experiment with the contract method in Dalton, Massachusetts, caught my fancy. Core curricula sounded good, and character education must have a place. Some ways must be found to better care for individual differences. So soon some of the Nevada teachers were writing detailed curriculum units to be taught on the contract plan. Thus programmed learning had its start.

Character education and citizenship called for much correlation of subject matter, and as the seven Cardinal Objectives came to be accepted as the goals of education, the whole curriculum came in for expansion and revision. Vocational courses such as shop, homemaking, stenography, bookkeeping, teacher training, and agriculture quickly came to be accepted, as did physical education and health. Likewise, art and music and a whole list of extracurricular activities became respectable. Indeed, a serious effort was made to have curriculum content and method that would accommodate the interests and aptitudes of every pupil. All this led to a demand for a new building with new features such as shops, band rooms, gymnasiums, and an auditorium with a modern stage.

The school board accepted a program for complete modernization of school facilities. The bond issue was for the maximum loan allowed by law and carried by a whopping plurality vote of the citizenry.

By the time the bonds were put on sale in the late second summer, I was away studying at the University of Missouri. There I ran across a new book written by John Guy Fowlkes, then a young man. The book suggested that the old plan of amortizing school loans after twenty years by having a sinking fund should be replaced by serial bonds, some of which were paid off each year. I brought the idea back and the board liked it. So Nevada, Missouri, was one of the first school districts in the Middle West to sell and amortize serial bonds.

The new high school went up fast, and the remodeling of the old building to accommodate the newly organized junior high school was completed before the year was over. The new and remodeled school buildings made the town a sort of showplace.

Following the example of Nevada, a new music program had sprung up all over southwest Missouri. The Nevada staff decided to issue invitations to a music festival. Competition would include male chorus, mixed chorus, bands, orchestras, quartets, and solo contests in voice, violin, clarinet, trumpet, and piano. The response was overwhelming, but the citizens of Nevada rose to the occasion and provided meals and lodging for each visiting contestant. Judges were sought from Missouri colleges and universities and medals were awarded to the winners.

After four long summer sessions at the university, I was awarded the master's degree and initiated in the honorary fraternity, Phi Delta Kappa.

While in Nevada I was active in church, fraternal, and community affairs. I was an officer in the Lions Club and for two years I was responsible for securing the weekly speaker at the Chautauqua-like programs sponsored by the chamber of commerce. Since I had gained a healthy respect for the railroad unions in Monett, I made friends with the union men connected with the railroads that passed through Nevada.

While in Monett I had joined the regional and state teachers associations and attended their meetings. Soon after moving to Nevada I was elected president of the Southwest Missouri Teachers Association and, about the same time, president of my college alumni association. But my big annual professional stimulation was the convention of the American Association of School Administrators—called in those days the Department of Superintendence of the NEA. Although the board authorized my going, no one ever suggested that the budget should have an item for such expenses.

Near the end of the first year I was faced with a salary problem. The secretary of the board called me in to the bank and said, "Mr. Engleman, you will be reelected superintendent at the next meeting. You should apply for a good raise. If you don't, the board simply will not raise your salary enough."

I said, "Mr. Carter, to ask for a raise is against my policy."

He replied, "Change your policy. Make the request."

That night Mrs. Engleman and I talked the matter over. Should we ask for as much as $300? We decided to ask for nothing. Imagine our delight when the board gave me a new contract with an $800 raise!

My favorite forms of recreation were fishing and hunting. Some of the staff, together with a dentist friend, constituted the sporting parties. Seldom did I fish without success, and hardly ever did I hunt without returning with the limit of quail. Rabbits were so plentiful that they just weren't counted.

For most of my life I have worked six and often seven days a week. I found that fishing and hunting served to break the stretches of tension that accompany administrative jobs, to relieve tangled nerves and taut muscles and restore my state of normalcy.

I have often believed the best way to test the character of a man is to go with him into wild virgin country with little food, limited clothing, makeshift shelter, and there meet millions of insects and raw, rainy weather.

One aspect of my experience in Nevada causes me much humiliation and distress. There were about six families of Negroes in the town, with about a dozen school-age children. I found them housed in a one-room school with a single teacher and hardly any equipment. After they outgrew the seats in this elementary school, they had no further opportunities for schooling since no one, black or white, suggested an integrated high school. And so far as I can remember, I did not attempt to do anything about it. Only twenty miles away in Fort Scott, Kansas, all schools were integrated and opportunities for blacks seemed equal to those for whites from grade one to twelve. In later years I was haunted by the fact that I had made little effort to improve the quality of education for Nevada's Negro children. Culture patterns are a blinding force.

One day while in Nevada a vice-president of a book company who knew of my interest in improved textbooks called on me. I invited him to dinner at home. Before the evening was over he invited me to accept a position as editor with headquarters in Chicago. I traveled there at their expense, but I finally refused the offer of nearly three times my Nevada salary. Although I was interested in the publishing business, I somehow couldn't give up work with children and teachers. Furthermore, my dream of leadership and fellowship in school administration had become an obsession.

Kansas City, Missouri, was only one hundred miles to the north, and its schools were nationally known for their excellence. Part of this excellence was due to the high salaries and the board policy which allowed the superintendent and personnel director to seek outstanding teachers and principals from any state. Thus, the system was not handicapped by inbreeding, and fresh, imaginative ideas constantly poured into the city.

I had a telephone call from the Kansas City superintendent one day, inviting me to pay him a visit and talk about an opening there. Accordingly, I cranked up the Model T Ford coupe, and off Mrs. Engleman and I went to the big city. The superintendent drove me out to Whittier, the biggest elementary school I had ever seen. The enrollment was beyond 1,200—K-7. He told me they wanted me for principal at $200 more than my salary as superintendent. In addition, they wanted me to teach extension classes on Saturday at the City Teachers College. On the dusty road home that evening, Ruby and I decided to make the move. One factor that affected my decision was the platoon organization that was being tried at the Whittier school.

My superintendent friends could not understand why I would leave the head role in a good school system like Nevada and seemingly become pigeonholed in a subordinate position in a big city. Even I had periods of serious doubts about the wisdom of my choice. While in Nevada, however, I had become greatly interested in the education of the younger child, and I believed a Kansas City elementary school would offer opportunity for me to study this phenomenon.

The teachers and principals in each of the five elementary schools of Nevada had monthly building faculty meetings where each of us took turns in producing a "demonstration" lesson. I had agreed to do my share of demonstration teaching even though I knew my associates to be better able to present model lessons than I. Naturally, I had to work very hard in preparation but I did, I believe, develop a spirit of comradeship which got me by many possible personnel conflicts. Since I attended all the building faculty meetings, I had five demonstrations to produce each month. Consequently, I developed strong interests in the learning and teaching problems at the elementary school level. I also had begun to see the need for a greater range and variety of curriculum instructional materials. As I reasoned and felt, the Whittier School job in Kansas City would give me a richer experience. I reasoned, too, that should I not like being a subordinate administrator, there would be opportunities to change back into the field of the superintendency. In addition, I had come to believe that the principalship could be made to be the most effective and important link in an administrative team. The Kansas City superintendent had assured me that I would have great autonomy of operation.

Before leaving Nevada, we were blessed with another baby girl, Nancy Lane. So the Englemans, composed of four, prepared to live in the city.

I reported weeks ahead of the opening and again began to study the total situation. I walked the length and breadth of the district getting acquainted with neighborhood businessmen, the regional firemen in the district department, the pastors of the churches, and, possibly of most importance, the director of a large Jewish orphans' home whose school-age inmates were enrollees in Whittier.

Next, I looked into every nook and cranny of the old, friendly school building, examining as I went all resources for learning. I was pleased to find more than I had observed on my exploratory visit with the superintendent. For example, there were three playgrounds—one for the kindergarten, first, and second grades with adequate swings, jungle gyms, teetertotters, etc., one playground for the older boys, and one for the girls. They were small, but high woven fences helped to contain the balls. There were two gyms, shops, homemaking laboratories, art and music rooms, an earth science and geography laboratory, and an excellent library manned by a well-trained librarian. The central office had an excellent service of many kinds of visual aids. The auditorium had a well-equipped, large stage and the down-front seats were small enough to accommodate early grades. Two teachers were on duty for drama and dialogue. There were showers, an "open air room," and a lunch room designed to further the health of tubercular students, as well as an adequate dispensary and nurse's room. Two rooms were specially designed and equipped for slow learners. These two groups were called "opportunity classes" and operated on a nongraded structure.

To make sure that *all* these resources were utilized effectively *all* the hours of the day, the school was organized and staffed on the platoon plan. The children from grade three up were divided into platoons so that for two quarters of each day they were with a homeroom core subject teacher, while for two quarters they were with specialists in such fields as art, music, dramatics, physical education, homemaking, science, and shop. The playgrounds were open from 8 A.M. until 5:30 P.M. and on Saturday. School opened at 9 A.M. and closed at 4 P.M. The school year was for a minimum of 180 days.

The schedule under which a platoon school operates is a somewhat intricate affair, and I spent considerable time before the opening of school juggling and adjusting it. Had I had a computer, it would have been easier.

Soon after school began, I became aware that when children worked with several teachers each day there was need for cooperation and correlation among teachers. The team teaching concept was imperative. The need for proper utilization of the specialists on the staff was obvious to all. All teachers had two thirty-minute rest periods each day, but as we studied the problems of relationship, subject matter, integration, teacher specialties, and coordination, we agreed to have planning and work sessions during many of these rest periods and during the noon hour. As we worked together, I gradually became the team leader and general coordinator. I also found myself greatly involved in relief teaching and in managing the movement of many supplies and some equipment such as visual aids. In fact, I had the great satisfaction of being accepted by children and teachers as a partner in many of their major learning projects.

Many techniques of cooperation and leadership, as well as fellowship, developed during the era of platoon schools could have been used to advantage later by those who sponsored the team teaching movement.

Libraries in Kansas City, Missouri—all of them, school and public—were housed in school buildings. In fact, the city school board was also the city library board. The head librarian and all school librarians were employees of the school board. This meant, of course, that the school library was a neighborhood center for adults, as well as children. The libraries were open evenings and Saturdays.

The PTA at Whittier was strong and grew stronger. Weekly study groups on child psychology met at the school with some of the staff and others from the central superintendent's office serving as specialist leaders. A fathers' club, too, was formed. It met at night, whereas the PTA met in the afternoon. There were special clubs, too, for the older pupils. The Boy Scouts was possibly the strongest of the lot.

Without doubt, the most stimulating and enjoyable professional experience I had in Kansas City resulted from the formation of a little professional club called "The Filthy Five."

Five of the male elementary school principals agreed to meet together every month. We assembled at alternate homes for a dinner prepared by the host. No wives were allowed. The purpose was good fellowship followed by a "no holds barred" dialogue that often ended near midnight in good-natured debate.

In turn, each principal presented a position paper on various controversial educational issues of the day; heated discussion followed. In order to bring a bit of levity and relaxation to the year's discussions, we agreed to take one night in the spring to join the gandy dancers and riff-raff at the ringside seats of professional wrestling. On that night we threw decorum to the winds and whooped and howled as the big grunters performed. It was because of this custom that we called ourselves the "Filthy Five."

Soon after assuming my duties as principal in Kansas City, I was invited to become a member of the School Masters' Club, which met monthly for dinner and a program following. There were over sixty members, consisting of elementary, junior high, and senior high principals. The superintendent was not a member. Since up to that time I had presumed him to be a member of all professional groups, I made inquiry as to his absence. I soon learned the story. Several years earlier the individual principals had made overtures for better salaries but had been rebuffed and, in some cases, harshly criticized. As one principal put it, "We simply realized that we could get nowhere as individuals. So we organized this club for principals only. Once we were united and could, in private, set out our welfare objectives with no fear of reprisals, we were able to get the good salary and fringe benefits which we now enjoy."

So I found myself in 1924 a member of a union of sorts, and for administrators at that. However, as I continued to work with them, I saw no evidence that their membership in the organization had any detrimental effect on their professional competence, devotion to duty, and commitment to the welfare of children. Perhaps it was this experience with a principals' organization that caused me to be charitable to teachers' organizations when they became more militant twenty-five years later.

Our trips to the annual conventions of the Department of Superintendence were made by commercial bus over dirt or gravel roads. While at the conventions, we usually secured rooms at the YMCA at the price of $1.00 per night. It was at one of these meetings in Cleveland that I met Professor Frank Spaulding and Professor Clyde M. Hill of Yale. They convinced me that I should make plans to go to Yale for my doctorate.

I had given some thought to further graduate study during my last summer at the University of Missouri, when I had taken a course with a visiting professor from Minnesota. Each week he had given a detailed examination and posted the scores on the blackboard the next day. Soon it had appeared that the contest for ranking scholars lay between me and a superintendent named Lawrence Hoback. At the end of the term the professor had called the two of us in and said, "You men have Ph.D. potential. Why don't you make plans to go to a great university and seek the doctorate?" So the seeds were planted.

Kansas City school officials placed much confidence in mental and achievement testing. Almost all of my 1200 children had been given the individual Terman Revision of the Simon-Binet tests. All were frequently subjected to achievement tests of many kinds. After the physically and mentally handicapped pupils had been screened into special classes, all other pupils were assigned to X, Y, Z groups. Roughly, those with IQ's of 70-95 and comparable achievement scores were put in the X grouping, those in the 95-110 range in the Y group, and those above 110 in the Z class. As the Whittier teachers and I worked with this plan, we decided it was too rigid a classification, so we introduced flexibility. From time to time we used other evidence and thus shifted children in and out of the groups.

It was during these years that I came to realize that the good teacher encourages creativity and stimulates special imagination potentials. He is able to detect emotional blocks and release them.

Naturally, there were disciplinary cases, and sometimes the principal was expected to assign or even administer the punishment. During my first summer as I prepared for the opening of school in September, considerable maintenance work took place. Among other things, electricians put in new light fixtures in my office. A wag among the older boys who wandered in and out circulated the story that the new principal was a stern disciplinarian. "Why," he said, "The guy is installing an *electric switch* in his office." I had the poor judgment to try corporal punishment on very few occasions. After one such experience, my emotional state was such that I resolved never again to manhandle or strike a child. I decided it never gets the desired results, makes a nervous wreck of him who does the administering, and almost always erects a permanent barrier between the pupil and the adult who administers the punishment.

I remember one occasion when I had tried everything short of corporal punishment on two or three children of a disorganized family. I thought peace reigned and was checking records in the office about 4:30 one afternoon when I heard the tramp of heavy feet followed by a babble of excited children. In he strode, the father of these disturbed children I had tried to redirect, brandishing a huge 38-caliber Colt revolver. He swore he would shoot me. I was in a fix indeed, and with many young witnesses to see my demise. My mind is not clear as to how we changed his mind and by what argument we resolved the conflict. Of this I am sure, when I got home that evening I surprised my wife with two complimentary tickets to the Shubert Theater which the man had gratefully bestowed upon me.

As a city elementary school principal, I was granted a free day on Saturday of full privileges in the central library, and the help of a special librarian when I needed her. Often I would call her by midweek and say I was studying a particular subject—whales, bears, Eskimos, whatever. When I arrived Saturday morning, tables would be covered with materials on my subject. By nightfall, I would have completed notetaking, and during the next few days I would write my essay and be able to hold the attention of pupils and teachers with my story. When I left Kansas City, I had material for several children's books which I never found time to write during the demanding jobs that followed. Incidentally, while still in Kansas City, with the help of colleague teachers I did write two books for children, *Airways* and *Seals and Fins*, both published by D. C. Heath & Company.

During all but one of my summers in Kansas City, I taught courses for teachers at the Kansas City Teachers College, the Warrensburg State College, and the Southwest Missouri State College. Teaching these courses forced me to study the new professional literature, and the mature teachers who took the courses stimulated me with their ideas and knowledge. One summer, however, stands out for its outright pleasure. Four of us principals, together with our families, journeyed over dirt roads 650 miles to Boulder, Colorado. One, the president of the Kansas City Teachers College, went to teach, the other three to take advanced studies in education and psychology. (I recall trying to master Kelley's difficult book on statistics.) We drove in deep mud to Hays, Kansas, and in stifling dust the remainder of the trip. Not one foot of hard-surface road did we find. On our first evening in Boulder a college classmate who lived in Loveland called on my wife and me and invited us to spend each of the next six weekends with him and his wife. They explained that they had a baby-sitter who could look after our children from Saturday morning until late Sunday. Their two little girls and our two, of the same age, would be cared for. Meanwhile, the four parents would explore a different Rocky Mountain pass, valley, or ravine each Saturday and Sunday. The glory of those clear days and the grandeur of the Rockies have remained our most cherished memories. Too, it was such a relief and joy to miss a hot, humid summer in Missouri.

During the fall of 1927 I taught a late afternoon class at the Kansas City Teachers College. It later was claimed by the civil aeronautics officials to have been the first course in Aerodynamics and Theory of Flight ever presented to teachers. There were 64 teachers enrolled, some high school, some primary, some kindergarten. Many in-school laboratory-type projects were introduced by these teachers. One high school physics teacher, with the help of high school students, built a wind tunnel.

We closed the course with a visit to the new airport. Through officials of the young Transcontinental and Western Air Line (later changed to Trans World), a Ford trimotor plane was made available and all 64 teachers took their first flight.

Soon after I reported in Kansas City, I. I. Cammack, the superintendent, left, and George Melcher took his place. Dr. Melcher was an austere man with pointed beard and piercing, cold gray eyes. He was demanding, but none in his staff worked such long hours or so efficiently. Almost all the principals were afraid of him and were most humble and respectful in his presence. For some reason, I liked him and saw a very human, kindly soul behind his facade. So I would sometimes boldly question his assumptions as presented in principals' meetings, and would present wry but kindly satirical remarks about his rigid standards, demands for hard work, and lack of recreational activities. Many principals believed he deliberately called meetings on the Saturdays he knew they had earmarked for trips or recreation. To the surprise of my associates, he took no offense at my remarks, and before I left he proved that he really wanted to play some and be accepted as a comrade. He agreed to spend long weekends on the vacant Engleman farm 150 miles away. There a gang of kindred souls, all principals, would fish and hunt, cook meals over the open fire, and sleep in the hay mow of the old barn.

My most unpleasant task at Whittier School was rating teachers. The superintendent and board had adopted a merit salary plan. Nobody except those who achieved the merit salary liked it, and only 10 percent were eligible. Each principal was given an elaborate checklist of qualities or competencies deemed important in a good teacher. He had to report on every teacher. When first told of the plan I considered it to be good, but when I tried it out, I became conscious of its flaws in validity and reliability. Before I got through my first ordeal of trying to compare the competencies and select the best five of a roster of 38, I saw the difficulty of comparing the kindergarten teacher with the art teacher, the physical education instructor with the man in the shop. Each, I came to realize, needed different competencies. Furthermore, I knew full well that teachers had their own set of professional values and standards which were often different and, in most cases, were more valid than mine. Since rating was demanded, I did it, but only after full confession to each teacher that I very much doubted my judgment and evidence. Generally, I asked a teacher to rate himself; then we would compare ratings and try to reach consensus. I learned that such rating practices imply superiority of judgment on the part of the rater and carry the suggestion of authority. I determined that for the rest of my career, I would shun the appearance of authority among my associates. Leadership must be sustained by knowledge, imagination, competence, not by authority of office.

By the time my seventh year in Kansas City had rolled around, my wife and I had saved enough money for me to take two years off and go to Yale in an attempt to get a Ph.D. Mr. Melcher, the superintendent, approved my leave of absence without pay, to begin the following year. I wrote the Yale authorities and was elated to be accepted and awarded a fellowship that would pay my tuition and $800. However, bad times were ahead. In February, the bank in which our family heritage and other assets and savings were located closed. A department store in which the remainder of our holdings had rested was foreclosed the same month. The family farm had become worthless, also. So I gave up temporarily the idea of further graduate study. The depression with all its despondency was upon us.

Before discussing the next educational era, I wish to summarize the period from 1919 to 1930 as I viewed it. My years (1919-1932) as high school principal, superintendent, and city elementary school principal came during the greatest educational upheaval of all times. The explosions, the excitement, the striving for change following Sputnik seem less significant. Surely the twenties were a time of deeper hope and faith in the power of education, more responsiveness to the tidal waves of social and scientific change, and a greater professional unity.

Because of new visions and new scientific findings in the preceding generation, the twenties found American educators all astir. *Action, change, extension, innovation* were in the air; and the revolution was led by new schools of education (Teachers College, Columbia University, University of Chicago, Stanford, Peabody, State University of Ohio, Yale, etc.). Almost anything in education which had been revered now was challenged, not by outside critics, but by the operators of the schools. Ancient history, Greek, Latin, and grammar were considered irrelevant to the problems of the times and to the diverse enrollments of the high schools. Subject content was measured against the Seven Cardinal Objectives and the immediate needs of the pupils and generally found wanting. Accreditation of high schools was wrested from the grasping hands of the university academicians and placed in regional accreditation associations whose controlling membership was in the hands of secondary school authorities and the "liberals" in the colleges and universities. No longer would the scholars in the institutions of higher learning dictate standards or determine the curriculum for the public schools. Nor were they to write the acceptable textbooks. In fact, the revolution to achieve a curriculum for all was so extreme that the leadership bordered on being anti-intellectual—particularly in the academic and abstract sense. This was a severe and dangerous turn of events, but the curriculum revisionists believed that the needed changes would never be achieved without throwing out the old leadership previously found among higher education scholars. The old establishment centered in the colleges was annihilated, and a new brand of public school leadership took over. Professional teachers' organizations at state and federal levels played dominant roles for the first time.

Likewise, "faculty" psychology and the ancient and accepted theory of transfer of training went into limbo. Since change moves slowly, the curriculum proponents found obstacles to content extension and the inclusion of new solid subjects. Even the teachers had few tools in their kit for handling the new program which society seemed to be demanding. So, inservice education of teachers spurted both in extension programs and in university summer sessions. Local school systems, basing their attack on the findings of the twenties, began major curriculum studies. Charters, Bonser, Babbitt, and a host of other professors of education wrote books, pamphlets, and guidelines for curriculum revision. And, indeed, the traditional college preparation program was nudged aside, in theory at least, to accommodate homemaking, industrial arts, vocational education, modern language, commercial subjects, health and physical education, and problems in American democracy. In fact, sporadic efforts were made to introduce character education as a special subject and, indeed, teacher training in a high school program for those to enter teaching in the elementary schools became almost universal in the middle west.

Practically all state and national conventions of teachers, specialists, and administrators centered their programs on the broadened curriculum and on ways and means to provide better instruction in schools facing up to the challenge of an adequate and suitable education for all.

But the curriculum was not the only battlement to be attacked.

The new educational psychologists were pointing out how much children differed in aptitudes and interests. They insisted that some were handicapped both mentally and physically. They said only a few had the potential to be geniuses. Over and over, however, the cry of the optimist was heard, insisting that every child could be reached in the classroom by the right teacher. Dropouts, for the first time, had the attention of the administrator. Age-grade tables were produced to show that some children were retarded in progress while others were accelerated.

Efforts to recognize the individual's progress included skipping whole grades and promoting semiannually. However, the individuals graduating from high school at midyear were not accommodated by most colleges. The teachers colleges went on the quarter plan, thus accommodating some midyear pupils and also permitting students to complete four years of college in three.

Many new structures and ingenious curriculum organizational groupings were tried. Most progressive school systems had "opportunity" rooms for those classified as disadvantaged, and divided the other students into three groups—X, Y, and Z—according to IQ scores. Track systems were common. Scholastic standards and types of work materials were likewise differentiated according to the rated ability of each group and in some instances of each individual child.

Core curriculums were advocated, while the project method, problem solving approach, and the Dalton Contract arrangement of pupil work schemes became popular. Mrs. Parkhurst's scheme of units as practiced in Dalton, Massachusetts, was the forerunner of programmed learning as rediscovered in the middle of the century. Carleton Washburn and his staff in a small system in Illinois perfected the commendable and successful Winnetka Plan. Accelerated schemes permitting most pupils to complete fifteen years in thirteen were developed. Gary, Indiana, Kansas City, Missouri, and Detroit led the way with the Platoon organizational structure. This was a compromise between the self-contained classroom plan and a completely departmentalized scheme. When properly supervised, organized, and administered, it might well be called the forerunner of the team teaching concept which appeared a quarter of a century later. The plan, too, had the advantage of utilizing all building and playground space to the maximum at all times.

In the twenties, too, the 6-3-3 plan of organization became popular. The writings of G. Stanley Hall and Brandenburg revealed the special problems faced by the adolescent. The junior high school seemed to give aid and assistance to the early adolescence period. The old seventh- and eighth-grade program had become repetitious and unexciting. The junior high school, with an enriched program, a departmental plan of teaching, and extracurricular activities suitable for early adolescents proved a major innovation of the times.

Although a few experiments with the junior college had been tried earlier, the serious efforts in a relatively few places to bring a "practical" college education close to home were rewarding in this decade. The advocates of the junior or community college, like those of the land grant college, believed the curriculum should have comprehensive objectives and should include vocational and technical goals. A new dimension of the junior college was its free admissions and its encouragement of older adults to return for further education. But the junior college seemed doomed to grow slowly or not at all.

Public school educational leaders, convinced that universal education could be made a reality, and aware of the limitations of the regular curriculum, introduced many so-called extracurricular activities. These programs, designed to meet the special interests and aptitudes of all children, were ordinarily carried on by extending the length of the school day. So club activities sponsored by the regular teaching staff covered everything from creative art and musical interests through dramatics, Hi-Y, athletics, and debating to special academic interests such as conversation clubs in Latin and Spanish.

The expanded curriculum called for changes in plants and equipment.

Science laboratories, shops, homemaking areas, health facilities, libraries, gymnasiums, and auditoriums were considered necessary in all new or remodeled schools. Forensics, bands, orchestras, and athletic contests were enjoyed not only by the students but also by the general public. Many school building projects gained community support because a gymnasium and auditorium were considered by the public as essential to success in the fields of athletics and entertainment.

As hard surfaced roads were built to meet the demands of the automobiles, school district reorganization and consolidation became a practical matter, so the enrollment for this period was phenomenal at the secondary level. High schools became larger, affording an enriched curriculum and a multiple-goal institution; the comprehensive high school approached reality.

Superintendents, for the first time, found a need to understand school financing. Budget making and purchasing during this decade took on greater emphasis, and the superintendent was expected to have competence as a business executive, not just as an educator. Colleges of education sought professors who could teach school finance, and knowledge of schoolhouse construction was added to the superintendent's talents. During the twenties, too, a new plan for liquidating school district indebtedness was introduced. Bonds were issued serially, and school boards paid off the school debt on a systematic and annual basis.

CHAPTER III

But back to my story.

In early March of 1932 the assistant superintendent of Kansas City, with whom I played golf, came to visit Whittier School. As he was leaving, he said, "Well, Finis, I guess you will be leaving for Yale in the summer?"

"No," said I, "we have given up the idea." I explained our economic state. I told him that we were financially stripped. He thought we should go anyway. Again, I told him that it was impossible to take a wife and two children to New Haven on no income for two years.

"But," he said, "you should see Mr. Volker. He would lend you the money."

Mr. Volker was a wealthy furniture manufacturer with a huge jobbers' outlet in Kansas City. He was also a well-know philanthropist.

"But I have absolutely no assets or securities to give him," I protested.

Mr. Parker returned a week later and said, "You will see Mr. Volker at 4:30 in his office. I have made an appointment and he is interested in seeing you."

Mr. Volker's roll-top desk was located among many others in an open armory-type building. As I approached, he stood and said, "You are Mr. Engleman. Mr. Parker has been telling me about you. Just how much money would it take to do your studies at Yale?"

"Well," I replied, "in my financial state, I will have to change my plans and go to Yale for only one year to meet my residence requirement. I would then return to save some money before going back the second year."

"How much would you need for this one year?" was his next question.

I thought for a moment and explained that with my fellowship and a few dollars in our checking account, we might make out with $1,000. Quick as a flash, he turned to his desk, took a pen and wrote. He handed me a check for $1,000.

"Why Mr. Volker, I can't take this; I can give you no security."

"Mr. Engleman, I don't want any security, except you. Mr. Parker has told me of your character."

I left with an agreement that I would receive the thousand dollars in ten installments with the first check arriving in September. So, financially at least, we were ready for one year at Yale.

During that whole year before going to Yale, I studied French and especially German. Since these two languages were required at Yale and since the only language I had studied in college was Latin, it seemed wise to pass the language requirements before I began my studies. The officials at Yale had given one of Yale's graduates, then a modern language professor at Southwest Missouri State College, the authority to give my examination. By April, I considered my competence in German adequate to take the examination. I had overestimated my knowledge and skill: I stumbled over Paulen's *Ethics* and failed. Doggedly, I went back to my German, and by July 1, I had passed the second examination. Only two months remained for achieving a respectable reading power in French. Even though I was teaching a full load at Southwest State, I "burned the midnight oil" as I struggled with French. At the end of the summer session we moved to Mrs. Engleman's father's house in Monett. At once, I drove out to a Waldensian French settlement to see an elderly friend whose native language was French. He agreed to tutor me. Thanks to his assiduous help and my long, long hours of work, I passed the examination on September 10, two days before leaving for Yale. What a relief it was to be entering Yale Graduate School with no unmet language requirements hanging over my head.

Then began a rather leisurely journey by Model A Ford to New Haven. Up to that time we had traveled little east of St. Louis. Our route took us to St. Louis, south to old Vincennes, and on to Louisville. When we reached Washington, we found quarters in a tourist home in Falls Church at $2 per day and enthusiastically explored the Capitol, the White House, the National Cathedral, the congressional buildings, the Library of Congress, Arlington Cemetery, Mt. Vernon, Monticello, and various Civil War battlefields. On our way north, we stopped at Gettysburg, Harrisburg, Philadelphia, and New York City. This trip was such a rewarding educational experience that it gave Mrs. Engleman and me a taste for travel which has taken us around the world and into many strange and interesting cultures. To us, traveling is a magnificent way to learn. Surely respect and admiration seem inevitable when one views and contemplates the Pyramids, the Blue Mosque, the Taj Mahal, the city ruins of Afghanistan, the temples of Greece and Rome and of Thailand, Japan, and China. Contact with the music, the art, and the literature of other lands brings the same kind of respect and admiration. America needs nothing more, culturally speaking, than an enrichment of our splendid Judaic-Christian heritage. While the values and cultures of Western Europe have sustained us as an isolated developing country, they are not enough for a world leadership role in the approaching twenty-first century. Somehow, American education must be supplemented by all the world's cultures.

We reported in at Yale upon our arrival and then, after two days of fruitless searching for a furnished apartment that we could afford, we rented a little four-room, unfurnished cottage in West Haven, backed up against a huge cemetery. We then visited second-hand stores for furnishings. Almost immediately after becoming settled in our tiny home, Yale professors began to call and welcome us. Never before, nor since, have we encountered more hospitable people.

The enrollment of the Department of Education was limited to fifty graduate students. A few were working toward master's degrees, but the majority were headed for the doctorate. My graduating group numbered eight and came from the East, the West, the North, and the South. They were mature people, all having at least the foundation of a master's degree, and having left high-ranking positions in colleges or public or private schools.

The program of the department was designed to give the insights and competencies needed for leadership jobs in the schools and communities of America. During the years the Yale Department of Education functioned, it graduated men who were appointed to positions of great responsibility. Some became state commissioners of education; some were appointed university presidents, some college presidents and deans, and some professors; still others became superintendents, principals, headmasters, and assistant city school superintendents. At least one graduate became U.S. Commissioner of Education.

The program was characterized by the participation of professors from several related disciplines. In addition to distinguished professors of school administration, psychology, philosophy, history, personnel, curriculum, and secondary and elementary education, scholars from the Institute of Human Relations, the Gezelle Child Study Clinic, economics, sociology, religion, and government were active in our seminars. There were more faculty members than students in some of the seminars I attended.

Another feature of our program was the insistence that students work on their own initiative and in independent study. The library was fascinating. In addition to the huge Penniman room with its unique stock of educational materials, the whole of Sterling Library was available. I was assigned a private workroom with a key. If I were involved in one area of study, I could hand to the desk a list of books to be used, and within a half day my shelves would be stocked with them. If the need arose, I could have them removed and another 100 put in their place within hours. I could also prowl in the stacks. I particularly enjoyed the great shelves of uncatalogued materials on the schools of earlier days.

Advanced students were expected to do studies in depth as part of the general seminar, and then write their essays. A major paper could be produced each month, or a long comprehensive study could take the whole year. I chose to do research and write on a series of problems which had harassed me as a principal and superintendent. My essays were graded by three professors, each of whom gave me criticisms and suggestions for improvement. Never before had so many scholars been made available for my guidance. Their office doors were always open. Never before had I been in an atmosphere where it was so respectable to be a heretic. Outside of the one convinced of a truth or a hypothesis, everyone else seemed to question. Penetrating doubt emerged even in polite conversation. Yale was, indeed, a place to learn and unlearn.

Since the Engleman budget was tight and since the new federal N.R.A. employment system was in effect, Ruby decided to take a job in the Malley Department Store at $13 a week. We could hire a maid for $7, thus saving $6.

After becoming deeply involved with my studies, it seemed highly advisable for me not to leave at the end of the first year but to continue in residence until I earned the Ph.D. With the help of the chairman of the department, I succeeded in getting an evening part-time job as associate director of the New Haven YMCA Evening Junior College. It would pay $1,800—enough, I believed, to see the Englemans through another year at Yale. But I had the obligation of my one year's loan from Mr. Volker. I wrote to him explaining the situation and requesting permission to postpone starting payments on my debt, but promised that I would send the first year's interest. By return mail came these encouraging and generous words: "Mr. Engleman, I authorize postponement for one year of your installments on the principal. There is no interest for the first or second year." I resolved that though I could never completely repay my indebtedness to this man, I would try to repay it to humanity by giving aid to members of the oncoming generation. My experience with Mr. Volker has served to sustain my confidence in the human race over the years, even when I have observed instances of man's inhumanity to man.

Because I had a sort of faculty status as a teaching fellow, and because we secured strong recommendations, we were awarded season tickets to the Yale Theater of the Graduate School of Drama, on condition that we write a careful critique of each play.

We took advantage of many other cultural advantages afforded by the university. Endowed lectures brought great men from afar. We seldom missed a Bergen lecture, and the Law School permitted our attendance when great jurists and politicians graced the campus.

The faculty of the department and candidates for the doctorate had two outings each year. In the fall, when New England foliage was at its best, we journeyed to Buckland, the home of the founder of Mt. Holyoke College, Mary Lyon. The home had been converted into a delightful old inn. In the spring, former graduates were included in a trek to Jug End Barn in western Massachusetts. There, the Saturday evening was devoted to an essay presentation by one of the postdoctoral guests, followed by dialogue and debate.

On alternate Saturday nights, the eight members of my class and their wives had potluck dinner at one of our cramped apartments. Everybody dressed—the men in tuxedos and the women in formal long dresses. We always procured a record player for the dancing, having fun on a very limited budget.

There wasn't much time, but Ruby and I found some for reading biographies of Tom Paine, Benedict Arnold, Thomas Hart Benton, Andrew Jackson, James Fenimore Cooper, and others. Our interest in biography has persisted to the present time.

The research dissertation caused discomfort for most students, distress and frustration for some. The standards were high and the readers severe; the final oral examination sometimes led to dismissal without the degree. Since I planned to continue in administration and curriculum work, the faculty seemed to expect me to choose for research a problem directly connected with local, state or federal administration. I had other ideas. For two reasons, I wanted to do an experimental study in children's reading materials. First, I believed that detailed information and firsthand experience with the learning process give one the best basis for many decisions he must make as an administrator. Second, I had written two books with informational content in conversational style. I had a hunch that this style was better for children than narrative-expository style. But the study not only had to be accepted as possessing the potential for revealing hitherto uncovered data, it also had to have a design that would produce the data for valid and reliable conclusions. Since I had thought about it for months before reaching New Haven, I was able during the first semester of the first year to present my proposal to what was called the dissertation seminar, held at intervals. The faculty attended in a body and candidates for the Ph.D. likewise were invited. After the student's presentation, the fur would begin to fly. Many times I saw ill-prepared students, or those with proposals that contained pitfalls they had been unaware of, come to tears and leave the rostrum deeply humiliated. After considerable discussion, my proposal was given the green light, but two interested professors followed me out of the seminar room and urged that I begin my preparation of materials at once.

My first big job was to go through children's literature at the third-grade and sixth-grade levels to find samples of appropriate length and in both conversation and narrative-expository style. Then, for each sample, I must write another version in the opposite style. Both must be found by a jury of writers of children's books to be similar in every respect except for literary style.

These steps completed, I went to a printer, even though my funds were meager, and had printed two thousand copies, together with four thousand tests of content for each of my seventy-six samples. The thirty-eight for the third grade were printed in larger type than those for the sixth, to stimulate reading conditions found in each grade. I wanted to discover whether children preferred one over the other, whether they understood content more accurately with one or the other, whether they read one faster than the other, and which they retained best. The materials and tests were given to 1800 children daily for thirty-eight days. The teachers were given methods of determining how many children chose each version and their reading speeds for each. After sixty days, the tests were readministered to check retention.

Needless to say, I found myself with quite a statistical study. In fact, there were seventy-four tables of critical ratios. The study stood the test of critical review, and on graduation day I found myself in the line of march to Woolsey Hall. The Ph.D. candidates were called to the platform to be vested one by one with hood and to be given a handshake by President Angel. I was so excited I almost tripped over the feet of President Franklin Delano Roosevelt, who was there to receive an honorary degree.

Next day, I relaxed and realized just how tired I was. For the past two years I had been under considerable strain, and during the past ten months I had averaged fifteen hours of work a day. I felt one tinge of disappointment: the new Ph.D. hadn't produced a new job. Jobs were scarce in any field in 1934. I consoled myself with the fact that I would be teaching summer school at Albany State College and that my old job was being held for me in Kansas City. Furthermore, I had an all-honors record in my graduate work at a great university, and the satisfaction of knowing that my mental horizons had been stretched.

The summer in Albany went well, and fall found me settling back into the routine at Whittier School. I wrote several articles for publication and found myself frequently called upon to make speeches. The superintendent entertained us more often and placed me on numerous working committees.

The following fall, I was telephoned by a reporter on the *Kansas City Star*. He wanted to know if I was accepting the job in Connecticut.

I asked, "What job?"

He explained that the Associated Press carried a message from Hartford saying the State Board of Education that morning had elected Finis Engleman as principal of the state Normal School in New Haven.

"If this is true," I said, "I will be on my way to Connecticut soon."

Again the phone rang. It was Mr. Melcher, the Kansas City superintendent, asking me to stop by on my way home. When I did, he urged me to wait a day before deciding. The Kansas City school board was meeting that night, he said, and they should be allowed the privilege of bidding for my services. I thanked him but explained that his board had been given the opportunity to bid for my services but had remained dormant, and that if I got confirmation of my appointment in New Haven, I would accept.

When I arrived home, the telegram confirming my selection was awaiting me, as were reporters from both Kansas City papers. I sent an affirmative telegram to Dr. Butterfield, the secretary of the Connecticut Board of Education.

When meeting that afternoon with Mr. Melcher, I had asked permission to leave at once if the report was true. He agreed for me to go when I had packed and completed obligations at the school. A frantic week began. The next morning's newspapers alerted a lot of people. Moving companies, real estate agents, automobile dealers, and many others called for business. Quickly, we agreed on a moving company. I traded the old Ford for a good secondhand Dodge. Financial dealings of many kinds were consummated. *All* the relatives in Missouri and Oklahoma arrived, dozens of friends insisted on entertaining us, and, of course, I worked full time at Whittier.

We were ready to go by the next Friday afternoon. We stopped at Whittier, where baskets of food were shoved in our laps as we said farewell to the faculty—that wonderful group of old and young who had taught me much.

CHAPTER IV

During my long career in education, we moved many times. The worst feature of leaving a community is parting with friends, but, on the other hand, the best part of arriving in a new community is the opportunity to make new ones.

Two days' driving brought us to Connecticut. I left the family in Hamden while I went to the commissioner of education in Hartford to report for duty.

Next morning, I reported to my office in the Normal School building at 2 Howe Street. I found a small but devoted faculty, together with the one secretary, waiting to greet me. As the months and years went by, their loyalty to the highest ideals in education, their cooperative spirit, and their scholarly effectiveness were proved over and over.

My first assistant, Genevieve Leary, was the director of teacher training. That meant that she was head of the professional program of the curriculum and general supervisor to the three training laboratory schools. These schools were, in reality, part of the New Haven system. The city compensated the state to the amount which they spent per capita for other schools, while the state, through the Normal College, added sums to raise salaries above the average and enrich the materials and equipment resources. The training schools were administered by the president of the Teachers College. The teachers were state employees, but the janitors, unfortunately, were subject to the authority of the city superintendent. Dr. Leary proved to be not only the director of teacher training, but also a sort of deputy president. She was a professional expert with great energy and extreme ability, and she advised me wisely on all important decisions. I have never known a person who could inspire students and teachers quite so effectively.

The faculty was female except for me and three others, two of whom were part time. There were about 350 students, all of them girls. This came as a surprise to me, because teachers colleges of the Middle West were coeducational, with enrollments of men often matching those of women. I immediately resolved to try to remedy the lack of sex balance in both faculty and students at Teachers College. During the next few years more and more male students were enrolled, but the salary schedules tended to make the addition of male professors slow. The male students soon made a place for themselves. The male quartet, the basketball team, the masculine debaters brought new dimensions. They also became good elementary school teachers.

Since I had made careful study while in Kansas City of the problems of learning and instruction for younger children, I had fairly well-formed opinions of what the teacher education program should be. To my gratification, I found that the curriculum pattern developed by the combined faculties of the four Connecticut teacher training institutions under the excellent guidance of Mr. Franklin Pierce was of a frontier character. Mr. Pierce was the state director of teacher education. Although there were no electives except when determining the grade level of teaching, the curriculum was well-balanced between the academic fields and the so-called professional ones. The professional foundation was a strong curriculum in child psychology and educational psychology. There was also a comprehensive curriculum materials and methods course, backed by two extended periods of carefully supervised student teaching. All students received general education in the social studies, English, science, mathematics, art, and music. At that time, no modern language was offered.

The student body was selected with great care. Admission was considered a privilege, not a right. No student was permitted to apply unless he ranked in the upper half of his graduating class. Usually twice as many applied as the 125 who could be accepted by the quota system. A selection team, including the president and the registrar, assembled all the personal and academic data on master sheets. These data included: (1) score on a mental test, (2) scores in academic subject tests, (3) rank in graduating class, (4) a recommendation for teaching by high school principal, (5) medical examination data, (6) observation and interview by a psychiatric consultant, and (7) a writing specimen. The team members individually reviewed the data and ranked the students in order of their preference. The rankings of the team usually agreed on the first 75 of the 125. The team then met and by consensus selected the other 50.

To determine those who would be advised to drop out or transfer, a form was given to each faculty member at the end of each semester. He was asked to list the ten students he had taught who, in his judgment, were least fitted to be elementary school teachers, and the ten he considered to have strongest potential for this career. The data were then tabulated in the office and used for discussions with the faculty. How revealing these data and subsequent faculty dialogues proved to be!

While at Teachers College, I continued a practice I had previously followed in dealing with personnel difficulties, either faculty or student. When a teacher was in difficulty or when I felt one needed help, I made it a rule never to request an appointment in my office. I always waited for the opportunity to see the teacher as he sat in his own room and chair. When serious personnel matters are to be discussed, I believed the one in the subordinate position should be made to feel secure. A teacher's office or his room is his castle, and any authority intervening to help has best chance of success when he is the guest. Furthermore, curious observers usually suspect something amiss when associates are seen reluctantly entering the door behind which legal authority is known to reside. Again, it is my belief that authority—even the appearance of authority—should be shunned by school administrators. This does not mean that administrators shouldn't make decisions or structure management for orderly achievement. But the authority of knowledge, of wisdom, of human understanding, not the legal authority of office, is the authority of distinction and success and, in fact, the only authority in which colleagues can place their trust.

With students in trouble, too, I resisted calling them on the carpet. Rather, I sought opportunity to engage them in friendly conference on the athletic field, in the gymnasium, in the corridor, or sitting on the stairway steps. No person is likely to resolve his personal problems when in a defensive posture or attitude.

In the thirties adolescent girls began to smoke. It became obvious to me that girls and boys, too, left the campus to loiter at nearby "joints" and smoke. We discussed the matter in faculty meetings and with student leaders. Finally, we agreed to establish a coed lounge with smoking privileges. In order that the commissioner and state board would get the story straight, I carefully wrote a report on our policy and why. I was told some board members raised eyebrows, but the policy was approved. Faculty members, after observing the lounge in operation, agreed that it had solved some problems.

For several years, a plan proposed by the commissioner of education had been in effect in Connecticut. Of the four normal colleges, only one, the Teachers College of Connecticut, had a four-year program and granted a degree. The other three had no graduates. They simply transferred all juniors to the New Britain Teachers College for the fourth year. Hardly anyone liked the plan, and the students at Willimantic, Danbury, and New Haven, where they had developed loyalties and school spirit, resented the whole scheme.

In 1936 the legislators from the three regions began to feel the pressure. They came to visit and said they were going to make all four schools into four-year colleges with degree-granting privileges extended to all. Even at the Teachers College of Connecticut at New Britain, there was greater unity and cohesion.

I have believed since arrival as president that the college should attempt to serve the community in many ways. Accordingly, during the late thirties I found funds to bring a strong man from an Illinois university to head a new evening school and adult education department.

Within a short time after the college had four-year standing, my formal inauguration was held, with the state board, the governor, and prominent Yale personnel present. Speaking of the governor, I wish to say that rarely did the governor of Connecticut interfere politically with education, either higher or lower. Dr. Wilbur Cross, a former dean of the Yale Graduate School, served as governor during the early years while I was president. He was exceedingly interested in the public schools and in the teachers colleges. He gave several lectures in our little college and proved to be a staunch friend. He was at his best when sipping a Scotch, smoking a big black cigar, and discussing Shakespeare.

It was an edict of his, however, that caused me great mental turmoil and could have ended my stay in Connecticut. Tax revenues during the depression continued to be short. The governor was pressed to find funds to support state services. As a result, he told all agencies, including the state board of education, that they must cut their appropriations by a large percent. The state board passed the directive along to its several units. My budget had already been restricted unbearably by the commissioner. I went to work on my budget, however, and finally came up with a saving beyond that demanded of my unit. When I presented my figures at the next board meeting, much to my amazement the commissioner stated that I would have to cut another 10 percent. I looked at the board in distress and again presented my facts of savings. The situation was embarrassing because the commissioner had reduced my budget without telling me. I was operating from a different base line from that of my boss, and the board at first didn't see my predicament. So the chairman of the board, a strong supporter of the commissioner's views, said, "Dr. Engleman, please take your records to Mr. Pierce's office and return after you have achieved the commissioner's request."

I was terribly agitated, but I tried to hold my composure. When I got to Mr. Pierce's office, I began to cut again. I first took out my own salary. I was convinced that the college couldn't run without a minimum faculty, and we were at a minimum. It could, however, survive without a president. I then found other services that brought the total to the figure demanded. At that minute, Mr. Pierce came in and asked to see my next recommendations. When he saw that I was headed for resignation, he said, "You can't do that—I won't permit it. Go back with your other reductions and I will ask them to accept."

I returned and told them that the figures were not reduced as much as the chairman had demanded but that if the New Haven budget were to be cut further, they would have to do it, since I believed the only further cut that would not destroy the college would be to leave the presidency open. With that, I arose and excused myself and drove home to dress for the junior prom which was being held that night. I was dejected and considered myself disgraced in front of the board. The juggling of figures by the central office infuriated me. I doubted that the board members had understood how I had been crossed up and that I was reducing my budget more than was demanded of other unit heads, including the central office.

About 11 P.M. a state board member made her appearance at the dance. She came to me and said, "Dr. Engleman, please cheer up. Every board member respected you highly for what you said and did. After you left, they restored a considerable number of your cuts."

The second crisis to face us at the New Haven State Teachers College came a little later. Governor Raymond Baldwin was elected chief executive. State revenues were at a low ebb, and other forms of taxation were avoided. The proposed executive budget was due for announcement. The new state commissioner, Dr. Alonzo Grace, came to New Haven to speak to the Rotary Club. After the luncheon, he called me aside and confided that it was his belief that our budget requests had been approved by the executive branch. Naturally, I was pleased. Imagine my surprise the next day when my secretary met me at the door as I returned from lunch and cried out, "The governor has just been on the radio, and he announced the closing of both New Haven and Willimantic Colleges." Telephone conversations with Hartford confirmed her statement.

The evening paper gave the Governor's reasons. The overall budget must be cut. The Governor alleged that New Haven and Willimantic had very high per capita student costs and their student placements were low. Furthermore, the state had too many public colleges. There was no indication that he had given consideration to the future status of students or faculty. Obviously, both were to be abandoned.

That night and the next day I studied his charges. Soon the data available showed his charges on all counts to be in grave error. Patiently, I waited for consolation and promise of support from the state board authorities. Not a word was said or written. I called the president of Willimantic and we decided to fight. Mrs. Engleman and I announced a "hard luck and tacky dress" party for the faculty. We served "sow belly and beans with corn bread." The faculty came in costume; the entertainment was frivolous and satirical. But morale and unity rose to new heights which were sustained during the next ninety days.

In the height of excitement and suspense as the legislature weighed the governor's proposal to close the college, the faculty proposed an evening party at the college to be attended by the faculty and representatives of all the four classes to build further unity and morale. Each class produced a satirical skit, and the faculty agreed to put on a "stunt." The faculty committee, as part of their skit, proposed that I appear in tights and swing from a trapeze suspended from the ceiling of the gymnasium as they sang "The Daring Young Man on the Flying Trapeze." I accepted the challenge boldly, but my heart faltered as I ran on to the floor in the presence of the students and saw that trapeze being dropped to where I could reach it only by a mighty leap. "What if I couldn't get aboard?" But those shouting, singing professors gave me the energy to climb aboard and swing lustily to the music below.

From that moment on, when I appeared on stage at a student assembly, they would break into singing "The Man on the Flying Trapeze."

I made charts—big ones. I would say to my audience, "The Governor charges ... but here are the facts." I would then throw before my audience in bold relief contradictory information. "It is said that our per capita costs are too high. Here are the facts and comparisons between New Haven, the University of Connecticut, New Britain, and Danbury." The charges against New Haven were false in every instance. PTA associations, Chambers of Commerce, Rotary Clubs, Kiwanians, and other civic organizations of southern Connecticut asked me to tell the story. The public was aroused, and faculty and students became further consolidated.

Soon legislators and friends of the governor got the correct facts. A resolution was proposed in both houses of the legislature requesting that the finance committee restore the budgets of both colleges. By that time, the governor realized that he had been misled. Although I never found out who misadvised him, I had strong beliefs on the matter. At any rate, the whole crisis served to unite student body and faculty in a common cause. Survival is a strong motive.

The teacher training program at New Haven was founded upon rigid admission standards, but the selection of those entering the junior year as teachers was based on still higher personal requirements. The first two years were devoted to academic foundations in such areas as social studies, English, mathematics, science, and fine arts. The third and fourth years were divided about evenly between professional experiences and studies such as psychology, sociology, curriculum materials and methods, and student teaching and the continuation of the first two years in academic fields. Possibly the strongest aspect of the professional experience was the opportunity to be guided closely by an expert teacher during the student teaching period. Correlated with this experience was a supporting program of reading and dialogue with specialists and experts on materials and methods in the several areas of the elementary school curriculum.

In the thirties, no colleges or universities in Connecticut conducted summer sessions for teachers. The state director of teacher education, with approval of the state board, decided to authorize a financially self-supporting summer session on the Yale campus. All scholastic records were kept on file in the state department and used for certification and in some instances for salary increments.

During the school year 1935-36, Mr. Pierce, the state director of teacher education, proposed that I organize the summer session, make all arrangements with Yale, employ the faculty, and serve as director. He felt that my office was so near Yale that I could handle both jobs during the eight-week period. I jumped at the chance. In addition to providing another educational experience, the salary of $500 would be a welcome addition. We selected most of the faculty from Connecticut institutions of higher learning: Yale, University of Connecticut, Wesleyan, Trinity, Connecticut College for Women, and all the Teachers Colleges. Some were drawn from out-of-state universities such as Rutgers and Syracuse. Yale University donated the space for offices and classrooms and made available at minimum charges, the Sterling Memorial Library and the men's dormitories, used mostly by mature women teachers doing refresher courses. I continued as director of the Yale Summer Session until the Second World War began.

Yale honored me by appointing me as a lecturer in the department of education. I met one graduate seminar each week of advanced students and sponsored the writing of at least one doctoral dissertation. Often on the weekends, when preparing to meet the Monday's seminar took the time I wanted for recreation, I regretted my assignment. But when Monday class time arrived, I was again stimulated by working and thinking with my small group of bright young men. It was my seminars during these years that stretched my mental horizons. All during my presidency and while I was State Commissioner of Education, I had the rank of full professor at Yale, but with a minimum stipend. The position afforded me a number of special privileges, such as membership in the Yale Faculty Club and the Yale Golf Course, reduced price for football tickets, and access to the Yale Library.

Mr. Pierce, the state director of teacher education and general supervisor of the teachers colleges, died suddenly in 1937. The new state commissioner of education, Dr. Alonzo Grace, called me immediately and asked me to take over the responsibilities carried by Mr. Pierce and at the same time to continue as president in New Haven. I explained that I thought it unwise for one president to have authority over other presidents. However, if it were made clear to the other college heads that I would serve as chairman of the group, with no specific powers over them other than as presiding officer in meetings, I would give it a trial. The plan worked, and the four of us did more productive planning and evaluating than any of us thought possible. I not only presided, I took notes, prepared agendas, and dictated our actions within hours of our adjournment.

The colleges had been given little power to grow and minimum resources. So it was during the period prior to the war that future building programs, programs of services, and faculty developments were designed at the monthly presidents' meetings. The complex multipurpose comprehensive college program that is now in full flower in the colleges was dreamed of and planned for by this team of presidents prior to 1941. A spirit of comradeship and unification grew, and old conflicts of special interests and struggles for prestige diminished. I have had few professional friends that I treasure more than Ralph Jenkins, Ruth Hass, Herbert Welte, and George Shaefer.

During my tenure at the college, I became somewhat active on the national scene. At the first meeting of the American Association of Teachers Colleges following my appointment, I was elected vice-president. Almost immediately, I was appointed to the Accreditation Committee. This took me to many colleges on inspection tours. Furthermore, I assisted in developing annual convention agenda. At that time no Connecticut Teachers College had been accredited by a national agency. New Haven asked for inspection and was the first Connecticut state college to be accredited.

I was asked to give lectures to college faculties and to staffs of school systems. Some of these addresses were revised, polished, and published in professional magazines.

The American Council on Education had a big foundation-subsidized teacher education study underway. They asked the American Association of Teachers Colleges to evaluate it. The Association membership selected Professor Carl Matthews of Denton State College and me to make the evaluation and submit a report. All these activities threw me in contact with college officials in many states.

Because of my involvement as an officer in the American Association of Teachers Colleges, my name somehow came to the attention of Mrs. Franklin Delano Roosevelt. Consequently, with a small group of teachers, college presidents and university deans, I was invited to dinner at the White House. Up to that time I had seen Mrs. Roosevelt only once, during my attendance at Yale when she spoke at an education conference in New York. The cartoonists had given me a bad image of her, and I had been prepared to dislike her. However, as she walked down the aisle and onto the stage, I was captivated. Never before had I seen a person so dynamic and humanitarian.

With this experience behind me, I could hardly wait to arrive at the White House. I have vivid recollections of that dinner with Mrs. Roosevelt.

Although I had violent nervous headaches periodically until after I left active school administration, my health was good and my energy boundless. However, the tensions of being president of a teachers college brought on a condition diagnosed by the family physician as beginning ulcers. He advised me to go to a famous diagnostician, who put me in the hospital for two weeks and ran many tests. Finally, he sent for Mrs. Engleman and asked, "What time do you folks have dinner in the evening?"

She answered, "Oh, about six, as soon as my husband gets home."

"Don't," he said. "Instead of having dinner ready, please have cocktails ready and don't eat until the two of you have a couple and relax."

"But we don't drink," she objected.

"Well, begin and try my prescription."

We reluctantly started a new family custom and two things happened—first, we became reacquainted and grew to like the relaxed social hour; second, I have never had a touch of ulcers since.

With all the problems that beset a teachers college administrator during the depression years, there were many qualities of the times that were sustaining and stimulating. Perhaps a description of the education of that era is permissible here. Even though the great period of discovery and expansion in the field of public education during the first quarter of the twentieth century was followed by the great economic depression, the thirties gave birth to our greatest social advances. The stock market tumbled, making paupers of millionnaires; banks closed, destroying the savings of millions; mortgages on houses and farms were foreclosed, driving a whole multitude from home and livelihood; factories closed and unemployment was rampant. Still, most Americans did not panic and dash headlong to anarchy.

Even in the midst of misery, doubt, and poverty, America clung to her belief in her basic institutions, the fundamentals of the free enterprise system, the democratic republican form of government, deriving its power from the consent of the governed, and, above all else, in the worth and dignity of the individual man. This country was further democratized, and economic class barriers were smashed. Instead of abandoning their government and democratic philosophy, Americans set vigorously to work to make it serve them better. Instead of deserting the public schools, they appropriated a bigger percent of the national income for education than at any other time in the nation's history. With an imaginative and convincing Franklin Roosevelt at the head, America's faith in her ideals and herself faltered hardly at all. Instead of destroying public institutions, such as the public schools, the people determined to make them better serve their purposes.

All this really encouraged the new philosophy that freedom to develop, freedom to be different, freedom to create, freedom to learn almost anything, and freedom to explore should be guarantees assured by the schools. Perhaps the writings of John Dewey more than anything else caused youth and adults not to forsake but to alter democratic institutions. At any rate the urge to enable all pupils to have equal opportunities and access to education at any level and at all ages went surging through the nation. The unique destiny of every man found support as never before. Education was extended upward and downward, and the curriculum was broadened to include a broad spectrum of subjects designed to meet almost all interests and inclinations of children, youths, and adults. Electives and extracurricular activities became major aspects of the school program. The arts, poetry, and drama took on new and enlarged proportions. Teaching methods designed to serve the diverse natures and abilities of children were introduced in great variety. Resistance to the formal testing and homogeneous groupings so revered in the twenties took almost belligerent form. Disciplinary methods with rigid teacher domination gave way to a belief in freedom and self-discipline. Freedom for children became the watchword in home and school. Student government at all ages took on new and enlarged dimensions.

The old seating arrangements in formal rows and the somewhat military routine governing pupil movements gave way to informal groupings and flexible arrangement of furniture and materials of learning. Likewise, self-direction, self-learning, and self-discipline became major goals of the schools. The whole community in many school systems became a laboratory for learning. The frog pond, the forest, the farm, as well as the factory, the transportation system, and local and state governmental operations were visited and studied. Outdoor education and camping received new status.

The great thinkers and leaders became responsive to this great cultural emphasis. The deep-seated desires of the common man that his child have opportunity, that his personality, wishes, and inherent freedom be protected even at a tender age, found supporters among the educational philosophers, the psychologists, the curriculum makers, and many teachers. Mental hygiene experts, psychiatrists, and guidance experts became part of the educational team. Indeed, the revolution in methods, goals, and curriculum was real, as was a new respect and sometimes reverence for the child at an early age. Humanitarian goals rose to ascendency.

During this period, the revealing Progressive Education Society's five-year study, under the direction of Dr. Ralph Tyler, was completed. Among its findings was the well supported claim that success in college was dependent more on how effectively a student achieved in high school than on what subjects he pursued. The study denied the long-held concept that one "prepares" for college by taking certain required subject matter. The study, of course, was acclaimed by those who contended that children should have freedom to choose what they were to learn and was denied by those who continued to believe that certain subjects not only were of greatest all-round worth, but that they also had "disciplinary" or transferable qualities. The school and college curriculum was greatly altered, and the freedom of choice through the elective system, together with the cafeteria offerings found in so many institutions, made for great diversity in the educational patterns possessed by high school or college graduates. Since older concepts of what education is of most worth were challenged, likewise, the instruments of examination and measurement took on many forms. Since the individual student was given more status as a measurer of his own educational progress, standardized examinations were used less often, especially by college admission authorities. Evaluators became more concerned with measuring interests, special aptitudes, creative powers, emotional qualities, and personal development. Although the policy of serving individual interests and goals and of granting much greater freedom had many desirable effects on education, it also led to vagueness of purpose with some teachers and some pupils and sloppiness in quality for others. In an effort to allow self-direction and access to special individual interests, some teachers did not give the guidelines many pupils needed.

The federal government stepped into the public education world in a number of ways during the depression. Youth out of school and out of work were given opportunities to work and study in the giant Civilian Conservation Corps. Problems of youth not being met by local and state education authorities were subsidized by Congress and directed by the U.S. Army.

Public works programs and adult and nursery school educational operations became extensive. New ideas were rampant concerning the nature and scope of education at these two age extremes of the school enrollment. Thus, in the period of material scarcity, when the practical aspects of education would have seemed to be the place of emphasis, the creative arts and the social sciences, particularly government, held high places in the educational offerings. Artists, actors, musicians, and writers were given not only instruction free of tuition, but also employment to ply their art.

School lunches, especially milk, were part of a renewed effort to make health a major objective of education. Cooperation among public health officials, leaders in welfare, mental hygiene societies, conservation authorities, and the schools reached a new high.

Another development which again reflected society's renewed interest in the individual man was the expansion of two-year Normal Schools to four-year state teachers colleges.

Another significant development in this era was the growing number of state teachers colleges that became state colleges with multipurpose curricula and greatly expanded resources in facilities and faculties. But possibly of greatest moment in higher education was a rapid growth in the number of junior colleges and community colleges.

The spirit of the American public during the thirties which gave impetus to the concept of human dignity and freedom of action and belief expressed itself in the areas of adult human relations. The whole philosophy of authority within the hierarchy of the professional staff underwent change. Supervisors began to operate "on call" in local school systems and in state departments of education. Administration moved toward a team approach with teachers assuming a professional role with more dignity, more rights, more freedom, and more responsibility. Group dynamics as a means of reaching decision and synthesis became popular. Professional organizations were formed to assure greater protection from authority and from abuse by those that tradition had supported. Thus, state teachers associations took on a new dimension.

The conviction that a free people could control and reshape the whole social, cultural, political, and economic complex found expression in many proposals for social progress. Some were sound and others were visionary, if not downright unworkable and dangerous to a free man, but the people were willing to try the new while not destroying all the old.

Charles A. Beard wrote a particularly valuable document for the Education Policies Commission, a newly formed education deliberative group. The title of this brochure, adopted unanimously by this group of distinguished educators, was "The Unique Function of Education in a

Democracy." This publication had a profound effect on the public schools for many years.

About the same time Dr. George Counts, a professor at Teachers College, Columbia University, wrote the controversial document, "Dare the Schools Build a New Social Order?" Other leaders expressed the same sentiment. The writings of Professor John Dewey, Bode and William Heard Kilpatrick were avidly read and their theories accepted by many. The central theme in many of these theories placed the individual on a higher plane, but at the same time related him to the society of which he was a part. They insisted that the individual had no obligation to society, but, with hardly any exception, the school leaders insisted that society's government must be responsive to the will of the individual citizen. Naturally, these theories, this spirit, reflected itself in a strong emphasis on the rights and special interests and aptitudes of the individual pupil.

It is not strange, therefore, that student government as a school policy found many supporters. Neither is it strange that young people clothed with power given them by their elders and with limited experience in self-discipline and the principles of justice over-exercised their newly given authority. But children and youth who were permitted to learn through doing succeeded in self-government to a surprising degree. Furthermore, their new freedom seemed to impose broader concepts of ethics. At any rate, the "honor system" was adopted as a policy in many schools and colleges. Thus, the individual was trusted not only to use good judgment but also to be ethical and honest when his own welfare was deeply involved. Some pupils faltered under the strain of some examinations, but reports of successes were more prevalent than those of failures.

During this period, too, the home and the school formed a much closer bond of partnership. The parent-teacher organization, formed more than a quarter of a century earlier, had a new birth of life. School after school formed local units. Not only did these organizations raise money voluntarily to supplement the purchase of badly needed materials of instruction, but they also formed thousands of mother study groups to learn more about child growth and development. Furthermore, they became strong and effective supporters of better school budgets, increased tax levies, and school building bond drives.

Furthermore, the popular concept that the mind of every child was improvable and that all children should have equal opportunity gave impetus to the trend toward compulsory school attendance. The permissible leaving age ranged from fourteen to eighteen. It should be pointed out that the purpose behind compulsory attendance laws was not so much to compel children to attend school as to force communities to give them the opportunity for an education and, of course, to keep them off the labor market.

In other words, the whole management, operation, and administration of schools became more democratic during the thirties. Even school boards began to be conscious that the times demanded personnel policies that were designed to achieve sound selection of staff, fair promotions, and reasonable assurance of the security of teachers. The old and venerable concept of benevolent despot rapidly diminished in administration and in school board policy during the depression years.

The Day of Infamy

Suddenly, on one quiet Sunday afternoon, the radio shook the nation with the report of the attack on Pearl Harbor. Americans suddenly realized that they, too, were in the midst of a world war they had watched with detachment. Almost everybody seemed to sense that our nation was in serious danger.

Almost all the male students of the college began to prepare for service in one way or another. Special curricula were designed and arrangements were made at once for flying instructions. Within six months, faculty members began to enlist. Mr. Artemus Gates, assistant Navy secretary for air, requested an interview with me. He had heard of my many contacts with college officials. He had also learned that I had Navy wings. He said the Navy needed me. Would I accept a commission as lieutenant commander and work with the colleges that had V12 programs? He wanted me also to counsel cadets toward the Bureau of Aeronautics of the Navy.

I went home and talked with the family. The patriotic fervor was so great that my wife and daughters agreed that I should "join up." The state board gave me a leave of absence for the duration of the war, and E. Ward Ireland was selected as acting president. Another unexpected chapter of my life was about to begin.

CHAPTER V

The Second Hitch—World War II

In due time, my orders arrived and I was directed to report to the Officers Indoctrination School at Quonset Point, Rhode Island. The winter of 1942 had come, so the outside drill and cold barracks made life for a forty-seven-year-old man a bit rugged. The program was quite similar to the one I had undergone at MIT in 1917. In a few instances, the courses of 1917 and 1942 were almost identical. For example, Seamanship, Navigation, and Naval History were much the same. Having passed these courses twenty-five years earlier with distinctly high marks, and being only mediocre at Quonset Point, I had earlier convictions confirmed about the lack of value to be derived from repetition of grades. For years I had doubted the wisdom of failure and grade repetition as school policy. Now I was convinced that a child would learn more in promoted grades than he would in failure and repetition.

But some courses, such as Courts and Boards, Navy Regulations and Airplane and Ship Instant Recognition, proved exceedingly interesting and helpful. To observe an air station first hand and to witness the coming and going of aircraft carriers opened new vistas also. I successfully met all standards by graduation time. Being stationed at Quonset Point Air Station gave me new and needed experiences with modern aircraft operations and the new role of airplane carriers.

A few days before my class was to leave, my orders arrived. I was to report to Chicago and prepare to carry out the duties previously discussed with the assistant secretary for air. All seemed well. I called Mrs. Engleman and she immediately made contact with friends in Chicago who would start a search for our living quarters.

On the morning of graduation, my orders were cancelled and new ones arrived. I was to proceed to Bremerton, Washington, for assignment there. I accepted the directive and tried to explain to the family.

When I arrived in Bremerton, I took my orders to the admiral, who had received no instruction as to my assignment. He, in turn, asked me to report to the naval district admiral in Seattle. I reported and, again, no one in that office could advise me what I was supposed to do. I was dejected and a bit deflated. Surely the navy had an important role for me. I reported back to the Bremerton headquarters and was advised to go to the navy shipbuilding yards in Tacoma and look over the situation there —especially the pre-commission detail of the "Baby" carriers. These useful vessels were being produced at the rate of one launching every two weeks. Crews and officers had to be recruited and trained at an amazing rate.

When I walked in to pay my compliments to the officer in charge of this important operation, I was met with the question, "Where in the hell have you been?" He explained the problem of recruiting men from the big pool of enlisted personnel at Bremerton and then putting them through the schools, such as gunnery, communications, small boat handling, catapult operations, plane handling on decks, and fire fighting. He had tried several officers as heads of this aspect of his operation, but they didn't seem to have the rank or the competence to compete with other officers recruiting and training men for mine layers, destroyer escorts, landing craft, and the like. He told me to go back to Bremerton and produce.

I did and had a wonderful educational experience. Urgency and production were essential. Since I had always been in a hurry, the assignment was acceptable and satisfying. The goals were clear and the time always short. Inefficiency in the training of men for any specialized service on a carrier man-of-war could mean loss of ship and crew. As I recruited and worked with men and officers, I tried to get across the conviction that lack of skill and lack of knowledge would mean self-destruction. Every enlisted man and officer must see his duty and do it.

I not only recruited, but also entered actively into the supervision and activities of these schools. I tried to put into practice everything I knew about teaching and learning. In cases such as the fire fighting school, where I knew nothing about the program, I wrote myself orders and reported for a few days as an enrollee dressed in dungarees to learn first-hand as a student.

The shipbuilders at Tacoma were most considerate and would permit men and officers who completed training before the ship was launched to come aboard and become familiar with the ship's intricate construction. Thus, the damage control officer could be assured that much of the crew knew intimately the arrangement of bulkheads, entryways, communication conduits, and the whole wiring system. The men who would use them studied the guns, catapults, small boat cradles, ammunition lockers, and the like as they put them in place. Having eight hundred men and sixty officers trained and ready to man a carrier every two weeks was a responsibility of no mean proportions.

In addition to directing the preparation of the enlisted men and petty officers, I helped officers as best I could. Some would finish school or overseas assignments weeks before the completion of their new carrier. Others would arrive the day of the launching. But I tried to know each group, even if only in a social way. I assisted in organizing them into an efficient administrative structure with spirit and morale long before the captain reported.

After several months on this assignment, it appeared that I would remain there for a long period. I looked about and found a tiny apartment overlooking the navy yard at Bremerton. I telephoned my wife about it, and she agreed to pack and leave at once. Within a week, the furniture was packed, the old country home in Connecticut abandoned, and she and our two teen-age daughters were wheeling their way westward in an ancient car, with rationed gasoline and retreaded tires. I knew their itinerary and had suggested they check general delivery at post offices along the route. This served a purpose as they passed midpoint. I got orders to go upon arrival of my relief to a North Atlantic base known only by the code name Navy #103. I wrote the family at a city post office general delivery in Idaho, suggesting they telephone. They did, and since my relief was not yet in Bremerton, it was agreed that they would come on.

Soon after their arrival, the furniture arrived by through freight, and we used the little apartment for about two weeks. When my relief arrived, we repacked the furniture, and I flew off to the unknown while the family headed the old Dodge back toward New York City. As I flew northward toward Navy #103, I saw my first convoy. Outside the harbor of Halifax the transports, ships, and escorts were forming. At that point I was not aware that planes from Navy #103 would assist this convoy to avoid the German submarines that, at that time, infested the North Atlantic. It was midafternoon when I put down at Argentia, Newfoundland, and was met by the man I was relieving. He took me to call on my skipper, Captain Harry Horney, who greeted me rather formally; but, from the first, we seemed to respect each other. Later this respect warmed to admiration and affection on my part, and possibly his too. At any rate, he took me in hand and taught me much about being a navy executive officer. Never before in my training to be an administrator had I been given so much precise advice and direction. Administration in the navy, I learned, could never be vague; the goals must always be clear. He was so concise, so thorough, so exacting that most of his officers had little affection for him and considerable fear. But I knew my lack of qualifications to be second in command of an advanced air base, and I treasured and valued his excellence of leadership and complete mastery of his job. If I succeeded as an officer in the Second World War, I owe most to Captain Harry Horney.

At the time I arrived, the possibility of attack on the mainland of the United States or Canada had diminished greatly, and the Navy air wing was moving eastward to Great Britain. The submarine menace, however, was still imminent. The navy base had the role of serving as a logistic center for airplanes and ships in the North Atlantic, to help escort convoys out to sea, to search for and sink submarines, and to chart the movement of icebergs in the North Atlantic. The air station, of which I was the executive officer, was a basic part of Task Force 24, which served that North Atlantic area from Newfoundland to Labrador to Greenland to Iceland. Though based at Argentia, my contacts and duties sometimes took me over huge geographical areas.

From the first, I liked my assignment. In my view, the executive officer of a ship or station has the most active and exciting job in the Navy. It is his job to execute the policies and general orders of the captain. Furthermore, he is the chief source of much of the data and information on which the captain makes decisions. He shields the skipper from the minutia, detail, and routine time-consuming matters. He, more than any man, is responsible for the training, discipline, and morale of the officers and crew. Likewise, he must review communications, coming and going, and it is he who alerts the captain of security problems and other matters. He must accommodate himself to a life of irregularity insofar as sleep and rest are concerned. He is on call at all times. Every activity of the base is his concern.

To do all this, the executive officer must be in daily contact with almost every operation on the ship or station, from education and training programs to the ship's galley and enlisted men's living quarters. He is president of the officers' mess and responsible for its decorum. Since Captain Harry Horney could ask more exacting and detailed questions about every operation than any man I ever knew, I was forced to become thorough in my inspections and precise in my administration. Carelessness or casualness, I learned, would lead to embarrassment before the skipper.

One part of the continuous inservice improvement of aviators was to keep them efficient and skillful in flying under all sorts of weather conditions and within the whole geographic range of Task Force 24. This meant continuous practice flying on instruments. A very valuable training asset for this purpose was the Link Trainer. Most flyers did not like this type of schooling and had to be checked to see that they got in their "time" with this valuable device. Others neglected their navigation, whether it be celestial or otherwise. Just keeping up with the codes in communications was quite an educational chore. I often thought as we worked in the freakish weather of the North Atlantic that the most valuable officer was the one who could go out in the face of a storm and manage to find his way back. Lost pilots were a headache of the worst sort. Navigation and instrument flying were basic, and both required continuous study and practice. But the pilots who had most at stake were in need of constant prodding to keep themselves in prime form. Often, it fell to me to do the prodding.

All my life I had found satisfaction in playing key roles where action was concerned. Being executive officer of this base during the heat of a world struggle proved to be exhilarating. The complexity of the total operations made my task an exciting and rewarding one. Furthermore, the air base with its many facilities, including a hospital and medical staff, often played host to visiting ships and planes, including some from Russia, our ally.

As a peripheral duty, I served as president of a general court martial for eighteen months. Since our zone was an active operational one, the court only met in evenings or on days when the court members could be freed from pressing duties. As the senior officer of the General Court, it was my job to see that the prisoner had a fair trial, as outlined specifically in the publication *Navy Courts and Boards*. A General Court serves as both judge and jury. I made sure that the specific procedures set forth in *Navy Courts and Boards* were followed and our decisions were seldom reversed by the judge advocate or the commander in chief. I also headed one court of inquiry, which gave me another educational experience. The court of inquiry resembles a civil grand jury in many respects.

Another responsibility falling on the commander of an air station is to keep the runways in operational order at all times. Luckily, we had a battalion of Seabees who lived up to their reputation in construction and maintenance. Their slogan, "The difficult we do promptly; the impossible takes a little longer," seemed to inspire both officers and enlisted men.

The Navy frowns when officers have informal friendly relationships with enlisted men. Since I had come to believe that leadership involves the utilization and freeing of talents within a total organization, and since as a school administrator I had received inspiration and ideas from teachers and mature students also, it was difficult for me to draw a sharp line between enlisted personnel and commissioned officers.

Close observation also revealed to me that chief petty officers were the backbone of Navy operations. Among them was stored the technical know-how that only special training and long experience could provide. This expertise had given them special privileges and sometimes too much power, which I questioned. I attempted to gain their confidence and also lessen their exclusive power over operations.

On late inspection trips through the enlisted men's quarters, I dared look into the chiefs' country. At first they looked upon such excursions as intrusions on privacy and special privileges. But since I was casual instead of official, friendly instead of austere, they soon became hospitable. Many midnight snacks were my privilege in the chiefs' quarters. At no place else on the base could food and coffee be found at all times of the day or night. How they managed to have refrigerators, electric burners, and steaks was a mystery to me until I noted that the chief electrician, the chief commissary steward, and several chiefs of the Seabees were aboard. They controlled food, services, and equipment.

My friendly contacts with these stalwarts of the navy made it possible for me to get technical and friendly advice that tempered many of my major decisions. I considered such relationships good administrative policy, but many admirals would have thought otherwise.

Since an air station has the duty of servicing any operational unit that might be assigned to it, barracks and mess halls became a serious responsibility. To have a continuous supply of equipment for men and machines and to be well-stocked with food and the personnel to prepare and serve it was no mean undertaking. The supervision of these service operations fell upon the shoulders of the executive officer, to a great extent.

The story told in the *Caine Mutiny* has special interest for me because I had a captain who possessed all the characteristics of Captain Queeg. In addition to having the emotional and mental quirks of the commander of the *Caine*, he suffered health damages resulting from service in the South Pacific in the early months of the war. Thus, he was incapacitated in many ways for the role of captain.

With full knowledge of the chief of staff of the task force, I made decisions again and again without the knowledge of the skipper. From my point of view, the safety of men was at stake. I did not seize command; I merely took over decision making for the air station. Wrongly or rightly, I overstepped the prerogatives of an executive officer, but I did so because there seemed to be no other way to preserve an efficient operational unit. Inaction would have been disastrous to men and to the operational program. Had I been court martialed, I have often wondered what testimony the chief of staff would have given. I wish to state, however, that as the captain's physical health improved, so did his mental health. No doubt he later became an efficient navy officer.

I became personnel director for all enlisted men at the Corpus base and satellite fields and for the whole navy complex at Pensacola. The job was almost wholly educational and guidance in nature. Soon I fitted into the routine of it, but the excitement of an overseas operating base was lacking. It seemed obvious that the war was gradually coming to an end.

Shortly before Hiroshima and Nagasaki, I had a telegram from the state board of education in Connecticut offering me a newly established job, deputy commissioner and acting commissioner. I declined the offer, explaining that my commitment to the navy was for the duration of the war. Then, suddenly, the Japanese surrendered, and immediately the state board offer was repeated. I accepted, provided I could get a release.

When I requested release to inactive duty, the chief of staff, realizing the serious personnel job now facing the armed services, refused to endorse my request. The request went in to the bureau of personnel anyway and within ten days I was released to inactive duty.

I am compelled to say that I had real affection and admiration for the navy. I feel greatly privileged to have served under orders during most of the two world wars. To completely surrender oneself voluntarily to the service of his country in a state of declared war is a deep and satisfying emotional experience. In my judgment, those who have not had such privileges are the ones who are underprivileged.

Part Two

CHAPTER VI

Administration at the State Level

Our biggest problem upon arriving in Connecticut was finding a place to live. In fact, the problem was not resolved for over a period of eighteen months.

Since the commissioner, Dr. Alonzo Grace, had already departed on a study project in occupied Germany, I was at once plunged into the role of acting chief state school officer. Within days, an agenda had to be prepared for a state board meeting. With the help of assistants, I did the job and attended the meeting at an old inn in the town of Norwich.

It started with a dinner and an evening session. The board had before it a study report on teacher education in Connecticut. The document was long and devoted almost altogether to the theory and philosophy of teacher education. In the entire report, not a word was said about allocating responsibilities, expanding to meet postwar problems, improving staff, increasing budgets, facilities, or modernizing buildings in any of the four colleges under the board's jurisdiction. I observed the rather haphazard dialogue of the board members and said nothing. About 11 P.M., the chairman turned to me and said, "Engleman, what do you make of this pedagese?"

I answered by asking them to go to bed and give me until 9 A.M. the next day to formulate recommendations. They agreed, and I spent an exciting night. Since I was convinced the study had no practical value, I threw it aside and began to recall the many projections and plans the four teachers college presidents had made before the war. I recalled some of the wise projections. I then gave consideration to the programs and lack of programs at the university and the private colleges. Next, I tried to foresee the demands for teachers that were imminent. By daybreak I had a program outlined for each college and a listing of building, faculty, and budget expansions which seemed imperative. I noted carefully the special areas of teaching for which no college or university was preparing teachers and specialists. I next noted the areas where expansion needs were pressing. The recommendations included immediate study to determine a ten-year building program. Naturally, if such expansion were attempted, millions of dollars would be needed. I felt the plan would have the wholehearted support not only of the teacher college staffs but also of the school boards and the Connecticut Teachers Association.

I caught a few winks of sleep, drank coffee and ate a hearty breakfast, and then won unanimous support of the state board for the huge expansion program. Thus began an expansion in these colleges that within twenty-five years produced two new campuses, unbelievable construction, huge enrollments, and multiple purpose state colleges. As an example, New Haven had less than six hundred undergraduates in 1945; in 1969 the enrollment had climbed to eight thousand, with a part-time and graduate student body of almost the same size.

At subsequent board meetings, the question of what should be the next steps for vocational education came up. In Connecticut, there were twelve vocational schools of secondary school rank, all operated and paid for by the state department. Our first recommendation was to build new state-owned buildings for each of the regions served by these schools. Previously, they had occupied makeshift buildings provided by the towns in which they were located. These were all inadequate and, in most instances, fire traps. Some were in abandoned trolley car barns, others in abandoned factory buildings. The construction was to be stretched over a ten-year period.

Another of our proposals was to modernize the curriculum. Although competencies in some of the building trades seemed little changed, other occupations were demanding skilled technicians and junior engineers. A study of Connecticut industry revealed the inroads of technology. One innovation would be to start three technical institutes at junior college level. All this meant much bigger state appropriations, but again the board agreed.

The state board in Connecticut also wanted to help improve the public elementary and secondary schools. I called together representatives of the State School Boards Association, the PTA, the Connecticut Teachers Association, and the Superintendent Association. I requested them to develop legislative programs, independent of each other, and bring them back two months later. They did, and we came to agreement on a four-point program which all organizations, including the state board, would support before the legislature and the public.

In order to achieve the goals we had carefully projected, it was obvious that a public information program would be needed. Groups within the general public were singled out for help. For the trade schools, the groups that readily came to the support were the labor unions, the Manufacturers Association, the Chambers of Commerce, and the Construction Complex.

Naturally, the goals for each year of the decade were not all achieved, but in some cases the goals were exceeded greatly. In fact, by the end of the decade the proposed building expenditures had been multiplied many times.

In September 1946, Dr. Grace returned and I became deputy commissioner. During this year I gave special attention to the teachers colleges, the new vocational program, and especially to the program in the small towns under the direction of rural superintendents. There were sixty-nine of these school boards, with only seventeen superintendents and seventeen supervisors to lead them. The superintendents were appointed and paid by the state board. However, they reported directly to the sixty-nine boards. Each man had as many as four boards to which he would report. Naturally, too, they felt a responsibility to the commissioner and the state board.

The thirty-four superintendents and supervisors were at a low ebb in morale when I first met with them. They had interpreted certain statements from the central office to mean that their jobs were on the block. Since my days at New Haven, I had done many things professionally in their schools and knew them to be responsible for Connecticut's superior rural elementary schools. In fact, these rural schools, in most cases, were superior to the larger town schools. Soon their morale went up and never have I been pressed so much to know more and more about the innovations in elementary education. They helped to give me a real refresher course in curriculum and instructional materials and methods. Each of them seemed to have something unique to contribute to my inservice education. Their daylong monthly meetings became the professional highlights of my busy schedule.

At the end of 1946-1947, Dr. Grace resigned to be dean of the University of Chicago School of Education. The board requested me to be his successor. By their action, I became the eighth state commissioner of education over a period of 115 years. The first had been the distinguished Henry Barnard, a contemporary of Horace Mann who, as I studied his record, I came to believe had been superior to Mann.

The pictures of all former commissioners were hung in the anteroom to my office. I at once moved Barnard's and Grace's pictures into my inner office—Barnard because of his great leadership when the public schools were beginning, Grace because of the intimacy of our friendship.

The commissionership proved to be very rewarding to me. It was almost completely removed from partisan politics. Since it was a public trust, it had to be political, but in the best nonpartisan sense. While serving as commissioner, I nominated all personnel to be appointed by the state board. They included state college presidents, deans, professors, directors of technical institutes, bureau heads, and the like. Not once did the board demand to know their place of origin, their religion, their politics, or their race. Professional and personal qualifications were all the board requested. I felt a responsibility to the board as my employer, but my greatest responsibility, I felt, was to the school children of the state and to the teaching profession that served them. Only infrequently was I ever challenged on these two positions, and then with little persistence.

Traditions in Connecticut are such that the other school administrators, and teachers as well, hold the state commissioner in high esteem. More than in most states, they look to him for leadership. Also, Connecticut is a small state and, therefore, has an intimacy not found in larger ones. As a result of these and other factors, I found myself closely involved in the programs of many towns—so much so, in fact, that I was seldom home before late evening. Fortunately, however, distances were so modest that I could leave a meeting in any corner of the state at 10 P.M. and be home by midnight.

While Dr. Grace was commissioner, he supported the formation of numerous citizens' committees for public education, which met and discussed issues and programs involving the public schools. They were related in many ways to the National Citizens Committee for the Public Schools spearheaded by Roy Larsen of *Time Magazine*. I gave them support too, but because they did not become action groups (or, if they did, their efforts sometimes overran the duties of a school board with legal rights) they gradually lost influence. Soon after I was made commissioner, a governor's study group headed by Norman Cousins came in to stimulate great citizen activities. The process of involvement which Cousins followed proved to be a tremendous stimulus to public education, and I was glad to give the group complete cooperation.

As commissioner, I soon relearned what I had come to know as a young superintendent: no administrator can neglect his board of control. They need to be given issues and programs about which to make policy decisions, together with much supporting documentary evidence. This means that great care must be taken in preparing the board agenda and that data of many kinds must give documentation to the agenda. When the timing suggests action, the recommendations of the administrator should be stated. Careful preparation before board meetings tends to ensure efficiency and save time. A school executive should never be personally offended if his recommendations are altered. He has a right to protest but never to be offended when his judgment is overridden. Of course, on some matters of principle, an action may be one he cannot live with in full conscience. Even so, an angry response is inadvisable.

Since I believed adequate budgets and sound financial accounting important, I introduced a new plan for making and approving budgets for the several units of the department, including trade schools and teachers colleges. Their entire budgets must be approved by me and the board and then submitted to the governor and the legislature. First, four-part forms were sent to all unit heads:

1. What old services would you recommend?
2. What old services should be deleted?
3. What old services should be extended?
4. What new services should be sought?

Their recommendations were discussed with me and sometimes altered by mutual consent. Then they were put in compact form and presented to the board. After careful review, they were usually altered somewhat and then approved and returned to unit heads.

With approved services before them and with agreed upon unit costs, they made up the dollar budget, and the same process was followed for getting board approval. Thus, the board always had before it the complete and desirable program of services. Furthermore, when money values were attached, the staff and board were forced to examine the options and determine priorities.

There were many critical incidents during the period I served as chief state school officer. Taking issue with the governor was not uncommon. One early December, Governor-Elect Chester Bowles asked me to visit him at his home overlooking the Connecticut River. I drove down in the snow to find him working on budget matters. He asked me what the state board's program was and I presented the four-point program referred to earlier: (1) buildings for the teachers colleges, (2) buildings for the vocational program, (3) aid for building in the towns, and (4) added state aid for operations of the public schools. He looked over the figures and said, "That is a lot of money. Before approving all that, I may have to have a study of need made." I explained that one of my chief duties was to make such studies and that the board's program represented our findings. He expressed interest but doubt. I insisted that one of the most important duties of the commissioner of education is to make a continuous study of educational progress and educational needs and to project programs to meet those needs. When he meets that obligation squarely and efficiently, outside studies are seldom needed.

Two days after his inauguration Governor Bowles invited me and the state board to lunch and asked the board to tell him its program. Of course, they repeated what I had told him. Again, he mentioned a study of his own. We left with doubt as to what he might support.

The legislature was in session, so I took the four bills to the legislators. Two senators and two general assemblymen—one from each party in each house—agreed to introduce them. It was our custom to seek bipartisan support on all educational matters.

The next morning's *Hartford Current* carried the story of the new proposed legislation. About 11 A.M. I was called to the governor's office. As I entered, I saw that his able, but not wise, young assistants were there to witness the scene. I suspected what was about to take place because one look at the governor proved he was angry. He stood as I approached his desk. "Did you introduce those four bills?"

I replied, "No, Governor, I didn't introduce them—I couldn't—but I gave them to the men who did."

This time he almost shouted, "You can't do that; it's against the law!"

"Now, Governor, I know what you refer to. It is the Cross Reorganization Act, but while that act prohibits your cabinet from introducing bills pertaining to finances, I am not a member of your cabinet. The act has never been interpreted to include the state board, nor was it so intended."

"But you just can't do it," he argued.

"Will you tell that to the state board?"

"Yes, when do they meet?"

Quick as a flash, I thought and said, "Tomorrow at noon at the Bond Hotel—will you be there?" He agreed, and I left with a disdainful look at the young sharpies—the advisors, the able but inexperienced men—who had come to witness the "kill."

When I got to the office, I called the members of the board and announced a special emergency meeting for the next day at 10 A.M. in my office. When they assembled the next morning, I told them the story. I recalled to their minds that I had asked them at the time of my appointment to whom I was to be responsible. They had said to them and not to a partisan leader. They now indicated that the policy had not changed and unanimously agreed to confront the governor at lunchtime.

The governor was on time, and we had a friendly luncheon conversation. Then the chairman asked the governor if I had correctly reported his position. He readily replied in the affirmative. Then the board, one by one, expressed distress at such interference. They told him that the state board had been autonomous and free to give leadership for over one hundred years. They said his example would be followed at the local level by mayors and first selectmen. In fact, he would wreck the schools of Connecticut. They insisted that if he persisted, they would take the case to all the people. He listened carefully. "I really want to help, not injure public education. You have opened my eyes—I shall never interfere again." He kept his word.

The legislature voted money for three of the four proposals, but hedged on the most pressing one—aiding the construction of new plants at the district level. They did, however, vote a tiny appropriation and then adjourned. In a few days, the governor sent for me and said, "What shall I do about this school building aid bill?"

"Veto the useless thing," I said. "The amount is so small that it will just cause squabbles and do more harm than good and get no needed school houses built."

He pointed out that my survey of need had been called exaggerated by some of the general assembly. He added that the survey instrument had been signed by superintendents and that that had brought doubts to some minds. Then he surprised me by saying, "Finis, if you will redo the study and have the study signed in each town by the mayor or first selectman along with the school board chairman, and if the need in this new study corresponds to your figures, I will call an emergency session of the legislature and we will write a new bill." I agreed with enthusiasm and he vetoed the worthless act.

The new study, when done and tabulated, showed the need for $10 million more than did the original, although each town report was signed by the officials mentioned above. I took the report to Governor Bowles. He immediately called the emergency session, presented the survey data along with a school building appropriation bill which committed the state to put up one dollar to match every two a local district voted, and with no limit. The governor continued to be of signal help on all educational matters, and our friendship has lasted. I consider him to be a true gentleman, a magnificent statesman, and an ambassador of great worth.

CHAPTER VII

One of the veterans groups resolved to insist that the state board enforce a loyalty oath for all public school teachers. The veterans' presentation before the board was vigorous and insistent. I expressed my opposition, but urged that the board not act hastily. I urged them to deliberate on all the pros and cons of the issue. They deliberated for several months. Meanwhile, I gave them all the data I could find. They reached consensus against the oath and selected a subcommittee to write with care the reasons for the decision. I was then requested to send the communication. In my judgment the board's reply to the veterans is a contribution to the thinking on this controversial subject. It read as follows:

> The State Board of Education has carefully reviewed the resolution (a copy of which is attached to this letter) adopted by the Department of Connecticut, Catholic War Veterans of America on April 28, 1951 and transmitted to the State Board of Education on August 2, 1951. The following action was taken by a unanimous vote of the Board.
>> "RESOLVED: That the State Board of Education does not recommend the use of the affidavit for the personnel in the educational system in the State of Connecticut and all subdivisions thereof, as contained in the resolution of the Department of Connecticut, Catholic War Veterans of America as transmitted to this Board under date of August 2, 1951."
>
> The State Board of Education further directed me, as its secretary, to point out to you that a majority of the Board based the decision upon the following convictions:
>> 1. *The requirement of the proposed oath is in our judgment unnecessary.*
>>
>>> We are convinced of the continuing loyalty of the teachers of Connecticut; we believe that in the absence of evidence to the contrary everyone should in justice assume that loyalty, and that any action which would stir justifiable indignation as well as distrust and insecurity within our teaching group should be avoided.
>>>
>>> We wish to assure members of your organization that we are aware of the many problems related to the fight against communism in the world today. We believe that our schools have been exceedingly effective in presenting the basic understandings regarding the characteristics of our free democratic society as well as the evil

qualities found in present-day communism. We have faith that the teachers of Connecticut will continue to render effective service in this vital area of the curriculum.

2. *The requirement of a loyalty oath is, we believe, already anticipated in actual practice.*

   a. The teachers' professional organizations—national, state, and local—have already declared their position on the employment of communists in their ranks. For example, the Connecticut Education Association, in a resolution adopted on May 12, 1951, stated the following:

   "Members of the Communist Party shall not be employed in the American schools. Such membership involves adherence to doctrines and discipline completely inconsistent with the principles of freedom on which American education depends. Such membership and the accompanying surrender of intellectual integrity render an individual unfit to discharge the duties of a teacher in this country. Communist organizations and communist front organizations should be required by law to register with the Attorney-General of the United States.

   ". . . the whole spirit of free American education will be subverted unless teachers are free to think for themselves. It is because members of the Communist Party are required to surrender this right, as a consequence of becoming part of a movement characterized by conspiracy and calculated deceit, that they shall be excluded from membership in the Connecticut Education Association."

   b. Teachers who are voters in Connecticut have individually subscribed to the following citizens' oath:

   ELECTOR'S OATH. (Sec. 3576 G.S. 1949). "You solemnly swear that you will be true and faithful to the state of Connecticut, and the constitution and government thereof, as a free and independent state, and to the constitution of the United States; and whenever you shall be called to give your vote or suffrage touching any matter that concerns this state or the United States, you will give it as you shall judge will conduce to the best good of the same, without respect of persons or favor of any man; so help you God."

   c. Existing sedition laws provide a positive method of prosecuting and punishing all violators. These laws are clear and concise; the Board believes that adherence to established legal procedure is a greater guard against subversive activities than would be the proposed loyalty oath for teachers. The statutes read as follows:

   Section 8346, General Statutes of Connecticut, Revision of 1949, "*Sedition.* Any person who shall speak, or write, print and publicly exhibit or distribute, or who shall publicly exhibit, post, or advertise any disloyal, scurrilous or abusive matter concerning the form of government of the United States, its military forces, flag or uniforms, or any matter which is intended to bring them into contempt or which creates or fosters opposition to organized government, shall be fined not more than five hundred dollars or imprisoned not more than five years or both."

3. *The proposed requirement, we are convinced, is unrealistic.*

   It cannot guarantee nor even promise to fulfill its purpose. Loyalty is a quality of mind and spirit and cannot be forced or sustained by any external means such as the swearing of an oath. Loyalty, lack of loyalty, or violation of loyalty will express itself in behavior. The behavior of teachers is observable. Their own professional organizations have assumed within the ethics of their professional codes forthright responsibility for the proper professional conduct of their members. Within such conduct must be assumed loyalty and allegiance to our government and respect for lawful authorities.

Local boards of education, the State Board of Education, supervisory officials including principals and administrative officials—local and state—are legally charged with the responsibility for maintaining professional conduct which must include loyalty to the government. The Board believes that the citizens of Connecticut may depend upon its teachers, supervisors, and administrators to safeguard fundamental American principles in the schools of the state.

4. *The proposed requirement, according to our interpretation, is discriminatory.*

It discriminates against one body of state citizens, against one body of state employees, and against one body of teachers in the schools of Connecticut.

The State Board of Education wishes to express at this time its sincere appreciation of the spirit of your organization in making this proposal. The Board will continue to do all in its power to keep our schools free of subversive elements and free to teach the best in American democratic values.

Textbook Censorship

Another still larger veterans group became inflamed and passed a resolution implying teacher disloyalty and demanding state censorship of textbooks. Many of the "Whereas" statements implied that teachers for years had been loyal subjects, but now were faltering and using subversive documents in the school room; therefore, the state board or some state agency should censor textbooks.

They sent the resolution to the board, in care of me, and suggested that they intended to make the same request of the legislature and the governor. I telephoned the executive officer of the veterans group and asked him to visit me in my office. When he arrived, I asked him if the resolutions committee had presented any evidence that teachers were subversive. His reply was in the negative. I next asked if they had presented any exhibits to show materials or books of a subversive character. The answer was "no" again.

"Well," I said, "did the resolutions committee advise with the veterans education committee?" He was unsure, so I enlightened him by taking out my wallet to show my card as chairman of that veterans standing committee on education. I assured him that I was angry at such irresponsible action by a presumably respectable organization of which I was an active member. I then demanded to see the executive committee of the Veterans of Foreign Wars. My request was granted, and before the meeting was adjourned they agreed not to pursue further the substance of the resolution.

The "Committee of Nine"

Shortly before I became state commissioner, the teachers of Norwalk, Connecticut, called a strike. My predecessor had the first teachers' strike in Connecticut history on his hands. He advised both board and teachers in a statesmanlike manner. A court decision was handed down prohibiting strikes but permitting bargaining, but the incident had stirred the public, the teachers, and school boards. Further trouble was brewing as the teachers associations became more insistent.

In order to study the problem and, if possible, reach agreement on procedure when teachers' rights and salaries were under consideration, I asked in 1951 that a committee composed of representatives selected by four state-wide organizations be asked to study the issue and make recommendations. This committee was chaired by an official of the state department of education and included school board members, school superintendents, and teachers, all selected by their respective organizations. After deliberating for many weeks, the committee made its first report and recommendations. No doubt, this was one of the first statewide efforts to establish a plan for school board-teacher negotiations, together with a procedure to be followed in case of an impasse. The committee came to be known as the "Committee of Nine." It continued to meet and revise its recommendations. As each revision was made and published by my office, the sponsoring bodies—the state board of education, the state education association, the state association of school boards, and the state association of school administrators—officially adopted the findings. The last revision, published in 1962, is entitled "Working Relations Between Boards of Education and Teachers Organizations." It is interesting to note that each edition expressed the philosophy that since the superintendent has responsibilities to both board and teachers, he should advise both. Subsequent legislation has outlined in detail the processes in negotiations.

After the recommendations of this committee were approved by the several statewide bodies, they served as a useful working model during the early days of teacher negotiations. They outlined a procedure for action in case of the board and teachers reaching an impasse. The following example shows how the procedure worked in one case.

The board and teachers in Hamden negotiated for weeks and

could not reach agreement. The teachers then asked the state commissioner of education to appoint a fact-finding committee which would give its findings to both bodies and to the public. This committee made one interesting discovery: the school board was not fiscally independent, but had negotiated as if it was. The selectmen really stood in the background but told the board of education what it could do. Publicity was given to this fact, and soon the selectmen were on the defensive. The public and teachers, too, knew with whom they must bargain. Shortly, an embarrassed group of selectmen released the board to negotiate a settlement. When teachers enter the negotiating arena, they need to know who controls the purse strings of education. Little can be achieved if the board is a mere buffer group.

The Department of Defense Sought Aid from the Schools

On one occasion, officials from the Defense Department, aided and abetted by the state civilian defense administrator, a retired general, besieged me to direct all school boards to build bomb shelters, store medicine and food, and take other precautions against possible atomic bomb attacks. In the midst of it all, something happened to stiffen my conviction that such activities would be like playing cowboy and Indian. General Omar Bradley visited the state and addressed a small group at the Hartford Club. A question period followed. I asked, "If two major powers were to engage in a shooting war, is there a likelihood that civilization would be destroyed?" The general gravely answered, "It depends on how desperate either might be to win. If either resorted to the atomic bomb, the next generation would be fighting with bows and arrows."

And this was before the hydrogen bomb—but still people believed man could hide from the effects of nuclear explosions created by a furious war. The experience with General Bradley gave me the strength to withstand the urging that badly needed money should be wasted on bomb shelters.

Later on, in Washington, I would be pressured by the Defense Department to have the American Association of School Administrators issue statements and directives urging that billions be spent for bomb shelters in the face of serious schoolroom and laboratory shortages. In spite of urging and downright pressure, I could not believe that bomb and fallout shelters should have high priorities in the education budget. To me, nuclear war means total disaster. The highest priority should be given to finding means of preventing a shooting war. I settled with the Defense Department by producing a brochure on coping with natural disasters such as fire, flood, hurricanes, etc.: a really useful document in the hands of local superintendents.

A Local School Board Problem

One morning my secretary announced that a delegation of six school board members wanted to see me. When they came in, one man carefully closed the door, and the chairman bluntly told me they had met secretly the night before and fired their superintendent. Before telling him, however, they wanted me to know of their action. I asked what the charges were. They found it hard to be specific. Teachers had been to see them, complaining that the superintendent wouldn't make decisions. Unlike the previous superintendent, he had asked the teachers to work in committees to study the total school offerings, to develop curricular guides, to study personnel policies, and to help set district-wide goals. Their own independence seemed threatened since broad policy might affect the sanctity of classroom autonomy. Of course, I knew the difference in the operational practice of the two superintendents. The previous one had done his own independent "thing," and each teacher had done his. There had been little coordination and hardly any broad policy. I sensed that each teacher wanted to be his own czar and felt little need for a democratic administration or for any innovative change. The board readily admitted that they hadn't presented the complaints to the superintendent, but had reached their decision a bit hastily. What would I advise? I seized the opportunity to point out that, in my judgment, they had fired one of the best superintendents in Connecticut and that when citizens of their town asked me what I thought of him, as I suspected they would, then my answer would be the same. Then I said, "You men, with no evidence of incompetence or immorality, will be in hot water."

"But what shall we do?"

"Rescind your hasty action," I said, "then call in the superintendent and frankly tell him what you consider to be his weaknesses. He will either convince you that his professional behavior is sound or will agree to make changes and improvements."

Ten days later I went to a regional high school conference in their town central building. As I crossed the campus in the evening dusk, I was met by the same board. They were smiling and said, "We did just as you suggested. We believe we have a fine superintendent and will have a better school system. Thank you."

Although I met with many teacher groups of the state education association and was welcomed into the council of their officers, my time was generously budgeted for working with superintendents. I helped them identify areas for further study. I encouraged them to set up regional drive-in centers where a dozen or more could meet periodically to share experiences and review progress on research studies. Since they needed someone to carry through their projects and to provide agenda and supporting data, the state department authorized them to select a department official to help them and to carry out their wishes. These regional groups made significant findings, and the individual superintendent grew in stature as he gave and received help.

In the spring of the year, it was my custom to write school boards concerning pressing priorities in education. On several occasions, I reminded them that their superintendent was the key to high quality education. I pointed out that sometimes school boards became so engrossed with teachers' salaries that they overlooked the most important employee, the superintendent. To neglect the superintendent's welfare in the end meant losing their most precious asset. Many superintendents expressed their gratitude to me.

Selecting a Site

Selecting a school site often causes much controversy. When the state board in Connecticut changed its vocational school policy and decided to construct state regional buildings, we realized that the problem of site was crucial. Previous sites had been accepted because some one town in a region had offered an abandoned building. Often the school was not in the best geographic spot, and always the site acreage was inadequate. Our first move was to determine comprehensive criteria and have them discussed and approved by the board. Then, in each instance, a strong committee composed of able laymen and professional schoolmen was asked to apply the criteria and recommend the best site. All went well until a particular recommendation advised that a new site be several miles from the town in which the school had previously operated. The chamber of commerce objected and the lieutenant governor, whose home was near the old site, appeared to protest. Local pressures forced the state school board member from that city to object, and, to confuse the whole issue, a dissident state board member took up the cudgel. I could see no good reason not to stick by the criteria and the committee's advice. I firmly recommended the acceptance of the new site, and when the vote was taken, the new location was decided upon. I did not lose the respect of the member who lived in the neighborhood of the old site, nor of the lieutenant governor, for that matter.

CHAPTER VIII

Although I had been involved in some educational activities on the national level for many years, my interest in the national scene began in earnest while I was state commissioner. I participated actively in the undertakings of the National Council of Chief State School Officers. In fact, I strongly endorsed the action to establish a secretariat in Washington. I assisted in the planning of several annual conventions. It was while I was president of the Council that a committee composed of Pearl Wanamaker, Lee Thurston, Mary Condon, Edgar Fuller, and me drove to Washington from Atlantic City to see the newly inaugurated President Eisenhower. The interview had been arranged by Senator Potter of Michigan. We wished to convince the President that he should set up an independent commission or federal board of education to help determine federal programs and federal policy. This autonomous body would function like the state board of regents in New York, the state board in Connecticut, and the city school board of districts like Kansas City. As we made plans in the Senator's office, I was relaxed, since I thought Lee Thurston, the chief state school officer from Michigan, who had made the initial contacts with Senator Potter, would make the presentation to the President. However, the committee insisted that the president of the Council of Chief State School Officers should be the spokesman. So I found myself in a Senate limousine headed for the White House with no specific supporting data or prepared statement. Upon arrival, we were taken into the Cabinet room and I was shown a seat facing the President's chair. Others were seated around the oval table. In front of me were a ball point pen and a blank pad. I quickly wrote a few notes on the pad. Almost immediately, the smiling President entered, shook hands with all, and in a friendly way looked at me and said, "What can I do for you?"

I plunged into the subject. I first told him of the way public education was controlled at state and local levels. I stated the belief that the federal government's role would undoubtedly increase. Then I stated our proposal. He asked a few questions and said he knew so little about education that he would have to seek further advice. He asked if we could return the following week to confer with his brother Milton, Arthur Flemming, Nelson Rockefeller, and Mrs. Oveta Culp Hobby. We readily agreed. As we left I noted that Mrs. Hobby, who was to become Secretary of Health, Education, and Welfare, was behind us listening intently.

The next week's consultation yielded no dividends. Of the four, Nelson Rockefeller showed the most concern for our proposal and displayed the most knowledge of the public schools and their administrative situation and financial needs.

In the fall following my return from the navy, I had attended a relatively small but representative conference at Chautauqua, New York, called by the National Education Association. The problem under discussion had been how to rebuild and strengthen the teaching profession, which had suffered severe depletion and debilitation in its ranks during the war. The available statistics on the state of the profession were alarming. The group present agreed that the profession must set to work assiduously to pull itself up by its own bootstraps. To spearhead the movement to retrain and recruit teachers and to raise standards, a new group was formed, the NEA Teachers Education and Professional Standards Commission, later to be called NCTEPS. An office for the Commission was authorized in Washington with a full-time executive secretary.

I was asked to serve as a consultant at the first conference of the Commission at the University of Ohio. Soon after that conference I was appointed to the Commission. I served two three-year terms and was chairman for two years. The commission held work sessions several times each year. National and regional work conferences developed. The strengthening and the promotion of teachers and the upgrading of public education were the constant goals. The Commission stimulated the formation of TEPS commissions in every state. State departments, school boards, administrators, and schools of education were deeply involved. New programs for training teachers evolved, higher certification standards developed, and the whole profession seemed to become involved with efforts to improve instruction. Some effort was given to raising salaries and bringing prestige to the profession, but the main thrust was to improve teaching and dignify it. A major accomplishment was the establishment of the National Council for the Accreditation of Teacher Education. My commission activity took considerable time, but it was an exciting venture in self-improvement.

As the teachers worked to improve their standards and competence, the school administrators entered the fray. Supported and stimulated by the American Association of School Administrators and by the W. K. Kellogg Foundation, regional conferences were held to try to decide what could be done to improve the superintendency. One of these conferences proposed that strong universities around the country be given grants to do research in school administration and to develop new and better programs for training superintendents. It also established a national committee for the advancement of school administrators, which included school board members, professors, local superintendents, and one chief state school officer. I served on this committee for fourteen years. The committee and its program had far-reaching results, giving support to the new accreditation association and to the improvement of training programs. It was this committee, too, that founded the Academy for School Executives.

Through the efforts of Commissioner John Desmond of Massachusetts and Commissioner Francis Spaulding of New York, a little organization was formed of the state commissions of the New England states, New York, and New Jersey. We met quarterly for two days with an agenda that included pressing issues common to all eight states. Once during the year, a conference was planned to which the state lay governing bodies were invited, too. From these conferences I learned very much, and I am convinced that public and private education was advanced by the concerted efforts of those involved.

In 1951 I was asked to be a member of an American delegation to the International Conference on Public Education at Geneva, Switzerland. The five Americans included the U.S. Commissioner, Dr. Earl McGrath. This conference, attended by delegates from forty-seven countries, was my first opportunity to work for an extended period with many other nationals. The experience gave me an intercultural interest which has persisted.

In 1955 and again in 1956 the Department of State asked me to return as chairman of the American delegation to the Geneva conference. By 1955, the conference had delegates from seventy-nine countries. Most of the new ones were from the communist world and from new countries which had emerged after the breakup of colonial empires.

Each country took to the meeting copies of a report on progress in public education. All were required to bring a copy in French and in English. In 1956 we were able to include also copies in Spanish and in Russian, which pleased the delegates who spoke those languages. It was the custom to have the heads of well-developed countries answer questions on their reports from the rostrum. When it was my turn, I was kept with my feet to the fire for three hours. The heat came from the communist world. Their questions were directed at our segregated schools, our unequal opportunities for blacks, our juvenile delinquency, our crime, and any other social ills they could think up. I had been warned by the Department of State that this might happen, so I was prepared. As I answered their barbs, I was also able to tell many admirable things about our society, our education, and our economy. Their persistence and often unfair observations, together with my unirritated posture, soon turned the tide in our favor. Never before had I tried to explain our failures in social justice to an audience that consisted of a majority of nonwhites and non-Christians.

When the ordeal was over, the leader of the three Russian delegations came to the steps and, through an interpreter, thanked me and asked if it would be possible for her delegation and mine to have an extended conference. I urged that they be our guests at our hotel headquarters the upcoming Thursday afternoon. She accepted, and then came our delegation huddle as to how we would entertain. We got fruit juices and soft drinks, Scotch, bourbon, and wonderful Swiss cheeses. The juices and soft drinks were not touched except by their women members and our lone woman delegate.

When they arrived, I pinned rosebud corsages on the three ladies and helped pass the refreshments. Immediately we were in concentrated discussions of the theory of education and politics. We soon saw that we were on a collision course on these issues, so we turned to instruction, school subjects, teachers, and children. This was, indeed, productive, and our congeniality expanded.

In the midst of our discussion of such subjects as consolidation, which they said was temporarily delayed because of the shortage of hard-surfaced roads, their leader turned to me and said, "In your discussion before the assembly you said the American federal government had played hardly any role in American education." I agreed, but she was not satisfied.

"Back at the time of your great President Lincoln, didn't Congress pass an act and make an appropriation for the establishment of state-operated colleges?" She was right, of course, I had overlooked the land grant colleges.

. "How about the research institutes?" She was referring to the Agricultural Experiment Stations. She next turned to adult education. I denied that Congress had ever supported adult education. When I finally understood that she was referring to the county farm agent and his female counterpart, I again admitted that they were federally supported adult education officials. She explained that she believed America owed her great industrial development to the land grant colleges, the experiment stations, and the adult educators, the county farm agents. She added, "You first had to free your people from the hoe before you could produce enough food, shelter, and clothing by the labors of a small proportion of your adult population. Only thus could you free the manpower for your General Electric, General Motors, and General Dynamics." The conference grew more friendly as they hurriedly brought gifts of vodka, books, and caviar. We were convinced that we had learned more about education, and we hoped we had advanced the cause of peace.

In the early years of the Eisenhower administration, Lee Thurston of Michigan was named U.S. Commissioner of Education. A few days later he invited me down to Washington for a conference in his office.

When I arrived, Dr. Thurston was already talking with Hugh Masters of the Kellogg Foundation and Francis Keppel, dean of the Harvard Graduate School of Education. His purpose in calling us in was that he believed public education needed a shot in the arm—it needed support from high places. What did we think of a Presidential Committee to study and report to the President on the next steps for improvement? He also believed that, as an asset to the study, a large White House Conference on Education, sponsored by the President, should be organized. We readily agreed that the proposal made sense. But how would such a major undertaking be financed? In answer to this, he appealed to Masters for aid from the Kellogg Foundation. Masters liked the proposal, but flatly said the Foundation had already committed all its funds. Then he took his departure.

We had a bite of lunch and reviewed the proposal again. I finally ventured to suggest that if the President really wanted something done, he could, no doubt, convince Congress to make an appropriation to finance the committee and its staff and also to pay the expenses of the delegates to a White House Conference devoted entirely to education. I insisted that the only democratic way to meet expenses and get representation for poor and rich alike was by an appropriation from public funds. In the end we agreed that such a proposal would be taken directly to the President by Dr. Thurston. Before the meeting closed, the three of us wrote the proposal and letter to President Eisenhower. I was then assigned the task of confidentially informing the executive secretary of the Council of Chief State School Officers. All arrangements in the states, such as choosing delegates, were to be handled through the auspices of the chief state school officers and state boards of education.

Within a short time, the White House Committee on Education was announced with Neil McElroy as chairman, representing the lay group of twenty-two, and me as vice-chairman, representing the eleven professional members. The Committee consisted of President Eisenhower, Marion B. Folsom, S. M. Brownell, Neil H. McElroy, Mildred C. Ahlgren, Ethel G. Brown, Ralph J. Bunche, John S. Burke, John Cowles, John A.

Hannah, James W. Hargrove, Albert J. Hayes, Margaret Hickey, Henry H. Hill, Oveta Culp Hobby, Mildred McA. Horton, James R. Killian, Jr., Allan B. Kline, W. Preston Lane, Jr., Roy E. Larsen, Thomas Lazzio, Joseph C. McLain, William E. McManus, Lorimer D. Milton, Don G. Mitchell, Frank C. Moore, Herschel D. Newson, William S. Paley, James F. Redmond, Martha Shull, Frank H. Sparks, Potter Stewart, Jesse G. Stratton, Harold W. Sweatt, H. Grant Vest, and Mayme E. Williams.

The White House Conference operations were under my direct supervision, while Neil McElroy presided at most of the plenary sessions.

Immediately before the first Plenary Assembly at 8:30 P.M., Neil McElroy gave a dinner in honor of the President and the Cabinet, with the White House Committee and wives present. A few days earlier, President Eisenhower had had a heart attack in Colorado. Vice-President Nixon, therefore, took his place and opened the Conference with a major address at this dinner. After the speech he joined us and said, "Gee, I am a bit tired. Could we go some place and relax, have a drink, and talk?" Mr. McElroy suggested that we go to his suite. There, we quickly assembled: Dr. and Mrs. Ralph Bunche, Mr. and Mrs. William Paley, Dr. and Mrs. Brownell, the McElroys, and the Englemans. I shall never forget the next two hours. Mr. Nixon and Dr. Bunche engaged in an enlightening discussion of the problems of South Asia. The Vice-President evidenced much knowledge, tempered with modesty. Usually, he urged Dr. Bunche or someone else to express opinions.

The President had announced a reception at the White House for all delegates. Vice-President Nixon switched the location to the National Gallery of Art. Since I knew so many of the delegates, I was placed first in the receiving line. Next to Mrs. Engleman and me stood the U.S. Commissioner, Samuel Miller Brownell and his wife, then the McElroys, and at the end, the host and hostess, Vice-President and Mrs. Nixon. The line dragged on and on for hours, but by darkness the handshaking was finished. Mr. Nixon turned to us and said, "Why not run down to my office and I will mix you a martini."

Time was short, and the McElroys and Englemans had obligations at a plenary session which would open at 8:30. However, within a few minutes we arrived at the Capitol. There in his office he told anecdotes about the chandelier and the yellow papers scattered about in his handwriting, and showed us official gifts he had received on a recent journey to the Far East and South Asia. When Mrs. Engleman suggested bourbon and water instead of a Martini, he handed her a glass on which was inscribed, "A rebel drink for a rebel." Somehow he had learned that she was a native of Arkansas. He was a charming host.

The Conference arrangements were very complex. We wanted 1800 people to hold face-to-face dialogue and reach consensus on the major problems on the agenda. To do this, we had hit on the unique plan of dividing all delegates into 180 round-table discussion groups on the first day. The topic was financing education. At the close of the day each of the 180 chairmen noted what he and the group believed to be the consensus.

These 180 chairmen met the next day in 18 round-table groups to continue discussing the topic of finance. On the third day, the chairmen of these 18 groups met in further discussion in two groups, and that night the two chairmen met and wrote the report which was given to the plenary session and voted upon.

All other problem areas were handled in a similar way, although there was some difference in the membership of the original 180 round tables due to the absence of chairmen seeking further consensus. All the original groupings were made by a computer with the objective of getting diversity in occupation and geographic region.

The Conference ran like clockwork. All consensus reports, including the most controversial one on federal aid to education, were approved by the assembled delegates, which came as a surprise to those who had publicly stated that the Committee was rigged against federal aid and that the Conference plans were designed to oppose it. While there was diverse opinion on all the problems among the Committee members, at no time did I see anything but fair play in Committee sessions or during the Conference. Never before had delegates from all states, representing a cross section of Americans, met and deliberated so long on educational problems. Never before had such a delegation calmly and deliberately voted the belief that general federal aid was needed and feasible. For me, it was a memorable experience.

After President Eisenhower had recovered, he met with the Committee on two occasions. When we finished our work and handed him the report entitled "A Report to the President—White House Committee on Education," Neil McElroy, Chairman, he expressed his thanks in his good-natured way. The report would be used for discussion by many thousands of persons as the several states held "Little White House" conferences.

On the day following the closing of the White House Conference, I met with the Chief State School Officers at the Hotel Woodner. There I read a paper on the need for guideposts for a national curriculum in the schools. This controversial subject was to be debated heatedly in later years. The manuscript was published that year in a contemporary professional magazine.

About a year before I was to leave Connecticut, the Secretary of Health, Education, and Welfare, Mr. Folsom, invited me to Washington.

He wanted me to accept a Presidential appointment as U.S. Commissioner of Education. He agreed to advance the pay schedule to match that of the Surgeon General. He also promised hands-off if I would accept the job, reorganize it, and develop a forward-looking program. The idea intrigued me, but I feared partisan political interference. I thanked him and took the matter under advisement. My chief advisor was my wife. It was her conviction that my independent nature could not survive in the partisan politics of office. Consequently, I wrote a letter of thanks and refusal. I liked Secretary Folsom very much and regretted exceedingly having to say no to him and the President. It seemed a tragedy that America could free the local school executive from petty partisan politics but keep the highest education official in the nation under the domination of partisan officials. I believed then, and I continue to believe, that a nonpartisan board should be established in Washington with independence to set policy and determine programs.

The *New Haven Evening Register,* a daily newspaper for southern Connecticut, was a watchdog of the public treasury. It seemed to oppose all expenditures for public education. Because I promoted such expenditures, the owner and publisher attacked me with front-page editorials.

One evening I arrived home about 6 P.M. The paper was not there. Evidently the delivery boy had overlooked us. About 8 P.M. Professor Mark May, director of the Institute of Human Relations at Yale, rang our doorbell. He came in and said, "Finis, that front page editorial tonight attacking you was worth a million dollars to you. Everybody with sense knows that what you support is good for Connecticut, and everybody with judgment knows that when the editor of that paper opposes something, it is likely to be good." My wife was hanging her head. She had tried to spare me by hiding the evening paper.

Possibly my most embarrassing experience as a chief state school administrator occurred on a muggy, foggy, morning in 1952. I was driving on a four-lane highway about 8 A.M. with headlights full on. As the traffic crept along, I fixed my attention on the taillights of a car just ahead with a New Jersey license. By turning my headlights down and by concentrating on the taillights, I seemed to have everything under control. If I could just be patient, we would eventually reach Hartford.

Suddenly a car swept around me and pulled alongside the one with the New Jersey license. To my surprise it was a local police officer who was waving the car to a halt. Naturally, I stopped too.

Then I could dimly see that he was writing the woman driver a traffic violation ticket. Since I had been following her and since I was feeling chivalrous that morning, I climbed out and approached the officer, saying, "What is the trouble, Officer?"

He whirled on me and said, "Don't you know the school bus law in Connecticut?"

Calmly, I answered, "Yes, I ought to know it. I wrote it."

Just as calmly, he wrote another ticket and as he handed it to me explained, "Back about two hundred yards you folks passed a stopped school bus."

Possibly we did, but the news was startling. Rather than risk being accused of trying to avoid meeting my responsibility, I did not contest the charge. So, I was fined and my license suspended. To my consternation, the *Saturday Evening Post* made a national story of it. Imagine receiving chiding notes from friends as far away as Fort Worth, San Francisco, and Milwaukee!

A few days before the White House Conference, I had a call from Henry Willet, superintendent of schools in Richmond, Virginia, and president of the American Association of School Administrators. He asked me to stop at the Mayflower Hotel on the way to the Sheraton Park Hotel as I went to the White House Conference. He explained that the Executive Committee of the AASA would be meeting and desired an interview. Since I had been serving on the Committee for the Advancement of School Administrators, I supposed they wanted my opinion of its progress.

When I settled in my chair, Dr. Willet asked, "If you were listing the major problems to be faced by school superintendents in the next ten years, what would they be?" I reflected a minute and began listing them. I could see people smiling so I stopped and said, "Have I said something wrong?"

Dr. Willet said, "Finis, we really asked you here to request that you become the executive secretary of the American Association of School Administrators."

I explained that while I appreciated the honor, I was satisfied with being commissioner in Connecticut. Furthermore, I would have good retirement in five years and, in addition, I considered myself too old to be their secretary. "What you need," I advised, "is a young and imaginative leader. Maybe I can help you find the man." With that, I shook hands and went to conference headquarters to help get things ready for the opening of the President's Conference.

I heard no more of the matter until the following February, just prior to the annual AASA convention. I was there with the TEPS Commission. On the Friday before the opening of the Atlantic City convention on Sunday, I was again telephoned by Dr. Willet. He asked me to stop by his suite at the Traymore early Saturday morning. When I got there, to my surprise, there sat the Executive Committee. Without delay, Dr. Willet said, "Since our conference at the Mayflower, we have thought a lot about our next executive secretary. You say you are too old and that we need youth. We disagree. In our judgment we need wisdom, statesmanship, and maturity. You have ten years of service we want. Won't you let two of our members come to your room tonight and tell you what we have to offer?"

Naturally, I agreed and awaited their proposition. Omar Carmichael, superintendent of schools in Louisville, and Clyde Parker of Iowa, came to see me at the Hotel Dennis. They took deliberate time to explain the role, the salary, and the benefits. I hedged and said I liked my job. Furthermore, I would have to talk to my wife. They said, "Call her up." I did so, and she readily expressed the belief that it was a desirable change. I said, "Would you be willing to give up that old Connecticut farm house and all your antiques?" Quick as a flash she said, "I wouldn't have to give up my antiques." Next day, after discussing the matter with Charley Carrol of North Carolina and Sam Brownell, then U.S. Commissioner of Education, I accepted, with the understanding that I would be given time in Connecticut to develop a legislative program and a biennial budget.

Before leaving Connecticut, I worked like mad helping the staff to complete projected programs. I was particularly anxious to complete construction of state-operated TV stations, but this I was unable to achieve. Proposed legislation, together with the detailed comprehensive biennial budget, was completed and approved by the board before my departure.

As my service as commissioner drew to a close, many ceremonies were held and many pleasant social occasions took place. The state board gave me a rather intimate dinner filled with thanks and best wishes and presented me with a beautiful inscribed silver bowl. The superintendents outdid themselves with a social affair at which they presented a huge sterling silver punch bowl. Teachers, administrators, school board members, PTA personnel, and supporting citizens gave a dinner at the New Statler in Hartford. The governor, with whom I had crossed swords, spoke facetiously. He observed that I should have been a dentist, since I had extracted so much money from the state for schools. I had intended only to express my thanks, but his statements irritated me, and I sarcastically cut him to shreds, much to the amusement of the large audience. I was a bit chagrined that I had allowed myself to chide the governor in public.

On the next day the columnist Alan Olmstead wrote a two column article in one of the Connecticut daily newspapers. The headline read

"FIGHTING FINIS ENGLEMAN HAS LEFT HIS MARK UPON EDUCATION IN CONNECTICUT." Olmstead wrote, in part:

"Future governors, legislatures, state Board of Education members and the president of the University of Connecticut all have some reason to breathe a little easier.—They can all say goodbye with a mixture of respect and relief. And, as they look to his future, they can feel some dawning sympathy for the President and Cabinet and Congress, now that Dr. Engleman is to move his formidable talents to the national field they deserve. But their feelings of sympathy for these national figures and institutions, which cannot really know just what is approaching them, are not likely to overpower the Connecticut figures who have had to deal with the flowering of Dr. Engleman's genius.

They will be too busy remembering.

There was for instance the time the legislature, following its own logic, decided that the steady decrease in actual number of schools in Connecticut, through town and regional consolidations, justified a token decrease in the number of supervisors.

Dr. Engleman was not always prescient, so the thing happened before he had his battalions called to arms. His task then became the formidable one of persuading the legislature to rescind its own economy. By the time the ensuing pressure campaign reached its climax, many legislators began to think they must have repealed education itself, so hot were the grass roots fires started against them. They repealed the economy at the first opportunity.

There was the time the state, and its governor, tried to face up to the issue posed by the fact that the state teachers colleges seemed to be developing into liberal arts colleges in competition with the University of Connecticut. The governor in question, it was understood, was firmly for restricting future expansion of the teachers colleges. That was before Dr. Engleman went to work. When he got through, the governor was on the side of the teachers colleges.

Also, there was the time another governor and a legislature education committee decided to see how far they could go with a plan for unifying the state's system of higher education, the effect of which was to make the University President top man for everything above the grade schools. The measure went fine, despite one of the best organized protest marches on Hartford in modern history, until, in the last clutch, it became apparent that the measure had somehow been altered as if to put the President under the jurisdiction of the grade schools. [insert—Really it was rewritten to completely centralize all public education—elementary-secondary-college—under the single State Board and State Commissioner.]

Then it was up to the University President to kill the bill, which he did.

Dr. Engleman in his Connecticut career fought hard, ably, resourcefully, for independence and for power. He expanded both, and we do not know that he was ever forced to yield anything. He has been something terrific and Washington is hereby warned, if warning will do any good.

We shall regret the absence of his mastery and particularly the absence of those fascinating long range duels. . . ."

The B'nai B'rith of New Haven held a dinner and gave me a citation for my work toward interfaith understanding.

Later, the state board called me back to receive its seldom given award for distinguished service to Connecticut. Still later, I was invited back to be honored by the dedicating of a multimillion dollar building on the Southern Connecticut State College campus named the "Finis E. Engleman."

Part Three

CHAPTER IX

Administration as Seen by the Executive Secretary of AASA

Four months prior to our arrival in Washington, Mrs. Engleman had visited the capital searching for living quarters. She found what she wanted and promptly signed the lease for rather spacious quarters in an apartment building at the corner of Connecticut and Wyoming Avenues. Consequently, when we arrived in September of 1956 we were able to get comfortably settled at once.

Between February and August I had made occasional trips to Washington to consult with Dr. Worth McClure, the retiring executive secretary. I also spent three days with him, Dr. Shirley Cooper, and Dr. Paul Misner at Greenbriar, West Virginia. At this meeting we planned major activities for the year ahead, particularly the dominant features of the Atlantic City Convention to be held in February.

My first several days on the job were given over to getting acquainted with the staff members and listening to each one talk about his work and his feelings toward the organization. My predecessor, Dr. Worth McClure, was an excellent organizer with a human touch that endeared him to the whole staff. Naturally, the morale of the staff was high. They immediately accepted me as a member of their small group. Instead of having 1,600 associates on the team as I had had in Connecticut, now there were three of professional background, four of the administrative assistant type, and eleven typists, secretaries, and bookkeepers. I found, however, that this small staff turned out an inordinate amount of work.

Once I became acquainted with the staff and the types of responsibilities they assumed, I turned my attention to a study of the history, goals and activities of the association. Although I had been a member of the organization for many years and knew a considerable amount about it, my horizons and scope of understanding increased immensely as I read the constitution, bylaws, resolutions, platform, annual reports, minutes of past meetings of the Executive Committee, and numerous publications.

Since one of the major meetings of the Executive Committee is held in early November, my attention was called to the necessity of preparing an agenda for it. The importance of planning for board meetings had been impressed upon me as a superintendent and as chief state school officer in Connecticut, so I did not neglect the preparation for the first official work session with the officers. Not only did I solicit suggestions from them, but I also deliberated with my new associates in the office. As a result, we developed a series of issues, topics, and programs which kept the board hard at work for two days. The agenda was supported by documentation and relevant data, together with the recommendation of the executive secretary where action was required.

The two day meeting of the officers and executive committee in November had special significance. At the close of their deliberations Mrs. Engleman gave an elegant reception, cocktail party and buffet in honor of the president. Two hundred prominent people of Washington, together with some from as far away as Chicago, were in attendance. This was only one illustration of the importance of the school executive's wife.

The policy-making and program-approval body of the American Association of School Administrators at that time consisted of four Executive Committee members, the president, the vice-president, and the president-elect. The meetings of this body always proved very stimulating and helpful to me. Somewhat unlike the boards of laymen with whom I had previously worked, these men could go beyond policy where necessary and could serve as professional sounding boards. Although every member recognized that his prerogatives fell in the areas of policy making and program approval, he was willing, when the secretary requested, to participate in discussion and counsel on matters of professional behavior and action. The high professional quality and the sterling character of the men who set policy and overall programs for the association during those years attest to the good judgment of the membership that elected them to office. At no time in my life did I have the privilege of working with an abler or more dedicated group of educators.

I recall one instance, however, when I momentarily had doubts concerning the board's will to "stand hitched." It happened early in my administration. Critics were reckless in their defamation and slander of the public schools. The spirit of the times seemed to give them freedom to vent their spleen for any and all reasons. I began to analyze their objections and found that they were confusing the successes with failures. In fact, many criticized the very outcomes sought by any good school. I wrote an article and at one of the early sessions of the board gave each member a copy. During the noon recess, they read it and unanimously urged that it be released as an AASA publication. By the next meeting, however, two members quietly suggested that it be delayed as an official publication since some critics would be angry. Naturally, I put the article aside. Two years later, however, a professional magazine publisher asked to see it and then requested permission to publish it. It is quoted below because I believe it accurately analyzes the critics of the fifties and the need for administrators to review their criticisms and inform the public.

THEY DON'T LIKE . . .

The successes, not the failures, of our public schools provoke the harshest critics. The schools are achieving what they were established to do—and some folks don't like it. Since the schools in America belong to the people and since schools have many improvements yet to be made, school administrators and teachers should seek advice and counsel wherever it is to be found. It is important, however, that the relatively few misinformed and destructive critics be identified—not for the purpose of suppressing them, but to identify them for what they are; not to satirize the questioner, but to prevent schools from being deflected from the goals they were established to achieve.

An analysis of the great group of Americans now discussing the public schools reveals that some take what's right with the schools and call it wrong. Either their sense of values or their lack of knowledge of what is done in the schools leads them to criticize the good as being bad.

Only by a careful look at what is said to be wrong with education can the sound and constructive critic be separated from the destructive critic. Caution is needed lest the able and constructive critic be rejected along with the others.

With the hope that the air can be cleared a little, an attempt is made here to identify those who see successes and mistake them for failures.

The founders of America's public schools firmly believed that education would level (or at least lower) economic, social and political barriers to opportunity. They maintained that only through universal education could there be freedom, free choice, productivity, a full cultural life, equality in justice, and a government that could be made to serve the desires of the electorate. Furthermore, these founders claimed that schools would be a means of developing the inherent talents of all people regardless of race, economic status, social origin, or religious belief. Society could best be served by the fullest development of the individual. In fact, they said the schools were the only means of reaching and holding the goals of America.

They Don't Like the Barrier-Leveling Effects

When the criticisms of some of the most vigorous and harshest critics are analyzed, it appears that they are really founded on the *strengths* of the schools, rather than the weaknesses. The doors some critics would lock are the ones many citizens would open. The fields the schools would plow and seed, some critics would have lie fallow. They believe neither in the same values as those listed by the founders of the nation nor in the methods employed by the people to attain those values. Schools, to them, have little or no place in man's struggle to attain justice, life, liberty and the pursuit of happiness.

They see tangible evidence, however, that the schools have gone a long way toward reaching the goals their founders expected them to reach, and the shortsighted critics don't like it. Results are showing. Now that education is giving the individual *the power to bring about such change,* there are some people who would desert that which they once supported, in the academic sense.

They Don't Like Free and Equal Competition

Today, more than ever before, the banker, the judge, and the industrialist observe that their sons are competing in surgery, in finance, and at the bar of justice with the sons of the janitor, the shoemaker, and the barber; and we hear from a few loquacious ones that they don't like it. The 1955 White House Conference on Education pointed out that "as long as good schools are available, a man is not frozen at any level of our economy, nor is his son." Schools free men to rise to the level of their natural abilities. So some find fault with the institution that did most to bring all this to pass. Too often they are heard to ask, "Must we build palaces for our public school children?" And say, "Why these public school facilities are as good as you can find in private school or college!" "Tuition rates in public colleges must be raised." Inherited privilege and socio-economic strata tend to be leveled by universal schools, and some people don't like it.

They Don't Like the Spread of Culture

A few whose families formerly had a monopoly on culture, as expressed in music, art, dance, theater and great literature, find themselves crowded and jostled by the many who now would participate. Now even the reserved boxes are crowded. The schools of America are producing millions who like symphonies, Shakespeare, great art, and good books. A half century ago such appreciation was for only a few. Some who criticize the schools feel that culture is somehow diluted and cheapened if enjoyed by all—what is so precious to a few can hardly be good for the many. The public schools in this respect have succeeded in spreading culture, and some people don't like it.

They Don't Like Tax-Supported Schools

Somewhat akin to the few just mentioned is another small group who, like the bitter antagonists of Thomas Jefferson, Horace Mann, and Henry Barnard, simply dislikes the idea of free schools for all children. The philosophy of these people conflicts with the right of society to tax them for other people's children. Their social philosophy, their concept of values, opposes the belief that schools without tuition should be available for all pupils. They see these schools serving all with public tax money, and they don't like it.

They criticize the schools for extravagance. They contend that the compulsory school age should be lowered. It is from these sources that the cry is often heard, "Why send others than the gifted to high school?" It is they who find fault with a broad and enriched curriculum. They would have the schools teach the bare bones of the three R's. It is they who call music, art and health education the "frills."

Even though the evidence grows that the economy which gave them their wealth is strengthened in large measure by the product of publicly supported schools, they somehow can't quite accept the principle that the support of public schools is everybody's responsibility. So they form clusters of opponents whenever a bond issue for schools is proposed.

They Don't Like Applied Education

Still others who might well be called the academic Brahmins of America see vocational education at both the high school and college levels taking on a state of respectability, and they don't like that, either. So long as vocational education was kept at arm's length from the academic studies, it could be tolerated; but now that it has a firm status, it is cause for alarm. Their caste would be sullied by any learning save the purely academic. Anything more modern than Virgil and Homer is labeled "progressive." The scholar to them can never dirty his hands.

For years, these few refused to accept science as a respectable discipline. So long as vocational education concerned itself with the semiskilled, confined its recruitment to the mentally handicapped, and served only "the trades," it was tolerable. But as life has become more technical, vocational education programs demand better brains and wider liberal bases. This change has made an old fact more clear. A good liberal education has many vocational features.

But the strict academicians would keep forever a wall between the education of the hand and the education of the head, and they cry, "We are making tradesmen of all!" "The schools, especially the teachers, are anti-intellectual!"

When the liberal arts themselves are used as they should be used—to interpret the universe and to give direction to man's behavior in it— there are those who shout that academic standards are being lowered and vocational education is being substituted for liberal education. Just what is liberating? What kinds of education best promote speculation, abstract conceptions, and inquisitive reflection? For them it is good to read *about* the Crusades; but to *study* the present developments and conflicts in the Near East is to depart from scholarship.

They Don't Like Economic Education

Still another success that irritated a limited number of citizens is the knowledge taught of economics and taxation. As never before, the supporters of public education are pointing out, even to students, the way to tax the productivity and economic resources for the support of the public schools and other general welfare services. Some people detest the very idea.

So long as the support of the schools is held to the local level, there is no way to tax fairly America's wealth for schools, and some critics know it but would hide the fact from others. Broader tax bases provide the only adequate and fair avenue for enough money to support education. Those who control these resources know that if school support is kept at the local level they can never be touched. But they see that courses in economics, political science, and taxation reveal sounder and newer ways of raising tax revenues. They become disturbed. As the trends move in the direction of broader tax bases, these few charge that local control is being lost and that school boards, administrators and legislators are ruining the schools.

They Don't Like Education for Active Citizenship

Schools were founded with the belief that education would give men in a democracy the knowledge and the know-how to live free and fruitful lives, to manage their government and the institutions of their society. The purpose of the new government, as stated in the Declaration of Independence, was to promote the general welfare, and to secure the blessings of life, liberty and the pursuit of happiness. Lincoln said it even more boldly when he characterized this government as being "of, by and for, the people."

During the last half-century schools have, in fact, helped accomplish these goals. The schools have prepared citizens to understand and meet their obligations as Americans. Students in the high schools have studied government, social movements, and economics and their effects on the people. Pupils in good schools have learned peaceful ways to human betterment. For this the schools should be thanked rather than spanked.

The purely academic studies where no controversy is possible have been in part supplemented by social and economic studies that give young people the tools and skills for being effective self-governing citizens. Thus democracy has been made to work. Evidence of anarchy and revolution is seldom found in America, simply because the schools have taught people how to bring about, through peaceful means, the evolutionary changes necessary to make their government their servant rather than their master. Social and political changes have been hastened by the education gained in the schools. Some modern "Crusaders" don't like it. Usually their attacks take the form of stating that textbooks are un-American, that socialist doctrines are rampant, that teachers are disloyal, or that moral and spiritual values are neglected.

Education Affects the Power Structure

Again there are uprisings against the schools by a few who see the control of education shifting from the old guard to a younger and more diversified clientele. Feudalism no longer controls the community, and knights are recruited to "save" the people. The P.T.A., citizens study groups, and young parents' clubs are stepping in to vote the school bonds needed, to insist that the finance groups and publicly elected officials help make available funds needed to elect school boards interested in kids rather than in restricting expenditures. Some folks see this happening, and they don't like it. They say that the radicals are out to bankrupt the district.

Any time the power structure within the community is shifted by new patrons, some critics arise to persecute the forces that brought it about. The great shifting of the population, the new phenomenon called suburbia, together with a phenomenal demand for new schools, intensify this struggle. The schools often are selected as the scapegoats. At any rate, some who see that new schools raise taxes don't like it.

They Don't Like Large Numbers in College

Then, strange as it may seem, another little group of citizens who carefully camouflage their real worry criticizes the public schools because too many high school graduates go to college. The colleges admit too many, they say.

Interestingly enough, most of this group went to college, and now it hurts to see the "exclusive club membership" being greatly expanded. Could it be that they fear a lowering of personal prestige by increased numbers? They claim the high schools do not adequately prepare for college, but admission tests and the scholastic results after admission belie their statements. Their allegations of poor preparation are contradicted by college board examinations, the number making honors, the deans' lists, and the percentage of public high school graduates who make Phi Beta Kappa. Recently an official admissions officer of Harvard said that half the membership of classes 25 years ago would fail today in competition with candidates of today. Critics see this increasing percentage joining the ranks of the "privileged" who reach college, and don't like it.

They Don't Like Attention to Individual Differences

Still another criticism of the modern school's success, or at least its partial achievement, comes from splendid but misinformed citizens who are usually strong supporters of the schools. They observe that two pupils in the same grade pass on to another grade when one obviously achieves superior standing and the other is doing poor work. They observe that one graduate of the local high school can spell, write and cipher much better than another, and conclude that the high school has no standards. From such casual observation, they are led to believe that schools don't really teach or make pupils work. Most of these people don't stop to think that the school serves all young people, that there is a spread of ability at every grade level, and that there is no way to "squash" them together. In fact, the good school widens the gap of achievement among students rather than sets one standard for all, but some pesons can't or won't understand this arrangement.

So the schools, by varied curriculums and by diversified standards, have tried to serve and to stimulate each pupil at every grade level. Some have taken calculus and Latin; others, the more simple, manual subjects. Some excel in music; others in science. The more successful the school is in doing all this, the greater the spread of differences at high school graduation time. Those who don't understand don't like it. The better the job with each individual child, the more severe the criticisms from those who are ignorant of pupil difference.

Individual differences are in serious need of better understanding by more teachers and, especially, more administrators, and of better explanation to all the public. If citizens could be made to understand that children differ as much in intellectual aptitude as in physical aptitude, fewer critics of school standards would emerge. Since they already agree that every child shouldn't be expected to pole-vault 13 feet or to throw the shot 50 feet, they could easily be made to understand that intellectual requirements must differ for the very same reasons as do the physical.

They Don't Like a Strong Teaching Profession

Again, there are some who get terribly stirred up over the fact that teachers have organized and have more power. They hark back to the day when teachers were hired from year to year with no assurance of security or continuous salary contracts. For them the times were sweeter when teachers were fired because of political pressures or petty official displeasures. The good old days when teachers were badgered by cranks and politicians are yearned for by those who want teachers to be beggarly servants. To them, the insecure teacher is to be desired. Servility on the part of those who teach their children somehow seems desirable. Strength from the profession, reasonable security, and a living wage mean more support, better budgets, and better schools, and some don't like it. So they rise and shout, "teachers' lobby," "pressure groups," and "politics." They often recall with eloquence that someone said, "All we need is Mark Hopkins and a log."

They Don't Like It—and It's Profitable

And of course the most despicable critic of all is the "professional mercenary." He is the miserable soul who recognizes that parents realize the importance of the school. He knows they worry about their children's reaching school age. He knows they believe education will make or mar the future of their children. He knows they fear a world that is more and more demanding of broad and special competence which the school alone can give. He capitalizes on this worry and fear and starts writing books on what is wrong with schools, knowing full well there will be sales to frightened parents. He explains just why children will be led astray by "modern" and "progressive" schools, and proposes oversimplified and sometimes invalid schemes for saving them. He often selects as his target the most scientifically sound aspect, which is often the newest. Often he will resort to dramatic descriptions of unusual or imagined instances. The very range of aptitude and behavior found in all public schools gives him ammunition to distort through use of the exceptional. Sometimes he will explain that teachers oppose discipline or that they let pupils study at random. Usually the "educationist" is the villain.

These writers often pose as scholars and imply that teachers and administrators are without culture or liberal education. Their motives are all too often profit motives. They are the professional vultures of our time. They may well be compared to the ruthless white traders who haunted the covered wagon trails of the West and sold guns to the Indians.

Still another group, closely related to the last, is made up of the overzealous, pseudo-education scientists, the promoters of gadgets and special methods of instruction or structured organizations. They say the teachers and administrators are reactionaries and are inefficient. They oversimplify the teaching tasks. They have *discovered* the quick road to rapid learning and *scholarship*. Unlike the true pioneer, the true scientist, they vigorously promote that which has not yet been validated and accuse the administrator who asks for evidence before adoption of being reactionary and resistant to needed change.

When teachers question and ask for proof, the promoters are frustrated and don't like it. Armed with many questionable "truths," they have set forth by sheer repetition and exalted manner to discredit the leadership of America's schools, teachers and the school curriculum. They set themselves up as saviors and present "new" images of "scientific" methods and "sound" philosophy and psychology of learning and just "what" constitutes proper structure, organization and curriculum. At the same time they present an inaccurate image of what the schools have been and are in relation to structure, materials, content and methods.

They Don't Like Intellectual Honesty

Last of all, the superpatriot and the supermoralist scourge the schools with gleaming swords and flying banners and martial music of saintly chant. If the schools dare search deeply for truth among the values of our culture; if the textbooks lay bare the weaknesses in our politics, our economic system, and our social customs; if pupils are critical and express dissent, the schools are branded as evil. Vehement propaganda which proclaims absolute truth, particularly in matters ideological, is demanded in the curriculum to ensure protection from the evils of foreign doctrine and the falsehoods of the enemy. The very freedoms and intelligent independence of thought which the schools would promote, these critics brand as dangerous and even subversive.

The sensible, logical skepticism which the schools seek to develop as sound preparation for the thinking man and intelligent choice-maker is criticized with loud demands for outright indoctrination for or against what they believe to be good or evil. Often these groups rally the patriotic and the devout, but more often the supporters are extremists with little balance and less knowledge of the great complex social, cultural, political and economic diversity which the teacher attempts to interpret wisely to the pupils. Again, what is right with the schools in terms of America's traditions and fundamental requirements for intelligent citizenship some critics brand as wrong.

They Sometimes Hoodwink School Boards

Boards of education often mistake these scattered but diversified false critics for the voice of the people and make unwise policy decisions. With criticisms coming from so many directions, it is sometimes assumed by school boards that there are great unrest and dissatisfaction with public schools, when in reality most parents of public school children believe the schools are soundly administered, wisely taught, and abundantly effective. Wise board members, however, do what this article attempts to do. They look carefully at all criticisms; accept and use the constructive; and analyze, classify and reject the invalid.

Beware of False Leaders and False Idols

The headlines schools are making today are healthy evidence of America's vitality and her belief that education is vital not only to the individual's welfare but to the nation's strength and security. So long as such faith holds and so long as we encourage diversity, independence and free speech, the public schools will be discussed and criticized. There is ample evidence that the typical American is still striving for the complete fulfillment of his hopes for the achievement of his son or daughter. Evidence, too, is adequate to prove that the teacher, the principal, the superintendent, have all led well in the past and are abler now than ever before. Their leadership must not now be surrendered to the "volunteers" who would coach from the sidelines, but who have never carried the ball. Neither should the partisan politician be permitted to make political capital out of public schools.

Administrators are trained leaders of American education. They should take pride in their knowledge, their training, and their particular scholarship, and should lead with confidence, courage and humility. In carrying out this leadership, they will thoughtfully and calmly set aside the ill-intentioned faultfinders from that great majority of critics who want to help the schools fulfill their destiny. They will join hands with the latter, but fight the former wherever they attempt to establish a beachhead. They will combat misinformation and false idols with accurate data and with a philosophy that is consistent with American democratic values. Their opportunity is unique. The superintendent, the school boards, the principals, the teachers, live on the same streets with all America. They have the direct ear of the people when they speak. Their ears can hear all the aspirations of all the people if they listen.

The AASA program of activities which occupied my energies was centered around speaking and counseling throughout the United States, chiefly with the state associations of school administrators, shepherding special commissions and committees, writing and editing bulletins, brochures, and major publications, and writing editorials for the *School Administrator*. As the years went by, many school administrators with special problems sought advice by personal contact, at the office, over the phone, during drive-in conferences and by letter.

Sometimes I was able to help a superintendent achieve visibility on the national scale. I recall one late afternoon during the annual convention in Atlantic City. I was trying hurriedly to get into a tuxedo in preparation for the evening session. A knock came at my door. There stood George Leonard, senior editor of *Look* Magazine. I invited him in. He realized my busy schedule but said, "Give me five minutes. I want to write a feature story about a superintendent and his daily activities. Please give me the names of a half dozen school systems, widely distributed geographically, that have forward looking superintendents."

I quickly listed a half dozen and led him to the door. But at the door stood Jack Hornbeck, then superintendent at Tilamuk, Oregon. Jack had attended a seminar I had once taught at the University of Oregon. Also, I had visited his schools.

I introduced the two men and Leonard turned to me and said, "Why wouldn't Hornbeck be a good man to investigate?"

I had admired Jack and his work, so I said, "Go ahead."

Three months later a splendid action story with Superintendent Hornbeck as the central figure appeared in *Look*. Today Hornbeck is superintendent in San Diego, California.

Planning seminars, conferences, and major conventions required time, imagination, and thousands of contacts. Developing policy proposals for board action, too, called for deliberation and writing by me and my associates. Many mornings before the clerical staff arrived, late afternoons when they had gone and on many Saturdays, two of my professional associates released our imagination and talents together to wrestle with current problems facing school administrators and to peer into the future to anticipate the emerging ones. Of all the hours I labored at AASA, those were the most refreshing and exciting and, in fact, the most productive. It was during these thrilling moments that we broke old tethers and found new directions for the organization. No dissent, no hypothesis, no criticism, no proposal was too extreme or diverse to escape our careful analysis and evaluation. On occasion, too, we spent evenings planning and programming in my home. Twice during these years when the heat of August in Washington fell heavy, two associates, Shirley Cooper and William Ellena, and I drove westward to the peak of Davis Mountain in West Virginia. There in splendid temperatures 3500 feet up, ensconced in a forest ranger's cottage, we planned and wrote. I prepared the meals, and they washed the dishes. The evenings were used to review our day's work and to program the work of the next day. Our production during those wonderful days on Davis Mountain was significantly satisfactory in both amount and quality.

One of the projects calling for detailed planning and much correspondence was the annual convention. During the fifties it was the board policy every third year to hold three regional conferences: in the West, the Midwest, and the East, while holding the national convention in Atlantic City the two years intervening. There was no other city that could guarantee all the resources for a meeting of the national membership. Careful evaluation of the objectives of the annual conference would lead to the abandoning of the regional meetings in 1961. However, to render more service to the membership finding it difficult to go to Atlantic City, more drive-in conferences were added, and circuit rides were instituted.

The work of planning and developing the annual convention called for agreement on the theme of the total conference and who would be asked to make the general session speeches, as well as alternates. In early spring the president of the association came to Washington to give his views on the nature of the program, the special features, and some national figures he would like to invite to speak. Early in the planning, too, the subject for debates, dialogues, panels, and round tables was determined. We solicited ideas from leaders in every state. Finding fresh and able talents to fill the two thousand program-participating roles was a most difficult task. It was always a temptation to repeat with old "reliables" who had often taken roles. Furthermore, the older men who had been active in the association for years were disconcerted if the program was printed and their names did not appear.

Allocating space for the many group meetings and accurately predicting the number who would attend each was most important when assigning rooms and halls. Hundreds of university groups and other allied organizations demanded suites, ballrooms, breakfasts, luncheons, dinners, cocktail rooms, and space for receptions. These, too, were controlled and allocated by our staff. Housing for the hundreds of educational exhibits by manufacturing concerns called for thousands of feet of floor space. To accommodate all and allocate specific space was no mean task in itself, and policing to make sure ethical practices prevailed called for firmness with diplomacy.

In 1961 we learned that Atlantic City had a closed-circuit TV cable connecting with nearly all of the hotels. A large percentage of all guest rooms had TV sets. We seized upon the opportunity to extend our services by contracting for TV time. Telecasting started at 6 A.M. and continued until 12 midnight. Naturally, the telecasting was off the air while other programs were underway, such as group meetings and the general sessions. The TV programs from the very beginning won the interest and enthusiastic support of those in attendance. With this additional feature, it was possible for one in attendance to be a listener and a viewer of programs for a twelve-hour stretch, if he so desired.

It was our goal to make the five days as full of educational information and stimulation as possible. We had great diversity of subjects, issues, and problems because the audience included local, county, and state superintendents, principals, school board members, professors, classroom teachers, specialists, and college presidents. The program and the exhibits of the newest in equipment and materials, together with dozens of award-winning architectural plans and drawings of recently constructed school buildings, constituted a magnificent refresher school for educators.

In addition to all this, it was found popular to have experts in many fields available for individual consultation, so scheduled time for meeting the experts became a feature. Likewise, recently made education films were run for several hours each day. In December 1961 I wrote a brief description of the upcoming convention program for the School Administrator House Organ. It read:

> Industry after industry has found it profitable in recent years to give time off and pay expenses necessary for top administrators to attend short-term schools for executives. Some boards of education likewise have encouraged superintendents to pursue programs of study. Is it not time for school boards generally to consider similar policies for their administrators?
>
> Nothing grows obsolete more rapidly than public education under the leadership of an administrator gone stale or unaware of the critical issues and changing demands on schools. Even the good superintendent who reads, travels, listens, and confers with the best local minds can be stimulated and made more competent by temporary absence from his daily work routine, and by induction into an environment of intellectual stimulation and deliberately planned contemplation.
>
> School boards everywhere should encourage their superintendent to attend the short, but intensive "school" to be held next February 17-21 in Atlantic City. Packed into this five-day school—the AASA Convention—is the most comprehensive and most diverse educational program ever prepared for superintendents of schools.
>
> The "faculty" (those who lecture, debate, demonstrate, present research data and interrogate) are drawn from great scholars and statesmen of this nation and some foreign nations. Instructional methods include television, visual aids, audio tapes, large group lectures, seminars, and individual seminars.
>
> The "laboratory" consisting of the very latest curriculum and instructional materials and equipment from more than 500 exhibitors can be matched by no other school or educational conference in the world. The "student" superintendents who explore and search out new knowledge in this great laboratory will go home stimulated, refreshed, and well-stocked with new ideas.

The curriculum for this intensive school ranges from the most critical issues in sociology, political science, and government economics and the humanities to the practical problems facing the school administrator and the research data which suggest solutions. The faculty is as large as is found in our largest universities and the student body will run beyond 20,000.

To develop such a diverse and comprehensive series of activities, to secure acceptances from persons invited to perform on the programs, to get their names and titles accurately printed, to allocate meeting space, it was essential to make careful division of labors among the small staff.

The Executive Committee showed its interest in international education by authorizing the secretary to invite all embassies in Washington to send their cultural affairs officer. Foreign students and visiting professors from many lands were invited to be the guests of the association.

Every staff member in attendance at the convention made out a time schedule, with a listing of where he would be in Atlantic City and what his responsibility would be at any hour. A central telephone clearing house was manned so that as staff members periodically reported they could be redeployed to assist with any emergency. Thus, as secretary, I had a "blow by blow" report at all times of all aspects of the giant operation. It was possible for me to shift personnel if the situation warranted change.

One of the great worries was travel mishaps that might prevent the appearance of a speaker for a big general session. My responsibility for the general session programs demanded that I be in touch with the travel plans of all major speakers. If they came in by air, I usually took a limousine to meet them. Naturally, I kept an ear to the ground each day regarding the weather. An incident with John Fitzgerald Kennedy serves to illustrate the problem. He was a U.S. Senator and was scheduled to speak at 8:30 P.M. His pressing duties in the Senate caused him to request a late afternoon flight. There was no commercial flight from Washington at that time of day, so I contracted with a private owner and operator to fly the Senator direct in a small twin-engine plane. At five o'clock I started to the airport to meet our guest, who was due at six o'clock. I waited and waited, but no flight came in. I checked with the flight control tower at 6:30 P.M. They had no report of the plane's approach. About seven o'clock, I learned that the plane had met bad weather near Baltimore and had landed there. Soon I had the Senator on the telephone. He said he was sorry, but he would have to cancel, since it seemed too dangerous to proceed. I insisted that he stay in a motel in Baltimore, hold the plane, and fly up the next morning. I would get a replacement for him that evening and he could speak in the morning. He said that he couldn't do that since he was having a luncheon meeting with the officials of *Life* Magazine in New York the next day. I explained the seriousness of canceling a speaking engagement to twenty thousand school administrators. Their disappointment would, in fact, turn to resentment.

"If you hold the plane, the weather is reported to be good tomorrow. You can fly here by nine o'clock, speak from ten to eleven, and we will fly you on to New York for your one o'clock luncheon." Reluctantly, he agreed.

Time was running short before the opening of the evening session, and the scheduled speaker was in Baltimore. I telephoned Mrs. Engleman and the staff leaders, asking that they locate the scheduled next-morning speaker and request him to shift to the program that was due to open within the hour. Since he might not be found readily, I also asked that they contact Professor Harold Hunt, past president, and have him stand by as a possible pinch hitter. Then I drove to the great convention hall. What a relief it was to find the speaker in the wings and agreeable to the shift in his appearance time.

On another occasion I became truly frightened. Vice-President Lyndon Johnson was the speaker for an evening session. The AASA president was Dr. Irby Carruth, superintendent from Austin, Texas. Since Mrs. Johnson was coming also, Dr. and Mrs. Carruth and Mrs. Engleman and I met the plane. The women rode in one limousine, the men in the other. All went well going into the hall. The back door was guarded, and we all hurried into the elevator which stopped backstage, but when we were leaving we were met by a mob of well-wishers at the sidewalk and on a dark street. I hurriedly escorted the Vice-President into the waiting car and closed the door, but he saw friends and well-wishers outside wanting to shake his hand. Into the crowd he strode, even though it was quite dark. The people were shoving and pulling to reach him. He seemed utterly unaware that there could be any danger, but I breathed easily only after we got him safely back in the car and were rolling toward the airport. That experience, together with his folksy conversation, convinced me that he was a true lover of mankind, with deep insights into human nature.

It was my privilege to assist in the planning and programming of eight annual conventions presided over by Paul Misner, C. C. Trillingham, Phillip Hickey, Martin Essex, Forrest Conner, Benjamin Willis, Irby Carruth, and Natt Burbank. Each one had its own special features, theme, and area of emphasis. From the many communications I received, and from our evaluation committee reports, it was apparent that thousands of school board members, administrators, and others had their educational, social, and economic horizons lifted at every convention. Possibly the most unique conference, however, was the one presided over by C. C. Trillingham. During the year preceding, as a result of Sputnik, critics had accused the schools of having no "tough" subjects such as mathematics and science. They said the schools were soft and the curriculum designed for fun and comfort. The reaction began, and it was evident that the school program of the humanities, music, art, and literature, was headed for a backseat, if not total curtailment. I felt that some counteracting movement was needed, and Dr. Trillingham agreed. We decided to plan a complete five-day program devoted to the arts, music, literature, drama, and the dance. The program had lectures, panels, and dialogue in the place of these disciplines in the curriculum and was highlighted by outstanding performing artists. Great poets read poetry, authorities on the drama appeared, literary critics spoke, a modern dance group and a great symphony orchestra performed. An outstanding modern painter gave a giant visual exposition, and Van Cliburn closed the conference with a magnificent concert.

Although the AASA president and I had some misgivings as to how such an emphasis would be accepted amidst the national cry for math and science, our fears were relieved when we heard the favorable acclaim. Indeed, those five days of restudy of the place of the humanities and the performing arts convinced the school administrators that the arts must maintain a strong role in the school program.

I recall well a meeting of a yearbook committee at the Mayflower Hotel. I was doing their secretarial work and editing. On this particular day, they all said, "Finis, can't you do something to stop the critics who are harassing and destroying the morale of teachers? Sputnik has driven much of the public wild."

As their deliberations began, I turned my thoughts inward. In a few minutes I thought of a Missouri Ozarks story. Then I started to write. At noon I gave my hurriedly written manuscript to C. O. Wright, a member of the committee, and said, "C. O., during the noon hour, look this over and tell me what you think."

When he returned, he urged me to finish and polish and publish. In the next two days, my three professional associates helped edit what I had written and gave me a few suggestions as to additional content. I gave the manuscript to a printer and the result was "Hogs, Ax Handles, and Woodpeckers." This publication was sufficiently pertinent to the immediate times that the demand for reprints from many states was overwhelming, and sufficiently satirical to silence many critics.

The regional drive-ins were increased during these years because of the favorable reactions. One of the AASA professional staff members, together with a staff representative of the Rural Department of the NEA, would meet with representatives from all the states of a given region. These representatives usually consisted of local superintendents, professors or deans, and personnel from state departments of education. The policy followed was to draw the program from the desires, judgments, and firsthand knowledge of the men in the field. Their pressing problems became the point of emphasis. The Washington representatives played the role of listeners and summarizers, following through with the printed program and digests. The host state administrators looked after all details of physical arrangements. These conferences, in my judgment, owed their continued success to careful planning and to the fact that their programs and talents were of "grass roots" origin. Furthermore, they served many who could not attend the national convention. Most credit for their effectiveness should go to Dr. Shirley Cooper who, better than any man I have known, knew how to release the talents of men in small communities. Bob Isenberg, too, felt the throbbing pulse of the rural and small town administrator.

The circuit rides served a different purpose. In a small region, usually within a single state, a superintendent would agree to play host to his neighboring school administrators, who would be asked to bring their problems and questions. One of the professional staff members from AASA headquarters would appear. The meeting usually opened with a run-down of contemporary educational happenings in Washington, new national issues, new legislation, new movements, and special activities of AASA. Then the small group would fire questions, raise further issues, express opinions, and enter into round-table dialogue. These seminar meetings raised the mental horizons and stirred the imaginations of many administrators.

It grew increasingly clear that joint projects were necessary between AASA and such other national organizations as the NEA, the National School Boards Association, the National School Business Officials, the Department of Classroom Teachers, the National Council of Chief State School Officers, the National Association of Secondary School Principals, the Association for Supervision and Curriculum Development, and the Department of Elementary School Principals. Occasionally, too, we joined hands with the Department of Health and Physical Education, the Mathematics Teachers, the Science Teachers, and the Teachers of English. Joint seminars with the Association of City Managers brought new insights into the relationships of education and political science.

The staff and officers played no role more important than that of giving direction and leadership to the officers of the state associations of school administrators and, at the same time, using them as sounding boards for evaluating the program of AASA. It was our philosophy that the best work for advancing the cause of public education would be done at state and local levels. Therefore, every effort was made to strengthen the state associations. We acquainted the presidents and secretaries with emerging issues and developments and stimulated them to get action from their organizations. An annual work conference of presidents and state secretaries was carefully planned, and half the expenses of participants was borne by AASA.

We planned these work conferences and selected talent with a view to lifting sights, exploding old worn-out hypotheses, and pointing to the future. The group was small enough—about 125—so that the program could be shifted quickly from plenary session to small group round tables. In 1956, it was clear to our board and staff that revenues for schools must be supplemented by federal funds, but the fear of federal control, together with just plain parochialism, lay heavily on everyone's mind. Not one in ten would approve of federal aid, but we brought in financial experts and presented the case. A few converts were made. In each succeeding year, the matter of adequate sources of revenue was studied. At the last meeting of the officers that I attended, in 1963, it was unanimous that the federal government had responsibilities for giving financial assistance to schools.

Possibly the strongest characteristic of these meetings with state officers was the participatory aspect. Although stimulated by speakers and proposals, they showed greater growth when discussing and deliberating in small groups.

Although continuous liaison was maintained with NEA on such matters as national legislation and national policy, the determination of AASA to operate with considerable autonomy seemed to produce a certain amount of coolness from some officials of the NEA. Occasionally, the governing boards of NEA and the annual general assembly would pass resolutions or regulations that offended the spirit of AASA autonomy. Possibly, the problem was made difficult because history and development suggested one image, while a literal reading of the constitution and bylaws of each organization suggested a different one. From the beginning, it was obvious to me that sooner or later the relationship between AASA and NEA would have to be clarified. It eventually was, when they voted to make themselves associated organizations rather than have AASA as a subordinate department. It was my considered judgment that a stronger leadership role and a more powerful influence on education and the federal government would prevail if both NEA and AASA operated with autonomy but joined hands as peer teammates on common goals. Two strong voices are better than one.

Since 1935, AASA and NEA had supported a national commission called the Educational Policies Commission. Vacancies on this body were filled yearly by a joint meeting of the executive committees of both organizations. The executive secretaries of AASA and NEA were ex officio voting members. For many years, this body produced policy statements that had far-reaching effects. Its membership was of the very highest quality, and each member had complete independence of action. Neither NEA nor AASA exerted any influence to control the statements issued by the commission. I had to resign as a regular member when I became an ex officio member upon acceptance of the secretaryship of AASA. During the first years I served, I was greatly stimulated by the caliber of personnel serving with me and by the nature of the issues we studied. For many years, the statements were rather profound policy declarations. In later years, the issues seemed much more nebulous and the productions more like small yearbooks than concise policy communications. In addition, the pressure to appoint members from certain strata of the profession rather than because of statesmanship and scholarship lessened the effectiveness of the Commission.

During my period of service on the Educational Policies Commission I found myself in vigorous but friendly dialogue almost all the time. I was perhaps most disturbed at one meeting of the Commission by a proposed statement called "The Central Purpose of American Education." The secretary, with persistent determination, favored a strong policy statement setting forth the belief that American education has only one basic purpose—to improve the intellect. Since I believed that public education was of multipurpose dimensions, there was a clash of opinions from the first, and so the debate raged. It seemed that the secretary's version was about to be adopted. I strongly urged massive alterations. Because my statements at that time give a reasonably accurate profile of the philosophy which has guided many aspects of my administrative practice, it seems fitting to present them, in part, here.

> ... This statement before us does not basically differ from the position set forth in previous versions. The persistent and enthusiastic determination to set forth *one* goal in education as central and overriding all others prevails in this document, although more subtly stated. I like much of the content because I, too, believe the effective man, the free American, should be a man of judgment with the will and the ability to make wise choices. I believe making him so is *one* objective but not *the* central overriding one of all American public schools.
>
> My observations are directly concerned with the heart of the document, pages 5 to 15. The assumptions and the accompanying arguments which contend that the power to rationalize is the central purpose of education and that other goals find their foundation and strength from this one purpose and subordinate all other aspects to this one central purpose is a statement of a half-truth, or so it appears to me. As we all know, arguing from half-truths always leads into difficulty. Throughout these long

discussions for many months, I have recognized the very great importance of having the schools contribute toward making men who can make good choices, men of sound judgment, and men who are deep thinkers. On this point I have firm convictions. I believe the school has a very great role in this although other segments of society contribute, including the home. But, I cannot in good conscience go to the extreme of accepting this goal as being so dominant and overriding as to obscure and subordinate all others.

I went to school when the school had just one central purpose—that of training the intellect and presumably making thinkers of its products. Because of this limited purpose more than any other single thing, only a very small percent of the pupils finished a high school education. Furthermore, I believe there is much evidence to prove that schools since that era have, with multiple purposes, *produced better thinkers.* It was only after the first World War, when a multiple purpose educational system was designed, that a curriculum pattern was broadened to reasonably well meet the needs of many pupils, not a few. It was then that vocational education, citizenship, worthy home membership, good health, ethical character, etc., became goals. If the schools now return to a single objective, or put such high priorities upon one objective, that all others sink into second, third, or fourth rate rank as was prevalent in 1916, and as this document contends, then our drop-out rates will increase; our curriculum pattern will become restricted and too limited to meet the needs of all pupils. I fear the Commission, while recognizing that schools need to have higher quality, better standards, greater scholarship in learning, has heard the critics who have never accepted the multiple purpose concept for American Education and who would say that 25 percent of those now in school can never achieve the goal of being rational men anyway, and therefore should be eliminated from the registration. In fact, this interpretation was given to a speech made by our Secretary in San Francisco when he pointed out that the Commission was producing a document that would set forth the rational man as the central objective of education in America. The reporter for the *San Francisco Chronicle* observed in a news story that the Policies Commission was at last coming around to the position of the University scholars and critics who recommended that the San Francisco public school board restrict its program to a very limited academic curriculum. This, I predict, will be the interpretation given to the document by all who believe in such a restricted concept for the schools of America. But school leaders who have sought broad curriculum objectives—including vocational competence and skill, and an appreciation of the arts as well, will be bullied and badgered with this document used as a club.

I may be wrong, but it is my belief that the development of rationality cannot be achieved except as simultaneous development takes place in physical well being, by the elimination of disease, by achieving emotional balance, by the growth of ethical character, with the acceptance of values, with the release and growth of creative powers, and with the liberation of the imaginative powers of man. None of these, including the state of rationality, is a discrete development, but is interrelated and interdependent. They do not and cannot be achieved separately. The biologists would term these relationships, symbiotic. If the schools attempt to separate these things into discrete compartments we revert to a psychology or philosophy of education that failed in China and in other countries of the world. Surely this Commission does not seek a return to pure scholasticism. Indeed, we should insist that the schools have a deep interest in, but not a preoccupation with, only abstract contemplation. No matter how concerned the teacher may become with abstract intellectual activities, these experiences alone have only a modest chance of success in developing great minds if a separatism or compartmental theory is followed. America by its multiple purpose approach has produced a new kind of man and a new kind of education. Its multiple purpose approach is its greatest asset abroad as well as at home. I don't believe we dare retreat from it. I believe that by selecting and emphasizing rationality as *the* central purpose we understate (possibly unwittingly) other objectives that also are and must be *threads running throughout any sound program*. This document very adroitly and quite appropriately points out the importance of the thinking individual in the development of the other values, but the document could with equal validity and adroitness point out that the rational man is rational largely to the degree that he possesses values, that he has creative power, that he has aesthetic appreciations, that he has emotional and physical balance. Thus the argument can be turned the other way, in my judgment. A good vocational program likewise, by its very objectivity, gives added meaning to abstract generalizations. In fact, some people would contend that the concrete must always serve as a foundation for the abstract. Equally valid arguments could be made that the central purpose is to make an ethical man, an emotionally balanced man, a creative man, because each helps make the rational man. Thus, we could contend that basic and central in our educational program are the establishment of beliefs, of appreciations, and of personal health and stability, etc. In a speech before AASA three years ago, John Ciardi, the literary critic, said:

"I seriously do not have the school system. I am concerned about the fact that it is *too rational*. Everything seems to go by reason, or the ideal seems to be reason. I wish there could be more recognition of the fact that the most important things we do in our lives are not rational."

In my judgment, the so-called rational man can and will have great limitations, *even in his intellectual stature,* unless the schools provide him with these other important aspects of life. Today in the eyes of many, the most rational human being on earth is the devoted and intellectually skilled communist. Moving to another field, we might ask the question: Was it Gertrude Stein or was it Robert Frost who wrote the most rational verse; or were they both rational, depending upon the values you happen to have? Is it DeGaulle, Nehru, Kasavubu, Kennedy, or Castro who is thinking straight today? Many rational men believe in and follow each.

I guess it is my belief that learning is a complex and intermingling kind of thing which helps people move toward multiple goals, all at the same time, with each aiding and abetting the other. I feel that the education process is a bit like a machine, say an automobile. We might contend that the drive shaft is the central controlling force which makes the automobile effective and yet you would not attempt to drive it with one wheel missing, the steering gear removed, or with no gas tank.

It would seem to me that the Commission should abandon rationality as *the* one central overriding goal. We should, I believe, state that the schools seek to achieve several goals which have a considerable degree of interdependence. We can give strong support to rationality without downgrading all other purposes.

Soon after becoming executive secretary of AASA, I perceived that the organizations with greatest kinship housed within the NEA building were administrative and supervisory in character. They were the Council of Chief State School Officers, the NCSSP, the DEAP, and the ASCD. These four organizations over and over faced similar issues and problems. Throughout my stay in Washington, there were few weeks that passed without thoughtful consultation with the various secretaries of the five organizations. Almost always, AASA had a major joint project underway with one or more of these organizations.

One exceedingly helpful cooperative enterprise was the annual conference and planning session held jointly with the AASA, the NEA, the Council of CSSO, the NSBA, and the National Congress of Parents and Teachers. Throughout these conferences, Wayne Reed of the U.S. Office of Education gave objective leadership, but without trying to dominate. Gradually, during the seven years I met with the five groups, they came to believe in certain national policies and national programs. To achieve this in the midst of fear of federal involvement in education was, indeed, a major accomplishment. It is encouraging to me to observe that five years after my last meeting with them, due in large part to the statesmanship of Forrest Conner and Ed Fuller, all five organizations agreed on a program of general federal aid. These two men achieved what I had so unsuccessfully tried to do.

I discussed earlier the efforts of the educational profession to improve itself during the late forties. When I began work at the AASA office, the Cooperative Program in Educational Administration was in full swing. In fact, while serving as commissioner of education in Connecticut, I was a member of the small commission of AASA that determined the cooperative program's policies. As executive secretary of AASA, I gave up my regular membership on the commission and became an ex officio member. About that time, too, the commission changed its name to the "Committee for the Advancement of School Administration." Its secretary then took on the additional title of assistant secretary of AASA.

With an additional grant from the W. K. Kellogg Foundation, AASA was ready, through its CASA, to make great strides toward the improvement of university programs designed to prepare school administrators and to raise the standards of the superintendent. Close working relations were maintained with university graduate departments of school administration and with chief state school officers and their certification departments. State associations of school administrators were deeply involved, as were school board associations. As judgments on standards were crystallized in the several states, the CASA presented this consensus to the AASA Executive Committee. After much discussion and study of the research done by the universities on competencies needed by the superintendent, the Executive Committee proposed an amendment to the constitution and bylaws of the AASA. The gist of the amendment clearly called for upgrading the standards for admission to AASA membership. In short, after a period of four years, all new members must submit credentials proving that they have completed an approved two-year graduate program beyond the bachelor's degree in a recognized university. At the annual convention in 1960, this amendment was adopted by the members, effective January 1, 1964.

Now that it had achieved high standards for its members, AASA had a further responsibility to help universities preparing administrators to raise their admission standards and to improve their graduate programs. There was slow progress in some graduate schools and hardly any at all in others. A program such as the Committee for the Advancement of School Administration proposed called for many resources, human and material. In fact, the majority of the resources of a large university were essential. Money, a great deal of money, was needed for the budget. The small or weak institution should serve only as a feeder, or not at all. It seemed clear that any program designed to give the competencies needed by a superintendent would borrow heavily from the behavioral sciences, government, economics, business, and personnel management, but to overlook the study of learning and teaching, the diversity of human kind, and the curriculum would be a mistake. The program, in many ways, must acquaint the prospective superintendent with the great scientific, philosophic, economic, political, and sociological phenomena on the horizon. For it is education, if properly designed and executed, that will prepare youth and adults to cope with the changing scene. Had the school administrators in larger cities recognized the impact of technology, transportation change, and communications on population shifts, the ghetto problem might have been solved before it became so serious.

Although I observed some exciting changes taking place in both content and teaching methods of many graduate schools of education, I must confess to considerable disappointment at the lack of urgency to improve on the part of many professors. It is my judgment that the organization known as the University Council on Educational Administration has produced the cutting edge for change in programs designed to train school administrators. Dr. John Norton of Columbia University was responsible for presenting the idea to representatives of AASA and a group of universities. It was he, too, who gave it a big boost by agreeing to share his grant from the Kellogg Foundation. I found the seminars sponsored by UCEA to be exceedingly profitable. Their films, case studies, and publications have also set high watermarks.

For selected superintendents, we attempted an inservice program that possibly later led to the founding of the AASA National Academy for School Executives. We invited administrators and some professors of school administration to attend High Horizon Seminars which were usually held at adult education centers on university campuses. To these seminars we brought experts who discussed great "breakthroughs" in science, politics, economics, sociology, and education. Vigorous dialogue was encouraged. The whole process was designed to disturb the complacent, to show the relevance of great developments and concepts to the role of the administrator. The response was enthusiastic. Almost all who attended reported that they had glimpsed new horizons and had been stimulated to meet change with change.

As I stated earlier, my work as executive secretary of the American Association of School Administrators took me to all fifty states. Often the occasion would be the annual meeting of a state association of school administrators. At these meetings, I spent considerable time listening to the presentations and discussions of state issues and hearing individuals pour our their hearts on local district problems. But my biggest effort was devoted to my speech to the group and to the discussion of questions that always followed. Although I frequently addressed my thinking to a special topic requested by the program committee, I was generally free to say whatever I chose. Consequently, my talk often became omnibus in character. Often the outline of the talk would include the following:

1. New developments in the American Association of School Administrators, with emphasis on new commissions, new publications, new services, and the continuing efforts to improve the university programs for preparing school administrators.
2. What is cooking in Washington?—Congress, Supreme Court, executive branch.
3. A reconfirmation of my faith and theirs that education plays the foundation role in a free society.
4. The issues and problems that must be faced by school administrators, boards, and staff, such as:
   a. How to make education cope with the changing world. Education and administrators dare not become obsolete. I tried to excite their interest in the relevancy of exciting phenomena in the scientific, economic, political, social, and cultural world. The emergence of a smaller, more interdependent world was stressed.
   b. The changing economic world and the obsolescence of the tax system. Even full-length speeches were given on this topic. A shift of support from local property tax to broad-based state and federal revenues was inevitable if schools were to have adequate budgets.

c. The growth in maturity of teachers. They must be dealt with on other than a paternalistic basis. Take their new power, their militancy in stride. Possibly they can achieve what the administration has failed to achieve.
   d. Technology, new structures: their assets and their liabilities in education. How can the computer, the data processor, be mastered and used?
   e. A plea for the freedom of teachers to deviate, to experiment, to try the new and fail without penalty. Administrators must stand ready and willing to share in their failures as well as their successes.
5. A final suggestion, always given: The administrator should keep close to the learners. The superintendent should know wherein the total program fails or succeeds in meeting the ideal set by the staff. Are all children respected, understood, developed, served? Where is the program weak, strong?

Although the pattern of the talk changed and certainly the points of emphasis shifted from state to state, I tried hard to shake complacency and, at the same time, strengthen commitments.

Some of the AASA publications caused controversy and sometimes criticism. Among them would be *Testing, Testing, Testing, Religions in the Schools,* and *Foundations.*

Testing, Testing, Testing was published jointly by AASA, the Council of Chief State School Officers, and the National Association of Secondary School Principals. The purpose of the publication was not to discount the need for evaluation, but rather to slow down excessive testing by organizations outside the school system, to stop testing that dominated the school program, to eliminate excessive pressures on children, and to try to ensure the validity of tests being used. High school and elementary school people hailed *Testing, Testing, Testing* with enthusiasm, but it aroused the ire of those whose business and position seemed threatened. Soon after it was distributed, I had an angry telephone call while attending a conference in Little Rock, Arkansas. The call came from a professor I had known at Yale, who had taken employment with a national testing agency. Even though his organization was in no way referred to in the brochure, he was quite disturbed—in fact, he approached the threatening stage in his first few sentences. I listened and listened, but made no attempt to break in. At last he ran out of words and I replied, "Professor, my mother many years ago had an expression that may fit the situation now. She would say, 'If you throw a stone into a pack of dogs, you can identify the one hit by the one that howls.'" He seemed to get the point, and I heard no more of the threats.

During the early sixties, goaded by the U.S. Commissioner of Education and others in the Office of Education, a few Congressmen, and a few test makers, and financially supported by the staff of the Carnegie Foundation, a movement was born to institute a national testing program. Those who supported the idea held that since the federal government was making monetary contributions, Congress was entitled to know just what returns were forthcoming from the money it contributed. Few who supported the idea had a clear grasp of the problem presented by a national assessment. Although I had proposed the need for national curriculum guideposts many years before, I feared the attempt to devise national tests that could measure the complex outcomes of education for the nation's children—particularly, since there was no semblance of a national curriculum.

Shortly before the movement started, I had spoken to the New York Parent Teachers Association on "Measuring the Products of Our Schools." The following are excerpts from the speech:

> I wish to open my remarks by indicating my strong belief in evaluating the products of our schools. Measurement of progress toward the goal set by the teacher, the school system, by parents, and, in fact, by the learners themselves is a very important part of instruction. Goals set by a test maker in Princeton or Washington are less valid. I therefore believe that a great deal of evidence, or data, must be gathered from many sources, including outside tests, teacher-made tests, and many kinds of observations by professionally prepared teachers. I think it is clear to anyone who has studied teaching and learning that the degree and quality of learning is revealed in many ways to the experienced teacher as he minute-by-minute, hour-by-hour, and day-by-day notes the behavior and responses of each pupil.
>
> Many school people are disturbed today because of what seems to be an overemphasis on the use of outside test instruments. Under pressure from a troubled nation, even a frightened nation, stern critics, harassed boards of education, worried parents, and members of the teaching profession, including many administrators, with a renewed personal desire to measure their own teaching, are committing outrages against children and making errors in sound educational policies and practices by the misuse of tests and the misinterpretation of test data.
>
> Sound evaluation of education is complex, and difficult. And if undertaken without observing basic principles and technically sound procedures it will likely lead to error. The hurry to improve quality, the struggle to pass tests for college entrance, or the urge to prove superiority on the part of a teacher or a school system in a few areas of learning, together with blind confidence in a formal and standardized written examination, may be the root of much evil in our schools today.
>
> This is not to say that we should stop using measuring instruments. Rather, it is to say that we must use care in the kinds of instruments used. Possibly the greatest danger arises when too few checks or tests, observations, pupil production scrutiny and examinations are used, rather than when too many are given. It is the blind confidence in and use of

standardized instruments which may not have been intended to measure what the teacher has taught which are most devastating. When validity is attached to an examination far beyond its author's claims, damage results.

There is a combination of specific conditions which has brought about the misuse and the overuse of instruments made outside the school system.

Among these conditions are, of course, the great fad of scholarships. The donors of scholarships, as well as school officials, usually depend on an examination—a single measuring instrument—as the means of choosing the winners. Many come knowing full well that few can be chosen. For example: During one year 550,221 high school seniors took one national examination to determine those who would receive scholarship recognition. Of this number, 1,008 received scholarships. This means there was one chance in 500 for these students to achieve the award of a scholarship.

Broken down in terms of time spent by these students, it adds up to one thousand man-years. The number of teacher-hours, the cost of transportation, meals, and other expenses run to many more dollars than were given out by the scholarship donors. The question might well be raised: Is this kind of examination gamble worth the effort? And let us remember that this particular test is only one of many that students take for purposes other than measuring what the teacher taught.

More than that, the same examination results are often published and the high school that happens to have one of the 1,008 students as a winner is credited with being a superior high school. These insidious and invalid comparisons between schools, on the basis of such limited kinds of information, are a serious threat to a broad program of education that goes beyond the purposes of this test. Also, examinations such as these often overshadow the importance of other examination test data plus observations of the teacher which may be much more valid in terms of measuring the mastery of a given subject, the quality of an individual school system, or in measuring the over-all educational progress of the pupils.

The public, generally, some teachers, some administrators, and a few over-sold promoters of tests are using the high school scores on a given national test for a few pupils and blunt averages of the total group to draw false conclusions on the comparative over-all quality of one school, or on one type of program against another. In most cases the data for such claims are invalid, unreliable, and seriously damaging to the school systems of America.

Then too, the promoters of tests, the multiplicity of test instruments, the emphasis on guidance by a specialized guidance officer, the urging of those with endless types of scholarships, the shouting for standards of a fixed, inflexible kind, the public clamor for proof of scholastic results—all combined—put the emphasis on formalized test instruments and restricted curriculum, rather than on an enriched program and the professional judgment of the school staff.

With your permission, I will now discuss a few rather fundamental principles or a few of the foundation conditions involved in the evaluation of education.

1. Tests, measurements devices, observations by teachers, anecdotal reports, and examinations of many kinds are fundamental to evaluation; and evaluation is essential and necessary, both to the teacher and the learner, as a part of learning itself. Thus, evaluation is an integral part of the teaching process and the learning process. It is essential for the underachiever, the emotionally disturbed, as well as for every learner of every subject.

2. When the learner knows and desires what he and his teacher are

trying to achieve, he almost invariably insists on knowing the degree to which he has achieved, or is achieving, his goal. Like the driver of an automobile, he is constantly checking to note his progress toward the place he is going. Satisfaction arises when his progress is known, and dissatisfaction results when he is lost on the road. Hence the child, above all others, wants to measure his progress. Learning is enhanced when the learner is kept in the light as to his progress. Thus arises the need for keeping him continuously informed about the degree to which he has achieved the purposes of instruction.

3. Good teaching, furthermore, involves the learner in self-evaluation, thus giving the learner the power to judge the quality of his own work. Often this aspect of teaching is overlooked. Some teachers seem to take delight in keeping a child in the dark relative to the quality and degree of success his learning is achieving. I recall an instance in my family: Nancy, my daughter, had entered a new school. She was ten years old. After three months had passed, I asked at the dinner table, "Nancy, how are you getting along in your work at this new school?" She replied, "Dad, I just don't know. We haven't had our report cards yet." My friends, can you imagine working to achieve something for three months and sustaining your effort when you have no means of discerning progress?

4. The extreme diversity of human talent—mental, emotional, and physical—together with the factor of uneven growth rates and uneven cultural backgrounds, suggests the need of continuous evaluation and the application of many kinds of checking instruments—some teacher made and some by others. Above all else, growth from a known starting point must be assessed so the base or starting point must be pinpointed. To withhold from the student the knowledge of his degree of development in skill, understanding, and knowledge for long periods of time stifles the impulse to learn and sometimes cruelly tortures the student. Let test results stimulate and help, rather than torture and embarrass. The satisfaction of developing a skill, gaining new and complex understanding, and achieving knowledge is a great motivation for more learning. This satisfaction can come only when evaluation is a continuous aspect of learning and teaching. Possibly there is no greater deterrent to pupil effort than to keep him in the dark relative to his progress.

5. Those who produce national examinations in subject fields may become, if they have not already become so, the true curriculum maker. Thus, the national test maker determines more than most realize what we teach locally. This is not only dangerous, but it puts the cart before the horse. Indeed, the tests should be made to measure what thoughtful, scholarly teachers have first determined as important to be taught to each child at any age. In other words, test what has been taught rather than teach what some test maker will say they will test. *Test for teaching, not teach for testing.* Now I am convinced there is danger when a teacher or a school system is judged good or bad by state or national tests. It is almost inevitable that teachers change their purposes so that they are drilling for the examinations, rather than teaching that which they, the local curriculum, or even a state course of study outlines.

6. Diagnostic tests, whether made by the teacher or the test maker, are likely to be most helpful to teachers and learners. Herein is an area that is exceedingly important. Here, the outside tests, if scientifically made, can perform a real purpose for good. Here, direction can be given to the learner toward those things which he needs most, pointing up where his weaknesses are and where his strengths prevail. I fear that today a great deal of valuable learning time is wasted and much money is spent

for examinations that have little or no relationship to the enhancement of pupil learning and progress. The good diagnostic test, like a good teacher's trained observations, is the exception.

7. I wish to emphasize again that when sound and efficient teacher-pupil relationships and roles are established, when both teacher and pupil know the goals, the minute-by-minute, hour-by-hour, day-by-day observations and applications of mutually accepted standards make learning and evaluation go hand in hand. Good teaching and efficient learning call for measurement and judgment of progress by both teacher and pupil. Hence, fear is largely eliminated. Thus, the child learner looks forward to the measurement of his effort, just as the archer looks hurriedly to check whether his arrow struck at 2 o'clock or 6 o'clock and how far away from the bull's eye. And just as the archer tries to figure whether it was the wind or the release of arrow that caused him to miss the bull's eye, the child becomes his own critic. So the learner is, in fact, watching his progress and adjusting his sights so that he hits the target in his learning. This, of course, is impossible unless both the teacher and the pupil know and accept the learning goal, the skills sought, the understandings to be achieved. Under these conditions, teaching is a joy and learning is exciting.

8. Again, may I warn that instruments, even for placement purposes, are dangerous. When long-time prognostications of learning ability are made early in school life, danger is inevitable. And when made with limited test data, they are likely to be insidious and invidious as instruments of good guidance.

9. No test instruments can be substituted for the dedicated and professionally educated teacher. The teacher's personal contact and skillful observations, his notes on the child's aptitudes, stages of development, and unique status, together with his idea of quality of daily production, cannot be superseded by any formal criteria for measuring learning and determining evaluation.

10. In my judgment, PTA members in particular should note that evaluation should have an emphasis on obstacles to learning rather than concentrating exclusively on what has been learned. I mean antagonistic attitudes of home and child; bad home environments; crime ridden neighborhoods, inadequate housing, poverty, racial animosity; physical, mental, and emotional handicaps; heavy teacher-pupil ratios; poor qualifications of teachers; unstimulating climates for good teaching and learning; obsolete tools for teaching; absence of personnel aides such as specialists and clerks, supervisors or consulting help; lack of community youth facilities; and above all, poor school boards. The parent-teacher association is possibly the greatest supporting bulwark of public education in the United States. I doubt very much if public education could have persisted during the past 25 years had it not been supported by the parent-teacher association. Thus, back of all these programs for advancing the learning and development of children is that group of parents and teachers who have banded together for better education. Let them take the little pamphlet published jointly by AASA and the NSBA entitled *Judging Schools with Wisdom* and insist that evaluation in their schools follow the principles laid down in it.

Soon the proposed national testing project was wrested from the hands of the early proponents, and a committee representing a much wider spectrum of American public education was put in charge. As a retired administrator, I continue to watch the project with considerable doubt of the outcome. Education is indeed very complex, with diverse goals. The school must constantly strive to provide a climate for individual fruition. Finding common denominators in the midst of such diversity makes nationwide testing exceedingly hazardous.

When I accepted the offer to be executive secretary of AASA, I explained that I had never been a partisan politician and could not function in Washington in that capacity. I further stated that the Executive Committee could not expect me to be a lobbyist in any sense, but the executive secretary—like every successful superintendent—should have skill in human relations with many groups, including legislative and executive bodies. In fact, he needs to have competence as a politician in the broadest meaning of the term.

Because public education by the mid-fifties was becoming of more and more national concern and because, as chairman of the President's White House Committee on Education, I had become better known in Washington it seemed advisable to keep in close touch with both the executive branch and the Congress. From 1945 until 1970 I knew all the U.S. Commissioners quite well. Those with whom I had closest communion were P. P. Claxton, John Studebaker, Earl McGrath, Lee Thurston, Samuel Brownell, Lawrence Derthick, and Frank Keppel. I must confess that as I found fault with legislation and administrative practices in his office, Mr. Keppel became cool. Since Howe continued many of the Keppel policies, we had less in common. James Allen and I worked very close as state commissioners, and he invited my counsel after going to Washington.

The President's office, too, was not inaccessible. While Sherman Adams was assistant to Mrs. Eisenhower, I could pick up the phone and call him instantly. The President was always gracious but infrequently responded with action that counted.

On two occasions, I had conferences of some length with President Kennedy. His concern for education was intense, although his follow-up in Congress was not as effective as was President Johnson's. I recall one day when Dr. Phil Hickey, Dr. Ben Willis, and I consulted with him about proposed legislation. He was enthusiastic and knowledgeable, but he seemed anxious to finish such practical business so he could give us a guided tour through his office. His pictures of navy ships were a primary joy to him, and being a navy participant in two world wars, I shared his enthusiasm.

On another occasion I made a visit with the purpose of inviting him to speak to the general session at the AASA convention. I was stopped by his administrative assistant, Theodore Sorensen. I sensed a sort of coolness from the man, and when I presented my invitation, he informed me that he thought it unusual that our organization would ask a favor of the President immediately after opposing parts of the President's legislation. I quickly replied, "We are not asking a favor when we invite him to speak to 25,000 school executives. We are bestowing one." That set him back a bit, and then I returned to his complaint about our opposition. We did oppose legislation that proposed to give public tax dollars to church-controlled schools, but that had been an AASA policy for nearly one hundred years. Furthermore, I explained that since President Kennedy's statement before Protestant clergymen in Houston, Texas, had expressed opposition to the use of tax funds for church schools, we considered our testimony to be consistent with his public statements. I have always believed that had I not been stopped at the door by his associate, the President would have given the speech.

As hearings were held on important education proposals in Congress, AASA was invited to give testimony. As a matter of policy and personal preference, AASA encouraged administrators in the field, rather than the executive secretary, to testify. My chief role was to analyze legislative proposals and write suggested testimony to be used by others. Naturally, I was called by a number of Senators and Congressmen to give private views on acts before Congress and on other developments in education.

Of all the members of Congress with whom I had dialogue, Senator Hubert H. Humphrey gave the most time, asked the most penetrating questions, and exhibited the most knowledge. Of all I dealt with in high administrative positions, Secretary Folsom of Health, Education, and Welfare was the most kindly.

In 1958 the Secretary of State asked me to serve as a U.S. delegate to the tenth session of the general conference of UNESCO in Paris. Before leaving, I was given an assignment to serve on a working subcommittee and was handed dozens of documents that must be read and digested before the conference opened. Mrs. Engleman and I left a week early aboard the old *Ile de France*. I did not enjoy the trip very much because all my leisure time was consumed reading dry, uninteresting UNESCO documents, and Mrs. Engleman was making slow recovering from a serious operation. The conference lasted two weeks. I found it tiresome, with too much time consumed in politics between the East and West while others played the ends against the middle. In fact, it was not nearly so rewarding as had been the International Conferences at Geneva. We did, however, make some lasting friends from the Far East, Middle East, and Europe. After returning home, I was appointed a member of the U.S. Commission for UNESCO and served for two terms.

The following year, two things happened to renew my contacts with overseas educators. A special conference on teacher education and vocational education was called by the UNESCO-sponsored Hamburg Institute of Pedagogy. The Institute sent me an invitation to represent the United States. Possibly, it was this contact that caused the director general of UNESCO to appoint me to the Board of Directors of that Institute. This post, which I held until after my retirement, gave me unequalled insights into comparative education, as well as the opportunity to make international friends and to accept varying cultural values.

My educational horizons were further lifted by my membership on the Advisory Board of the National War College. I was surprised to receive the appointment and more surprised to learn the character of the curriculum. I expected it to consist largely of military strategy, military tactics, and military government. Instead, it was given over largely to the great political, economic, and social issues in the United States and in the world, and the staff and visiting lecturers were capable of delineating, analyzing, and discussing such broad problems. In fact, most of the lecturers were world figures. As I read the efforts of many writers today who would discredit the military and who accuse the generals and admirals of being "dumb clucks," my mind rushes back to this program of the National War College which was designed to fit colonels to be generals and Navy captains to be admirals, as well as senior Department of State career officers to be ambassadors. Surely this program was not designed for the narrow-minded, the immature, or the mentally mediocre. Furthermore, although some members of the advisory board were nonmilitary—professors, college presidents, ambassadors—there was a strong sprinkling of generals and admirals. Their intellects appeared to match those of the nonmilitary and often were more flexible.

The demands were heavy on the staff of AASA, particularly on the executive secretary, to participate and speak at professional state meetings for teachers, school board members, and administrators. I traveled an average of 100,000 miles each year and spoke and consulted in all fifty states. Just the preparation of data and the writing of speeches consumed many hours. In 1956, I could write speeches during flights, but by 1963, the speedy jets cut down the time for work during transit. Reviewing and evaluating research proposals being submitted to the U.S. Office of Education for funding was another time-consuming activity. Many of these proposals were tomes resembling a doctoral dissertation proposal. My secretary would note the accumulation of these proposals and pack a huge briefcase with them for me to work on during flights. Somehow, I kept abreast of the flow, and I trust I rendered service to the Office of Education. Another activity, much more pleasant, was the writing of Christmas cards. While at AASA, I sent about 1200 cards, each with a personal longhand note. Again, my secretary would help out by packing a bundle for each flight in November and December. She would further help by addressing the envelopes. The messages I sent were short, but, in most cases, quite personal. Most of the AASA workers in the field received a "thank you" note at Christmas time, together with a friendly personal greeting.

Another practice throughout my period of work in education, one for which I was often thanked by associates and sometimes criticized by busy "executive-type" friends who learned of it, was my annual "thank you" note to my associates. This note, too, was in longhand. In it, I attempted to express my appreciation for special work done by each associate and to wish him a pleasant summer—with some rest. Possibly my time might have been used to better advantage, but I had enough positive signs, over many years, that I continued the practice until retirement. At any rate, most of these messages were written after the office was closed in the afternoon, during the evenings, on weekends, or while traveling.

I had one great emotional upset while in Washington. I had greatly admired my predecessor, Worth McClure, for years. Although I frequently asked his advice after taking his chair, he was exceedingly reluctant to influence AASA policy and at no time did he offer any suggestions without being asked for them. On August 20, 1962, I landed at the National Airport at four o'clock and hurried to my office. Awaiting me was a message saying Dr. McClure was dead. At once, the editor of *The School Administrator* entered my office, said her publication was ready to go to press, and asked me to write a statement. I shut the door and twenty minutes later handed her the following statement, which was placed on the front page.

A Great Leader of Men

Like a giant oak that has stood as a landmark, giving refuge from the heat of the day and providing a special character to a total environment, a great man serves his culture. Just as the complete worth of a magnificent tree is seldom appreciated until the ravages of time take their toll, so it is with a great man. Now that Worth McClure is dead, his role in improving education in America stands even more startlingly clear. His was a life filled with deep devotion to mankind, blessed with imagination, creativity, and depth of insight; and it was complete with a courage that never faltered.

Worth McClure, like the true leader of a great people searching for a special destiny, believed a responsibility was a sacred trust and that life had true purpose and personal significance only when devoted to the welfare of all men. For him there was no room for the defeatist, the weary, the despondent, the retreater, the cynic. He faced life possessing firmness without harshness, vision without daydreaming, confidence without brashness, and courage stripped of vanity.

Now that the great oak has fallen, let us recognize as never before the debt every educator in America owes him. Possibly we can honor best by resolving to emulate his signal qualities and by resolving to strive unrelentingly to be worthy of the mantle of leadership he has now passed on to us.

CHAPTER X

I wrote more than 50 editorials for *The School Administrator* while executive secretary, to give my views to the AASA membership on critical issues of the day. Although I signed none of the bulletins, brochures, or AASA official statements, the editor of *The School Administrator* insisted that I initial my editorials. Possibly, she feared she might otherwise bear the blame for the weak ones. Here are samples:

Editorial, September 1963. *Education for Elegance*

Vern Sneider's delightful and kindly satire, *Tea House of the August Moon*, raises many questions about human values. Western civilization might well be enriched by the commentary on those values found in the incident when all work ceased so that everybody could enjoy the wondrous natural drama of a setting sun and the bewitching beauty of the approaching night.

Here were people receiving and enjoying a "life-adjustment" education of simple but magnificent proportions. Here again was proof that man's greatest treasures are to be had by looking, feeling, and listening.

Although the great Western poets, essayists, artists, and composers have reflected deep understanding and appreciation of the beauty and power of nature, Western education seems to do far too little to open eyes and ears to that which the world of nature is eager to give. Frost, Shelley, Wordsworth, and Thoreau with pen; Dehn, Monet, and Homer with paint and brush; Beethoven, Debussy, and Copeland with musical note bring to us all vicarious experiences of infinite worth.

But our education places far too little emphasis on appreciating and understanding the great creative artists and their masterpieces, far too little on their interpretation of truth and beauty.

What teacher leads his pupils into the woods and along streams just to look and listen, to smell the fragrance of pine and cedar and newly cut grass, to feel the rush of wind on cheek or the ripple of water on bare feet?

What teacher breathes into his pupils the living, moving beauty of light, shadow, form, and design with which the world is so full?

What family in the warm summer evenings looks for the appearance of stars and traces their movements, or on cold winter nights watches the eerie flash of the northern lights, or on almost any evening listens to the stillness or to the whisper of winds that rise and fall?

How many people living around Isak Dinesen were prepared to see Africa like this: "There was no fat on it and no luxuriance anywhere; it was Africa distilled up through six thousand feet, like the strong and refined essence of a Continent. The colors were dry and burnt, like the colors in pottery, the structure of which was different from that of the trees of Europe; it did not grow in bows or cupolas, but in horizontal layers, and the information gave to the tall solitary trees a likeness of palms, or a heroic and romantic air like full rigged ships with their sails chewed up, and to the edge of a wood a strange appearance, as if the whole wood were faintly vibrating. All the flowers you found on the plains, or upon the creepers and liana in the native forests, were diminutive like flowers of the downs, only just in the beginning of the long rains a number of big massive heavy-scented lilacs sprang out on the plains. The views were immensely wide. Everything you saw made for greatness and freedom and unequalled nobility."

Why can we not all see and smell and feel and listen as did Isak Dinesen?

F.E.E.

Editorial, February 1963. *New Wine for Old Bottles*

President Kennedy recently said: "Education is both the foundation and the unifying force of our democratic way of life; it is the highest expression of achievement in our society; ennobling and enriching human life. In short, it is at the same time the most profitable investment society can make and the richest reward it can confer."

To play this magnificent role in our contemporary society, public education must be sustained by teachers, specialists, and administrators who are on the frontiers of new knowledge and new research and who are steeped in the cultural heritage as well. The deadly aftermath which inevitably follows the teaching of knowledge, concepts, and dogma which are no longer valid presents neither a foundation for strength nor a profitable investment to society nor a reward to the individual. An obsolescent teaching makes of education a false Maginot Line. There is hardly a greater disservice to man or nation than that of teaching untruths and obsolete concepts and outmoded values. The teaching profession is faithful to its deepest commitment only if it strives to keep its methods and content consistent with the discoveries of modern man.

The knowledge, insights, and interpretations essential to a teacher in almost all disciplines or fields of knowledge half a generation ago are completely inadequate today, and, if transmitted to children and youth, will unfit rather than prepare them for life.

The teacher or administrator who operates on the assumption that the education he received in college 25, or even 10, years ago is still adequate is hiding his head in the sand and unwittingly betraying his pupils and insuring ultimate public distrust of the whole profession. Entering the classroom to direct the curriculum content with only the knowledge of a quarter of a century ago is to be like the general or soldier who today would march boldly forth with the blunderbuss or cutlass.

If the teacher with obsolete knowledge, skills, and understandings is dangerous to society, the seriousness is multiplied when the profession is led by a superintendent or principal who carries the dead weight of an educational armor of a former era and has not the vision, imagination, and insights which open his mind to the newness in the world. Today's administrator is obligated to bring to bear all that the relevant disciplines possess on the great social, economic, and political issues and problems of the day. His must be the statesmanship that helps develop public policy. His must be the leadership that helps the staff develop the new curriculum.

Colleges and universities which have assumed responsibility for preservice education of the teacher and administrator must hurriedly accept a still greater responsibility—that of continuing the education of all in the profession. This latter task is much more difficult than the first one. It means that tailor-made programs must be made available.

In some fields the first task is to scuttle, to destroy, to abandon much that the professional worked and studied hard during his preservice period of preparation to master—assumptions that he and his professor had found true. Generalizations and concepts formed as a result of these studies must be re-examined and in many cases cast aside. Revised models must take their place in the intellectual and emotional framework of professional competence.

The second step in some areas is to master selected relevant new knowledge. At the same time, those in the teaching profession must re-examine the complex configurations in which man's knowledge in any field has been grouped, and they must work out methods for achieving deeper insights. The teaching profession needs better understanding of the methods of research, experimentation, and inquiry which others have used, and it needs to find ways of adapting those methods to its own approach, research, study, and experimentation. Reevaluation of the teacher's own realm of knowledge and its relevance to the school program is of pressing importance.

For the administrator, it seems imperative that he must not only seek out new research findings and take action in the areas where he must make decisions but he must also be sensitive to great contemporary social, economic, scientific, philosophical, and political issues which face mankind, particularly within the culture of America. His inservice study should supplement his previous education and experience by revealing areas of knowledge most likely to throw light on those issues and to give guidance toward their sound and appropriate solution. Thus the findings in social anthropology, psychology, philosophy, economics, political science, history, literature, and the arts open many doors that lead the administrator to be an interpreter of issues, a dependable leader of his profession, and a shaper of public policy.

Supporting the profession in its desperate struggle to raise its own competencies should be school boards and legislators who encourage rather than discourage. Sabbatical leaves are imperative as school board policy. Activities such as workshops, study and work conferences, research, and writing should be stimulated by boards of education. Education for members of the staff should be considered as investments guaranteed to bring heavy dividends, just as investments in education for children and youth are good economic ventures.

Unless the public as well as the teaching profession accepts the imperative need for massive continuing education for the teaching profession, education fails and the nation's rightful destiny is denied. Herein lies a must in the field of adult education.

F.E.E.

Editorial, November 1962. *Roles and Responsibilities*

Never before in the history of education has there been so much stir within and among organized education groups. Never before have individual educational workers and various organized groups struggled so vigorously to clarify roles and find their rightful responsibilities and prerogatives. Never before has there been so much confusion as to goals and relationships.

Welfare seems to take precedence. Organizational patterns and procedures for determining welfare goals are shouting for recognition. People and organizations are being thrown off course, and the unity of purpose and the mutual respect essential to the welfare of both pupils and those in the teaching profession are in danger of being impaired.

While relationships, roles, and practices relative to developnig and securing agreement on welfare goals are in flux, one thing does seem clear: the members of the teaching profession are demanding a positive role in discussions that affect them, their working conditions, their salaries, their welfare.

One aspect in the matter of welfare is a deep-seated determination on the part of many members of the profession to have recognized status as self-determiners. As professional maturity develops, the staff member is no longer content to accept the rewards handed down by an individual or an agency, whether done benevolently or by legal authority. The same welfare provisions take on different values, depending on whether they are bestowed or whether they are worked out cooperatively with all concerned.

The second aspect is the conflict between groups in the profession which have strong ambitions to be the single mouthpiece. The jurisdictional problem is new among teachers, professional organizations, and its solution is difficult.

As new roles and changes in responsibilities emerge within the total profession, much depends on the wisdom, care, patience, and unselfish judgment of many people. Change is due in many school districts, but the good practices already present should not be thrown overboard in the scramble to accept a pattern found in industry.

Unless the profession finds ways to unify on those issues and problems which are common to the kindergarten teacher, the high school math teacher, the principal of the high school, the principal of the elementary school, the psychologist, the guidance officer, the assistant superintendent, and the superintendent, it will lose its strength and all segments will get hurt. This can be achieved without destroying in any way the organizations that have specialized professional interests, such as the Association for Supervision and Curriculum Development, the NEA Department of Elementary School Principals, and the NEA Department of Classroom Teachers.

Unless common needs are identified, a dog-eat-dog period is likely to emerge. Then our special professional interests will become special selfish interests and those without deep interests in public education will cut us to pieces.

As now structured, most welfare matters in education, especially salaries, are handled locally. Education is quite different from an industrial or a commercial enterprise. As the Educational Policies Commission pointed out 25 years ago, public education has a unique function and in most respects its control is unique. Its dividends are not available to be plowed directly back into the enterprise. Sources and extent of revenues vary greatly from district to district.

Furthermore, the school board is interested in a better quality of schooling for every child, not in holding down salaries to increase dividends, as is usually true in industrial management. Democracy at its best reflects the will of the people as they select board members charged with the responsibility of providing a good education for every child.

If the American people want good schools, they want good teachers. If they want good instruction, they want good school boards which will provide it. If the teaching profession assumes that parents and school boards are opposed to reasonable wages and good working conditions, it will be on false ground. Better is the assumption that if the board is well informed it will carry the appeal to the people for better financial support.

I believe that more often than not the school boards seek to be on the same side of the table with the staff. I believe the profession should seek to move all of them to that side rather than force them to assume the role of opponent. When their compelling purpose is good schools, board members will work diligently for better budgets and for better staff welfare rather than yield to selfish forces or hide behind legal prerogatives.

The superintendent, like any staff member, is an employee of the school board, but he is not a mere agent of that body. His first and overriding allegiance is to his personal and professional integrity and to the making of wise judgments in terms of his extensive professional preparation and experience. He has an allegiance to the goals, professional concepts, and ethics of his profession that transcends other commitments, such as immediate contractual relationships or expectations from his employer. His dedication to public education, which his education taught him to understand, to organize, and to administer in ways most likely to achieve the best educational rewards for pupils, will not permit flagrant compromise.

Although he is a devoted member of the professional group and is deeply concerned with the success of his associates, his allegiance to the learner transcends his loyalty to his associates. In most instances, he will find that his associates have similar value commitments.

This ideal of service does not place the superintendent in conflict with his colleagues; instead, it puts him on the team in a special role. His very concern for pupil development makes him a determined champion of those environmental situations which his associates desire, such as respectable and pleasant working conditions, satisfactory work loads, instructional materials and aids, living and saving salaries, security, and specialist assistance.

If he ever loses his interest in the welfare of his colleagues, if he avoids taking up the cudgel for improved teacher welfare, including adequate salaries, if he is deflected from a statesmanlike and independent role in decision making by any force from within the profession or without, his leadership role will decline to a low level. And, within our total structure, I see no one who can possibly succeed him as adviser to the board, as stimulator of public support, or as overall professional leader of the staff.

More than anyone else, the superintendent must know sources of revenue and likely sources of increased school income. More than anyone else, he has a responsibility to keep the school board informed and to advise it on staff matters and financial matters. More than anyone else, he understands the overall needs of the school system. More than anyone else, he should understand that the success of the educational program and the educational welfare of pupils are related directly to the welfare of the staff.

Surely he is not to be pushed aside with all other professional personnel while a lawyer or a classroom teacher meets with the school board, the mayor, or the governor to achieve the welfare needs of either the total profession or a segment of it. If this happens, the good school board will be likely to dismiss the professional superintendent and get a lawyer to represent it.

The superintendent who meets his responsibility to the school board and the professional staff knows that policy structure and machinery must provide opportunity for staff members, teachers, supervisors, principals, and specialists to play roles in the development and acceptance of professional working conditions and welfare. It is the responsibility of the superintendent to assist the staff members in ways satisfactory to them to have a machinery for studying welfare problems and for developing welfare proposals and presenting them to the school board for consideration and action. School board policy should support such cooperative staff planning and action.

AASA President-Elect Natt B. Burbank has said, "The superintendent should take the leadership to see that salary problems of teachers are presented fairly and fully to the school board." He should, in fact, continually keep the board informed of the welfare status of all staff members and of the developing needs pertaining to salaries, working conditions, sickness and hospitalization, and retirement. He should also take the leadership in developing and establishing a plan for permitting grievances to be fairly adjudicated.

Only as school boards, too, continue to study the effect of welfare provisions, including salaries, will they be in a position to act wisely on any new provisions brought to their attention for approval.

F.E.E.

Editorial, June 1962. *Who's Irresponsible?*

For several months 18 thoroughly competent, courageous, dedicated, and professionally experienced school administrators exchanged ideas on the paramount issues confronting the American Association of School Administrators—issues that merited attention as possible resolutions for 1962. Since the adopted resolutions of the AASA in a major sense set policy for the organization, these men accepted their roles on the Resolutions Committee with feelings of deep responsibility.

On Friday and Saturday, February 16 and 17, the committee deliberated, analyzed, debated, and restated resolutions until unanimity prevailed. The resolutions were printed and distributed during the AASA convention in Atlantic City. On Monday, February 19, they were discussed in an open hearing to which all members were invited so that they might present their views. On Wednesday, February 21, the resolutions were presented to the membership at the open business meeting and were unanimously adopted.

The first resolution reads in part:

The Association urges the Congress to move immediately to enact needed legislation, providing federal financial support for *public* elementary and secondary schools.

The Association believes strongly that any program of general federal support should encompass all grades from kindergarten through the fourteenth year. It further believes that the cost of an adequate program of education will increase substantially in the years ahead and will approximately double in ten years. It is essential that a substantial program of federal support be established if the widely acclaimed goal of an adequate educational program is to be achieved. To accomplish this it is necessary that legislation be enacted now to provide direct grants to the appropriate state school agencies in the amount of at least $200.00 per public school pupil per year.

While the resolutions were being discussed, the United States Secretary of Health, Education, and Welfare, in an off-the-cuff statement, branded the school administrators with irresponsibility for proposing such a resolution and suggested that superintendents go back to their teachers for more learning. Editorial writers in some newspapers have echoed his charges of irresponsibility.

To be called "irresponsible" is a serious matter, especially for a school administrator who carries the heavy responsibility of teaching ethical character, sound citizenship, and productive living to every child regardless of race, religion, or cultural status. Responsibility is the heart of good education.

The contention in the resolution that greatly increased sums of money must be spent if high-quality programs are achieved throughout the nation is supported by every responsible commission or study group reporting on financial needs for the nation's schools. Witness, for example, the conclusions of the White House Conference on Education report, the Rockefeller report, the Killian study. Yet, none of these groups has been charged with irresponsibility. Possibly such charges are not leveled except when a reasonably adequate source of revenue is recommended.

Broad Tax Base Necessary

Increased budgets for public schools must come from public tax sources. There are only three tax depositories: the local or county, the state, and the federal. Since approximately three-fourths of all tax dollars go to the federal treasury, it is not irresponsible for a citizen to conclude that some of his dollars in Washington might well be returned to the local treasury to help pay for his schools. Indeed, since he knows that tax resources at the local level often are very limited, is it not a responsible act to conclude that universally high-quality schools in the future are exceedingly unlikely, if not impossible, without using the broad tax base available only to the federal government?

Would it have been honest and wise for the committee to ignore the vast differences in the geographical distribution of wealth taxable by state and local education agencies? Would it have been a responsible committee to have accepted present resources as adequate and to have ignored the fact that approximately 75 percent of all the people's tax dollars is in the federal treasury and that a majority of the citizens, according to reliable polls, desires some of it returned for use by school boards at the local level?

Funds Needed Through 14 Years

Furthermore, they peered a bit into the future and saw that our scientific, technical, and complex society requires that many youths pursue their studies in colleges and universities through at least the fourteenth grade and at public expense. Would it have been realistic for the committee to have assumed that present sources of revenue would prove adequate?

For those who charge irresponsibility, let us ask the question: Where can school boards get money to double their budgets in a relatively short time? Here are the alternatives.

First, they could look to the federal treasury for approximately half the increase as did the Resolutions Committee of AASA. They could then turn to local and state sources to find the additional dollars. On the average, approximately half the school revenues presently come from local property taxes and almost half from the state treasuries. If these state-local ratios are maintained, the local tax revenues would have to be increased only 50 percent and state legislatures would have to increase revenues only 50 percent.

The second alternative, evidently the one preferred by the critics of the Resolutions Committee, would leave full responsibility to state and local agencies. Here again choices could be made. If either of these agencies assumed full responsibility for the needed increase it would have to increase its tax revenues 200 percent. If they were to continue present ratios, each would have to raise its revenues 100 percent. Do school boards believe the property tax will yield this increase, or do governors think states will find such an increase from state revenues?

Superintendents, school board members, and critics of the Resolutions Committee should study carefully these possible tax sources from which it is possible to get the huge sums of money which almost every thoughtful person believes we need. Realism and integrity suggest that the Resolutions Committee showed great vision and wisdom rather than irresponsibility.

F.E.E.

Editorial, November 1961. *Limited Quantity Means Limited Quality*

The story is often repeated of Robert Louis Stevenson's observations that the village lamplighter seemed to be "punching holes in the dark."

Teachers, the leaders of public education, long ago assumed the role of lamplighters where the souls of men cry in darkness, ignorance, and fright. Although they sometimes possess inadequate wicks and insufficient oil, those who operate our schools have consistently and continuously punched holes in the dark.

The darkness of ignorance, prejudice, and incompetence shrouds the world. Every individual, whether he has 10 talents or one, has the potential to penetrate this darkness and to throw light on a segment of the universe.

Light of great magnitude is necessary for some segments; but light of lesser brilliance, like that so helpful in a cellar or a photographer's darkroom, is also of great worth. When the lights from many individuals are put together, brilliance like that of a fluorescent-lighted highway dispels the darkness.

When a light goes out or when a new one is lit, the degree of darkness changes. Thus universal education gains full support from a law of nature.

If education is to have quality, it must have both quantity and diversity. The modern, complex world demands more diversity of human competence than ever before. Through quantity, which public education assures, the greatest number of samplings of potential talents of a diverse character may be found and developed.

But diversity in human competence is attained not alone by locating diverse human potentials, but also through the diversity of educational programs that nurtures all those diverse potentials. No simple, restricted curriculum can possibly develop the interests and latent capacities of all pupils. A vast scope and range of subject content are indispensable if the school is to serve contemporary society adequately.

Hence, the development and use of technological teaching and learning devices, the application of democratic values, and insistence on the full development of the average as well as the academically gifted are not inimical to scholarship, mental power, or cultural achievement.

The worry of some highbrows over "Masscult" is to an extent an alibi for their doubts and confusion about the relation of art and culture to a democratic society.

Emerging in America is an educated public—enlarged and enlarging—which has a common culture and tradition. This public must be both the source and audience for such continuing cultural advances as our civilization may make.

Jacques Barzun has said that we have undertaken what no other society has tried, in that we do not suppress half of mankind to refine part of the other half. Rather, the refinement must be public and general if our civilization is to be democratic as well as great.

F.E.E.

Editorial, September 1960. *Do American Educators Resist Experimentation?*

One of the wisest and fairest education writers, in the September 6, 1959, issue of the *New York Times,* wrote: "There are signs that even conservative educators acknowledge the need for daring experimentation. . . . The sounding off barrier against new ideas has been pierced. . . . The lock step has been broken." Another writer, in the March 1960 issue of *Phi Delta Kappan* stated, ". . .We must rank education as a relatively undynamic, unprogressive industry."

Such statements are typical of the observations of many who seemingly do not know the history of education in America. Since education is a social institution, rapid change which would affect the whole of it is impossible to achieve with the same alacrity as is possible in shifting to hybrid corn by the farmer. When compared to changes made by other social institutions, however, American education seems to be relatively out front in matters of change.

Due to the extreme autonomy of private schools and to the fact that they have often been established to try out a new theory, their curriculums and their methods have often been diverse and unusual. Public education also has been diverse and unusual. Public education also has been experimental to an amazing degree due to decentralized and independently operated school districts undergirded by the American freedom to be different.

Unlike European centralized school systems, American schools have been diverse, flexible, and responsive to the changing needs of the communities they serve. The very free democratic spirit that created American schools gave them at the same time freedom to develop programs and teaching methods restricted only by lack of imagination. Furthermore, the fact that the schools belong to the people and therefore are responsive to individual citizen and group ideas and pressures brought innovations, both good and bad.

Likewise, the teaching profession was trained in a galaxy of diverse general colleges, liberal arts colleges, teachers colleges, and universities. Thus diversity in curriculum content and method was afforded those who later would teach.

Although history reveals unevenness relative to what school districts have done in trying out the new, the over-all evidence is encouraging. A glance at nationally recognized experimental schemes such as the Lancastrian System (teacher aides), the Oswego Plan, the Batavia Plan (multi-track), the XYZ Grouping (gifted), the Platoon Plan (better utilization of staff and buildings), the Winnetka Plan (core curriculum plus individual attention), the Dalton Plan (student responsibility to learn and individual contract), the Kansas City Seven-Five Plan (Grades 1 through 8 in seven years, and Grades 9 through 14 in five years—acceleration), the Non-Graded Primary Plan, the One Subject Per Semester Plan, the Springfield (Vt.) Plan, the Work-Study Plan (long before Khrushchev started his), the Team Teaching (described in 1935 by McGaughy), the Honors Plan (for gifted), the Upgraded (for mentally handicapped), and the Open Air (for tubercular) proves that American education as a social design has had considerable flexibility.

One of the most violent attacks on public education today is leveled at experimentation with curriculum content, new methods, new instruments for reporting pupil progress, and new concepts of the nature of the individual pupil. The history of education in the United States clearly shows that individual instructional methods have been experimented with by thousands of teachers with full approval of boards of education and administrators. Those who now imply that American education has been controlled by conformists, by people who resist experimentation and change, simply don't know the facts.

Let us hasten to say that it is undoubtedly true, however, that our times demand greater efforts than ever before in research, in experimentation, in imagination, and in devotion. Our first responsibility probably is to *hold on* to those structural schemes and those methods that our diverse experimentation, together with our sense of basic values, suggests to be desirable and educationally sound and to resist a retreat to those our experience and research show to be inferior or failures.

Furthermore, our search for the most appropriate curriculum for developing the intellect, strengthening the moral fiber, liberating the mind, and developing individual competence for high level citizenship participation and individual effectiveness should go on unceasingly and with a feeling of urgency. The critics should never deter the administrator from those paths which he has so effectively followed in building the American schools; nor should they put him on the defensive even when he goes about setting the record straight. It is his responsibility to intensify experimentation and research.

He should have the courage to make needed changes faster than was necessary yesterday. But the administrator also needs the courage not to rush headlong into imaginative but fantastic schemes.

F.E.E.

Editorial, February 1959. *Let's Use Sense About Homework*

All of a sudden a lot of teachers, supported by scared administrators, have gone hog wild over homework. Some now think it a mark of superior teaching to load pupils, even in the early grades, with meaningless tasks which make them misinterpret what schools are for and cause some parents anguish as they try to do the jobs for their children.

This is not an indictment of homework. Any intelligent American knows full well the importance of thorough and comprehensive education, because of his knowledge of what the new world demands of every citizen he, too, senses the urgency for quality education.

An often overlooked truth, however, is the fact that children like difficult tasks if they make sense to them. In fact, when the work of the school becomes important to the learner, he is likely to insist on continuing the pursuit of it after school hours. When the work of the school is not accepted by the pupil as important, assigned homework is not likely to be fruitful. Consequently, the first prerequisite to effective out-of-school study is to have a significant program *in* the school and the development of an interest and thirst for learning—then the pupil will seek out the tasks to be carried on outside the classroom. When good education programs and good teaching go on *in* the school, nothing can prevent school work from continuing *out* of the school.

But some adults, mostly people who have never understood children or are now too old to remember what they once knew, are demanding that school teachers be slave drivers and pile on work for work's sake. They shout for toughness, stiff courses, and a lot of sweating over meaningless memory gymnastics and spirit-breaking skills of the animal-learning type. Some folks feel that if the learning is frustrating, time-consuming, and obscure, some sort of disciplinary results will be obtained that are good.

So much is being said about stiff courses and tough taskmaster teachers that even good teachers are acting as if they knew nothing of how and why children learn. So some pupils are assigned homework when they have no home in which work can be done. Others have assignments which neither they nor their parents have the resources to do. And, worst of all, the work that is done is not checked and evaluated by many of these "tough" teachers.

It is high time that school administrators look into what is now going on relative to homework—not to stop it, but to make it serve the purpose of better education; not to mollycoddle children, but to see that they are treated with the individual attention and respect to which they are entitled; not to interfere with good teachers, but to give them the counsel and special assistance they may need.

F.E.E.

Editorial, March 1959. *Why Not Ask the Teacher?*

Self-appointed appraisers of today's education shout from every housetop. Nonplaying quarterbacks are trying to call the signals for education. Boards of education and administrators are asked by disturbed parents: "What is the situation?" "Are children running wild in classrooms with no discipline?" "What do kids know about American history?" "Do they still teach the multiplication tables?" "Do children take only easy courses?" "Is science a neglected area?" "Is handwriting no longer taught?"

Everybody seems to give the answer except the person who knows—the teacher.

Although there is a general shortage of teachers and some of them are ill-prepared, there are many good, professionally-trained teachers. Wherever they are, answers can be found to questions on how good are our schools. In fact, there is no other place to turn for valid information about the present status of American education. The teacher is the only person who knows *enough* to give reliable answers.

It is the good teacher who really knows what is attempted in the way of learning—knowledge, understanding, appreciations, and skills. He knows most about what is set as the goal of learning each day, each week, each month, each year. He has more at his fingertips in the way of measuring pupil progress each day, week, month, and year, than all the admirals, testmakers, and surveyors put together. Likewise, he knows better than any others how diverse pupils are in interests, cultural backgrounds, and potentialities. Yet he is being overlooked or ignored.

Learning and the irregular growth of children call for every-hour observation and checking. The teacher, with the child as collaborator and partner, is in a position to *know* what is going on. It is the teacher's concern, the teacher's trained power to observe, the teacher's skill in using many testing instruments, and the teacher's continuous skill in correlating all sorts of data that result in valid and dependable evaluation. It is the good teacher, too, who has noted the analyses by specialists. Indeed, it is the competent teacher who can put the total mosaic together and so judge the quality of education.

Why can't parents and other responsible persons join up with the teachers rather than listen to prejudiced, irresponsible, incompetent, and careless critics who look at the "elephant's ear" and proceed to shout that the animal is a fan?

F.E.E.

Editorial, May 1960. *Let's Quit Apologizing*

It's high time those of us in the teaching profession quit apologizing about incompetence among us and raise our heads in keeping with the dignity and responsibility of our calling. One of the chief reasons the public places a moderately low value on the services of educators is the lowly value set by many educators themselves. If medical doctors had bowed their heads, ceased to be proud of their calling, and admitted incompetence when it was discovered 50 years ago that many of their members were meagerly trained in charlatan institutions, their great profession would be weak rather than strong today.

Self-respect, self-confidence, and pride in one's calling, when coupled with continuous effort toward greater competence, demand and get the respect of the public. The phenomenal rise in the qualification standards of teachers and administrators since World War II is ample evidence of the emergence of a great and devoted profession. An attitude of confidence and dignity, together with righteous indignation at unfair and untrue implications from those who would wittingly or unwittingly bring scorn upon us, should characterize our behavior. Humility we must retain, but courageous self-respect and an unwavering pride and confidence in the essential worth of teaching should be our hallmark of distinction.

So let's stop the groveling and apologizing and act the part of members of the most complex, socially significant, and difficult profession on God's green earth. If we don't place value on our professional competence, few others will do so.

F.E.E.

Editorial, February 1961. *Are Public and Private Colleges Exchanging Places?*

America in general has long believed that the total society is best served by two kinds of higher educational institutions—one, publicly financed and publicly controlled; the other, privately financed and, within broad limits, privately controlled.

Each of these types has characteristics needed by a democratic society. Each will fulfill its historic destiny best if the one continues to be characterized as public, responsive to public need, with little or no tuition or fees, while the other is characterized by a special service to students who prefer the program of great freedom from public control, and reliance on private sources of income from students, interested citizens, or institutions.

Furthermore, the nonpublic institution may be free to promote a given religion without doing violence to the principle of separation of church and state. The other must not promote any given religious belief.

In recent years, however, it would seem that both institutions have deviated from their earliest roles.

The public universities and colleges are gradually raising the tuition and fees, thus breaching the principle that they are in reality open to all who qualify scholastically, personally, and physically. Slowly but surely the public institutions of higher education are raising financial barriers for those who seek admission. This policy is being encouraged by legislatures, college administrators, and even scholarly survey committees, such as the one recently headed by Dr. Heald in New York State.

Furthermore, the report by the New York committee retreats from America's historic support policy in two respects. First, it recommends much higher tuition rates for public colleges and at the same time proposes a most far-reaching policy of giving public tax revenues for the direct support of private or church-controlled colleges. Thus, in one fell stroke the committee would hasten the trend to take public colleges out of the reach of much of the public and to bridge the gap between church and state. The intent seems to be to make it more difficult for a youth to attend a public institution and easier to receive his education in a private one.

But the issues are closely related to education at all levels. If it is sound to move toward having students finance their education through tuition in a public institution at the thirteenth grade, it is not difficult to reach the same conclusion at the twelfth, eleventh, or fourth. Likewise, if it is sound public policy to support with tax funds a church-operated school at the thirteenth or higher grade level, it is an easy step to go the whole way to the kindergarten.

These trends also appear in both the administrative and legislative branch of the federal government. At first glance it may appear that the nonpublic college is the gainer, but a long look suggests exceedingly great dangers and losses to it if its long-cherished privileges and independence are still desirable.

School administrators and the public generally should be alerted to what is happening in public policy at the higher educational level, because policy can hardly be set at one level without its affecting policy at all levels. Furthermore, expediency or impulse should not be allowed to determine far-reaching public, social, and political policy. At few times in our history have we needed such calm, penetrating, and logical analysis of our old and new practices as they relate to a new world with some old values.

F.E.E.

Editorial, March 1961. *Don't Lose the Individual*

In the early twenties the research findings and testing instruments of

Terman, Thorndyke, and others—together with the whole "scientific movement"—struck the American schools. Not since that time have American administrators so seized upon ability grouping as a panacea for quality education as they have today.

It might prove valuable if those who make plans for improving instruction would study what actually did happen with attempts at homogeneous grouping in the schools from 1920 to 1930 and, in fact, what has happened in this area since. Many school systems have experimented widely with ability grouping for 35 years. Considerable data on the merits and weaknesses of grouping are available.

One discovery revealed by these experiments seems clear: Homogeneity does not actually prevail after groupings are made, no matter what criteria may be used for selection. Only a reduced range in deviation has been achieved. Vast differences still remain in the aspects measured, and sometimes other qualities not measured are found to be even more heterogeneous because of the grouping.

It should be remembered also that, whenever groupings are made, some persons in the group will always be more like many in another group than like many in their own. Furthermore, the actual degree of homogeneity will change sharply after enough time elapses for individual growth to take place—which may not take long.

Homogeneous grouping at best can merely cut down the range of differences, and then only on those special aptitudes, knowledges, skills, or potentials which are measured by the grouping instruments.

Possibly the greatest hidden booby trap in a scheme of homogeneous grouping is the likelihood that teachers will assume that the individuals in a group are all alike and that they will teach accordingly. Likewise, the administrator may falsely assume that, after grouping, the teacher's task is made simple, and a single standard of achievement may be expected.

Over and over again teachers must be reminded, whether teaching homogeneous or heterogeneous groups, that the individual still must be taken where he is and directed from *there*. He learns as an individual. Any gifted child is quite different from other gifted children, just as any handicapped child is different from all other handicapped children.

Administrators should help keep teachers sensitive to their responsibility to the *individual* and should give them the working conditions (including groups of manageable size and flexibility of structural organization), the environment, and the instructional tools to achieve good instruction for each child.

If used, grouping should be designed to further the American dream of giving every individual the opportunity to realize his full potentials. Thus, any administrative arrangement for class or group management must have the interests in mind of the elusive and changing average child, as well as the extreme deviate. American values must be supported by the public schools—not unwittingly deserted in order to minimize the effort necessary to achieve them—to make teaching a simple, routine task, and to make learning a standardized procedure.

F.E.E.

Editorial, September 1961. *Let's Change the Structure of Education at the National Level*

Public education in the United States performs a unique function. This unique function was recognized early in the history of public education. Since schools were established to give equal opportunity to all children, America established a special plan for governing them. Legally, education is a state function; but control has been delegated largely to local school districts, with lay citizens acting as boards of education.

With few exceptions, the parents of school pupils have insisted that public education be above partisan politics and have established methods of selecting board members on bases other than partisan politics. Extensive powers have been vested in these boards of education; in practice, the boards determine the policies and programs of the schools.

In the past two decades, as states have assumed larger roles in education and state boards of education have become more extended in scope of operation, people in the several states have insisted more and more that the state boards of education, too, should be selected on a nonpartisan basis, and that the boards in turn should choose the chief state school officers and set their salaries.

The state board of education, as an educational agency with a professional staff of no partisan political allegiance, owing no responsibility to any segment, determines the over-all program of the state department of education; and, with the advice of the chief state school officer, determines educational policy for the state and gives nonpartisan advice to the state legislature and to the governor. It bears no partisan allegiance to the party in power. It attempts to understand educational problems and needs and assumes responsibility for fair administration and for developing public support.

On the federal level, the nation is getting its policies made, in most cases, not by careful deliberation of the implications that should be considered for any broad social policy, but by numerous action bills submitted in Congress by vested interests within and without the government, with dangling amendments which contradict most of the policies which have previously held true in the state and local communities. As long as the federal government played minor roles in public education, little concern about its political relationships was necessary. However, the sudden growth of personnel due to the National Defense Education Act—60 percent of all U.S. Office of Education personnel now work on NDEA operations—is stark evidence of the growth and power of the federal government in education.

A Powerful Office of Education Should be Removed from Politics

Recently a school reporter interpreted remarks of the U.S. Commissioner of Education to mean that he intended to take a positive leadership role in shaping the goals and program of American education. If such is the situation, then his position must be removed from the partisan political scene, or American public education may be seriously damaged.

For the federal government to assume an increased role, particularly in the administration and development of educational programs, without removing its agencies from political domination, is a serious threat to public education at state and local levels. If federal operations in education cannot be made independent of the control of either political party or of vested interests, every effort should be made to keep the U.S. Office of Education weak and limited in participation.

Yet, as the nation becomes more interrelated and interdependent, with communication and mobility of population greatly extended, it seems almost inevitable that the federal government will play a larger role in the educational affairs of the nation. Evidence mounts to support the belief that greatly increased financial support and strong professional leadership at the national level are necessary if public schools are to maintain high quality.

If this be true, it would seem that it is high time for an independent, national board of education to be established and given the power to propose and execute educational policy and to direct the activities of the growing U.S. Office of Education and other related national educational bodies such as the National Science Foundation.

If it is sound to govern education at the state and local levels by independent lay boards of education, surely it is equally sound to have the educational activities and policies of the federal government under the control of a similar independent, nonpartisan body.

The national board should be appointed by the President for a period of at least nine years, with long, overlapping terms. This body should be given the authority to select the U.S. Commissioner of Education and to set his salary. As a national body responsible for acquainting the nation with the needs of the schools and for determining policy on the national level—independent of partisan politics—this board could do what is needed badly at the national level—set policies in a deliberate fashion. This board could then, of course, make its appeal to all arms of government, particularly the administrative and congressional arms, and to representatives of all parties.

With a President such as our present one, anxious to strengthen education, now is the time for educational leaders everywhere, as well as laymen who are interested in the sound development of education in this country, to propose for action by this Congress a plan which would meet the specifications indicated above.

Possibly the American Association of School Administrators, together with other national organizations—such as the National School Boards Association, the National Education Association, the National Congress of Parents and Teachers, the Council of Chief State School Officers, the National Association of Secondary-School Principals, the NEA Department of Elementary School Principals, the Association for Supervision and Curriculum Development, the Association of Childhood Education International, and the American Vocational Association—should seek the support of the President and the Congress for changing the federal governmental structure for education.

F.E.E.

Editorial, October 1963. *Scholarships vs. Adequate Public Tax Support*

In recent years America has resounded to the siren call of scholarships. Like the Irish Sweepstakes, the odds do not seem to count; the lightning strike, the lucky coupon, the hex-marked number are irresistibly appealing. Although the use of scholarships as a supplement to sound financing of higher education should not be undervalued nor should generous donors be discounted, scholarships must not be substituted for inexpensive tuition charges for all.

Great industrial organizations and wealthy individuals seemingly get much more humanitarian satisfaction from giving money for scholarships to a relatively few than they do from paying tax dollars for the education of a much greater number.

Some state legislatures, federal officials, and congressmen seem to believe that spending tax dollars on scholarships to both public and nonpublic colleges is the most sound and adequate method of providing equal educational opportunities at the college level.

Secondary Policy Should Set Example

If America had attempted 75 years ago to solve the secondary school problem by scholarships to be used in the then prevalent private academy rather than by public taxation to establish tuition-free public high schools, this country would never have had universal education through the 12th grade. The policy America adopted for secondary schooling should become a reality for collegiate education.

In recent years the issue of giving equal opportunity to all in low-tuition or tuition-free public colleges has been blurred by scholarship programs which are given out-of-proportion status because of the out-of-proportion publicity, competition, and testing involved. The glamour of massive testing programs to discover the few geniuses worthy of scholarships blinds the public to the fact that hundreds of thousands were in the great group of able youth who "didn't quite make it."

Furthermore, it sometimes happens that the greater the number competing for a scholarship, the greater is the emphasis given to winning it. Thus, a high school principal loudly boasts of the one scholarship winner and toasts to the ceiling the donor, while 250 others in the graduating class, with the help of their economically pressed families, somehow make the grade and find the funds to go on to college also. If the time of students and faculty which is spent on taking and grading scholarship tests is worth half the prevailing minimum wage, the costs of taking and administering the tests exceed the value of the scholarships.

It has been suggested that the people and industrial firms which gain public acclaim for their generosity in giving highly publicized scholarships might better go on the public forum to ask for bigger appropriations and heavier tax levies to make low-tuition public colleges available to millions of worthy youths. No greater error can this nation make than to deny to many of the able, but not necessarily the academically brilliant, the opportunity for higher education. The very nature of the contemporary world calls for many, not a few, well-educated citizens. To leave the potentially most valuable national asset undeveloped is to court disaster.

All this is not to discredit scholarships, those who get them, or the individuals and organizations who give them. On the contrary, they are to be commended. However, scholarships are not, and cannot become a substitute for low-tuition colleges and universities. They must not confuse the issue.

Scholarships from private funds for students in private, high-tuition colleges and universities should be encouraged. But the public colleges and universities should receive public tax appropriations sufficient to provide free tuition, or at least tuition reduced to a bare minimum. The public colleges should be financially supported so as to allow them to achieve free tuition status just as was done three-quarters of a century ago with the public high school as it evolved from the restrictive, high-tuition private academy.

F.E.E.

Editorial, June 1963. *Crosswinds and Irregular Tides*

The superintendents of schools and the boards of education of 30 years ago had little influence brought to bear upon them other than that of the local power structure. The compass they steered by was their values, their knowledge, and the modest influences of their immediate community environment.

But today there are strong forces from beyond that must be reckoned with. Crosswinds and irregular tides bring gusty storms and heavy waves that threaten to throw education off course. The superintendent who pilots the modern educational enterprise needs new charts, new horizons, new sounding devices, new navigational knowledge and skill, and even new ports of call.

Unless the school administrator and his staff are sensitive to the pressures from outside their community and are capable of evaluating and accepting or rejecting those pressures, their educational program may be dashed upon the rocks.

Science and technology have revolutionized transportation, communication, and the whole economic system. The phenomenon of a nation filled with apprehension, indecision, passion, rash actions, insecurity, and fear should not be a surprise to the school administrator who is aware of the compression of time-space spans of scientific and social change during the past quarter century and the signals loud and clear that portend still greater acceleration by the year 2000.

Tax System is Obsolete

The local, isolated, self-sufficient, and autonomous community has largely disappeared, giving way to a greatly enlarged community where interrelatedness and interdependence are a necessity, but at the same time leaving school budget planners with an absolute and inadequate tax system with which to provide needed revenues.

Although the world demands a cosmopolitan outlook, the intermingling of cultures, and a tolerance for conflicting values, the great preponderance of the people still holds to parochial views. Insecurity and fear are components of our times and express themselves through men and groups of men who are hurrying toward what they believe to be an assurance of security and a retention or achievement of their particular purposes. They assume the role of educational quarterbacks, but usually with only one signal for the one play they are convinced will score.

It is the developments of our times, together with the social, economic, religious, and political conflicts that a suddenly shrunken world presents, which now permit and produce the outside influences playing upon the schools. If evaluated and understood, the sound and helpful influences can be used to speed education on a true and efficient course and the unsound and devastating ones can be ignored, resisted, and cast aside. What are these new forces from outside the community that need to be understood, evaluated, utilized, or resisted in whole or in part? From what do they stem and whence comes their impetus?

Human Race Longs for Freedom

Among these influences are the violent longings of the human race for freedom and dignity, personified by the founders of America, but recently erupting into world proportions. This almost frightening suddenness of change brings pressures from the extreme right and the extreme left. But, in the main, it is the welling up on a world scale of what Henry, Adams, Madison, Jefferson, and a whole company of early Americans who established our nation and its foundations thought and were bold enough to urge society to try.

The federal goverment and its many agencies such as Congress, the White House, the Supreme Court, the National Science Foundation, the Atomic Energy Commission, the National Aeronautics and Space Administration, the Department of State, and the U.S. Office of Education today influence the educational program to a considerable degree. Some of the effects are good and some are bad. The most serious fault lies in the fact that there is no nonpartisan, independent body responsible for developing and maintaining policy and for coordinating the whole federal effort. Almost everything done in education at the federal level is based on expediency, special interest, or the special prejudices of individuals or groups.

Because there is little or no accepted educational policy at the federal level, Congress responds to a babble of voices. It passes legislation which adds to the conflicting and unsound policy which its previous actions have tended to establish. Although almost all congressmen profess to believe that the federal government should not control education, their special, piecemeal, categorized legislative proposals suggest that they really believe federal officials alone can be depended upon for knowing what is best for the public welfare, education, and the national interest.

Armed with special grant power for aiding certain aspects of the curriculum or for bargaining to influence both students' choices and the program offering, federal agencies present a difficult situation for the local officials who have been charged traditionally with controlling and operating a school program with autonomy and with responsibility for student guidance.

As long as federal administrative officers and Congress presume to know the specific educational needs of the nation's public schools and as long as they show distrust in the very principle they profess to support, piecemeal, control-laden legislation will be proposed and passed, while the greatly needed general operation—uncontrolled federal financial support—will go by the board.

Since patterns of federal operation and control are rapidly crystallizing, the time is urgent for educational leaders at state and local levels, including school board members, to establish a commission which would study with the various agencies of the federal government, both executive and legislative, the ways by which the federal government can best cooperate with and serve public education in America. Publication and dissemination of agreed upon policies and practices to guide future relationships would indeed be timely. Unless this is done, empire builders among the federal civil service personnel, academic and commercial special interests, and partisan or selfish politicians will make a farce of the principle of state and local control and at the same time will split the educational program into isolated, unrelated parts rather than make it a unified, powerful guiding force.

Other national forces that affect the school program and that need to be understood and evaluated by local and state school officials are:

The findings of educational research.

National testing services.

Writers of dramatic attacks on modern education.

Organizations with extreme right or left views.

Angry, hostile, and prejudiced, as well as calm, friendly, and objective operators of newspapers and magazines.

Inventors, promoters, and salesmen of instructional devices.

Foundations.

National professional organizations such as the American Council on Education, the National Education Association, the Council for Basic Education, the American Association of School Administrators, the Council of Chief State School Officers, and the Association for Supervision and Curriculum Development.

National professional organizations such as the Chamber of Commerce of the U.S.A., the AFL-CIO, the American Farm Bureau Federation, the American Medical Association, and the American Legion.

Television and the powerful voices that use it.

College entrance programs.

The state of public opinion and positions on matters of public policy, national and international.

These and many other national or even international forces now must be reckoned with by local school officials.

Plans, policy, and machinery for dealing properly and sanely with these and other influences call for wisdom and statesmanship at the local district level. Only breadth of insight by local authorities on both educational matters and the great social issues of the times can sustain the commonly accepted principle of local and state control of public education. If the superintendent, staff, and local board cannot interpret the times and sense the nation's needs and develop programs that serve both, it seems inevitable that the concept of local control and local determination in educational matters will be destroyed.

Men of grander stature, wider vision, more abundant courage, and greater professional competence must man the school superintendency of the immediate future. In turn, they will fail unless supported by school boards of independence, wisdom, and devotion to getting the best schools possible.

F.E.E.

Editorial, May 1963. *Is Education on Course?*

Within recent years two major phenomena which are destined to affect public school administration have developed in the United States. Both stem largely from the fact that there is no local community in the old sense of the word; increasing mobility of population and advances in technology, communication, and transportation have made the whole nation interdependent and interrelated economically, politically, socially, and culturally.

The first phenomenon which is growing out of this development and which affects the administration and operation of schools concerns the shift in the economics of school support. Educators, school boards, and others interested in public education should be aware of America's changing economy, and they should be aware that local taxation no longer provides the preponderance of funds for school support.

The local property tax is proving both inadequate and unfair as a source of revenue. Within a few years local school systems have come to depend for almost half their budgets on state and federal resources. Tax revenues themselves have shifted. Whereas 30 years ago nearly 75 percent of all tax revenues flowed into the local treasury, now only 15 percent resides there. As state legislatures and Congress appropriate more and more of the local board's budget, there will be less and less control exercised by school boards over promoting and raising the revenues which sustain their budgets unless school board members and other interested citizens concern themselves with influencing the action of state and federal legislators on educational matters.

Without responsibility for raising revenues, without the opportunity to affect the sources of revenue, and without some assurance on probable total revenues, the local board cannot with confidence negotiate contracts with business firms or with school staffs, and this state of affairs is becoming a frightening reality.

Unless policies are adopted which allow local boards to deal directly with tax-raising agencies outside the district, such as the state legislatures, and unless local school authorities have reasonable estimates of how much money will be made available to them from state and federal sources, staff groups will feel that they must negotiate not only with local authorities but with state and federal agencies as well. Herein lies one of the great developing issues of our time. Unless the issue is resolved, the concept of local autonomy and local control of public schools will be in jeopardy. Unless reasonably stable policies and principles are adopted by state legislatures and by Congress, state and national organizations will likely be the determinants in teacher contracts rather than local teachers' organizations, principals, superintendents, and school boards.

In fact, welfare matters such as salaries, retirement and hospitalization benefits, and other working arrangements will be determined by state and national fiscal authorities rather than by school boards unless school boards become sensitive to what is happening and unless legislatures agree to make substantial appropriations needed by local districts and to transmit such funds to local school boards without restriction as to use.

The situation in Utah serves as an indicator of things to come. When recently the Utah legislature not only refused to lift sufficiently the limits previously placed on local tax levies but also failed to make adequate appropriations to provide requested raises in teachers' salaries and other badly needed educational services, the state education association's membership agreed to suspend all discussions of teacher contracts at the local level. The traditional role of local administrators, local teachers, and local school boards was abandoned in favor of negotiations between the state legislature and a state-wide organization of the profession.

Unless the shift in revenue sources is recognized by school boards and unless some legal policy is adopted at the state and national levels to provide funds and at the same time protect the autonomy and adequacy of local board operations, the future of American educational operations and control will be drastically altered. Of this evolving phenomenon school boards and professional staffs as well as legislators should take serious cognizance.

Authority is Assumed

The second phenomenon is the growing sensitiveness on the part of many citizens to the fact that public education must be guided toward the national interest. The goals of the nation must be served by the public schools. Some people in both the administrative and legislative arms of the federal government contend that they know better how the schools should operate to achieve this end than do local or even state authorities. Consequently there is a growing tendency for the federal government to assume authority for the curriculum and the budget previously delegated to state and local authorities.

These phenomena, together with other evolving forces, will unquestionably affect the course of American education. Both the shift of financial support and the concern for education as an instrument of national purpose can result in a better quality of education. The way in which they will be utilized to affect the administration of schools is an uncertainty, however. Unless the wisest of leadership is provided, the quality of education will deteriorate.

Casual examination suggests three possible outcomes as related to administration and control.

First of all, local school boards can alert themselves to the possible effects on them and can seek to retain their traditional autonomy by influencing state and federal legislators and administrative agencies to formally adopt policies and practices which guarantee local independence. Such policies then could govern the distribution of appropriations for educational purposes. Even so, eternal vigilance would be needed to head off violations. Insistence on no violation of such policies could even result in no appropriation, depending on the membership and mood of a given state legislature or Congress.

Second, the interrelatedness of local, state, and federal resources may demand a team approach with ground rules, roles, and responsibilities established and agreed upon and formalized. There is considerable evidence to commend this plan, but how it could be developed, who should lead, and what governmental structure would be needed present a challenge.

Third, the developing forces and practices can be ignored by educational leaders and by school board members and be allowed to take their slow but sure course of erosion.

F.E.E.

In recent months the city superintendent has been under such severe criticism that I felt it necessary to express my opinion on his effectiveness in today's city schools. The following is an editorial which I wrote for *The School Administrator*:

The Big-City Superintendent: A Man of Many Talents

Don't tell me the city superintendent has failed! Don't indict him for being obsolete! Don't replace him with a neophyte!

The hue and cry of critics, faultfinders, reformers, newly visible experts, and just frightened people is heard in legislative halls and all about and finds written expression in respectable and not so respectable publications.

The faults of society, so they say, are the faults of the public schools. The inability of the schools to meet mounting expectations and greatly multiplied enrollments can be laid at the door of the school administrator—so it is said. To solve the problems and save the schools, some writers and speechmakers say, "Remove the prevalently school-oriented, professionally educated, broadly experienced administrator and replace him with a finance expert, a managing wizard, a spiritualist in business, or just a sharp politician. Some are saying that the school executive needs nothing except managerial skill, a hard-nosed ability to play politics, and courage to make quick big decisions. The new administrator—they claim—needs neither experience in teaching, acquaintance with pupil learning problems, knowledge of the diversity of teaching roles and problems, understanding of school organizational structures, nor organized information in the fields applicable to school administration.

Although the city schools face almost insurmountable problems and new emerging issues for the most part have developed at explosive speed, it has not been because the school program has been weak and poorly administered but because the phenomenon of a changing social, political, scientific, and cultural society has brought new dimensions to education. Changes in expectations, cultural patterns, values, ethnic groupings, and family life have literally engulfed the schools with new and pressing problems that take time and money and retrained personnel to solve. Even with the mounting problems and increasing militant demands that teaching rise to new heights, the public grows in its faith that education holds the key to individual happiness and success. Although many new problems remain unsolved and many successful innovations have not yet been adopted, never before has this nation or any nation engaged in such wholesale efforts to make the dream of universal education a reality and to change rapidly the curriculum patterns to meet children's needs. Never before has the drop-out rate been so low. And much of this success and little of the failure can be attributed to the skill, the devotion, the understanding, and the overall competence of the school administrator.

Much of his success is due not to his youth, not to his manipulatory qualities, not to his training in business management, not to his engaging in partisan politics; rather, his success can be attributed to his deep devotion to public education and his broad training in the arts and sciences, coupled with professional training programs that acquaint him with school organization, societal phenomena, school curriculum patterns, teaching problems, and the nature of learning. His training has taught him how to engage in politics *without* being engaged in petty partisanship. Few leaders in public life have as much formal training for recognizing, analyzing, and interpreting the power structure, the community value systems peculiar to contemporary culture, and the onrush of science, technology, and social change. Even in matters of community growth trends, changing industrial needs, program planning, and budget making and control, he has had to be adept and imaginative to survive.

His experience usually includes teaching at various levels and administration at the building level. For years he was successful in dealing with staff and public. His training in public relations equals that of leaders of other public enterprises.

Thus, his educational training as well as his teaching and administration experience gives him the special competence and value system suitable for making decisions on educational matters and broad public policy. Without a basic understanding of the problems of the classroom, administrative decisions will be wrong. And decision making is at the very heart of sound and imaginative school administration. He who does not have the relevant education and experience is poorly prepared to administer a school system. Likewise, it will be a sorry day for education when the superintendent is tied to the coattail of the vote-seeking mayor or the local political boss. Indeed, he may work with them but not for them.

Both political parties are his clientele—as are the League of Women Voters, the PTA, the Chamber of Commerce, the Council of Churches, and the labor unions. With all these and others, too, he associates as the independent spokesman of the whole education system. His role is the most complex and the most harassing of all public leadership posts, and the last quarter century has proved the city superintendent's skills and power over and over. Our present revolutionary and militant times compound his responsibilities and his problems. But to proclaim that he is failing is to deny the facts. Furthermore, to state that his position is of short tenure is questionable. Occasionally, the city superintendent has been replaced—usually because he has offended the conservative power structure and on occasion because cultural change overwhelmed him. But a check of the big cities (Fort Worth, San Antonio, Kansas City, Denver, St. Louis, Tulsa, San Francisco, St. Paul, Chicago, Minneapolis, Boston, Cincinnati, Los Angeles, Milwaukee, Portland, Seattle, Omaha, Dallas, Atlanta, Buffalo, Columbus, and a host of others) shows a surprisingly long tenure for the superintendent.

Don't accept the carelessly made statement that the superintendents have failed and must be replaced by a new "breed of young cats" trained to be business executives and change agents without knowledge of what needs changing or competence to judge the effectiveness of innovation. All professional educators, in the big city especially, must know that change has accelerated and that society has made new demands which the schools must somehow meet. No one is more sensitive to this than the superintendent. Furthermore, he has not quit; he has not been cowed; he has not retreated though he has often been maligned, threatened, and harassed.

We should be thankful that as the city has changed character, as its leadership has fled to the suburbs, the superintendent, in the main, has kept his faith in public education, stayed on the job, and helped guide the task of developing new instructional goals and molding new leadership. The militancy of many of the emerging leaders, together with the impatience of the culturally deprived, serves as an irritant as well as a stimulant. Since the average city superintendent was trained in the philosophy that every child can be reached and must have opportunity, it is not surprising that he has exhibited patience with those who are impatient.

He knows better than most that it is time for large efforts to be made to provide enough skilled and deeply committed teachers and exciting experiences to meet the diverse needs of every pupil. Possibly no group of educators has pooled its resources so vigorously as have the city superintendents for self-reeducation and for depth analyses of their problems and for adequate understanding of the contemporary, social, cultural, and technological scene. For years, they have supported joint data-gathering surveys and research, and for years they have met regularly to analyze the findings and to seek professional renewal.

Yes, the public schools—particularly in the city—are in trouble as they face poverty, deprivation, and anger. But the fault lies not wholly with the schools. It lies with a people upset by technology, beset with cultural turmoil, and awakened to a better destiny. The schools will shape that destiny, and the city superintendent, more than any other person, has the responsibility, the commitment, and the competence to give the leadership.

F.E.E.

During the late sixties, great publicity was given to the fact that many students found the schools unsatisfactory and dropped out. Believing that there are two sides to most questions, I expressed my views on the subject in the following editorial in *The School Administrator*, September 1965.

Do Not Indict the Dropout

Let us not make capital offenders of school dropouts. Not all of those who leave school are guilty of social crime or bad judgment. It is right that the American public should be alarmed at youth unemployment, juvenile crime, and gang disturbances. But these problems will not be solved by forcing every adolescent to stay in the schoolroom.

Many school authorities have long contended that, ideally, the school program and the school environment should be sufficiently diversified and imaginative and so expertly managed as to reach the interests, aptitudes, and range of individual differences of all boys and girls. Realistically, however, that ideal has not been reached and probably will not be for a long time. Resources—both human and material—must be multiplied many times over if the goal is to be achieved.

In the meantime, let us stop pointing an accusing finger at the youth who chooses to find for himself a better environment than his present school offers. Let us be reluctant to say that he who drops out before high school graduation has taken a giant step toward delinquency and a life of unproductive idleness and crime. Let us hesitate to say, "There is no place except the school where youth can live, learn, and work." There is much truth in such a statement for most youth, but our present-day schools are not necessarily good for every child.

World of Work is Not All Bad

Neither is the community and the world of work all bad for all youth. Eight thousand educators heard Helen Hayes, as she received the 1965 American Education Award say: "I never got a diploma in my life.... The theater was my school."

Let us not condone or encourage dropouts except in rare cases, but let us condemn "force-ins," where the school offerings and the professional services are harming rather than helping a particular youth. Surely, for some, the community has more to offer than does the school.

For many young people, however, the choice is to either walk the plank into a turbulent, unfriendly community sea or be incarcerated in a school which, for their natures and potentials, is stifling. This situation is a crime against adolescence and an indictment of the professional competence of school and community leadership.

If school guidance officers, teachers, and principals knew enough about potential dropouts, if they knew enough about students' interests, longings, and aptitudes, if they knew enough about the educational potentials of the business and cultural facilities in the community, the dropouts might find themselves and develop their potentials outside the school.

Workable Partnership Is Difficult

It would be good, indeed, if school and community leaders were to seek together the answer to the most appropriate environment for these youth. But a workable partnership takes thought, time, and a rearrangement of resources—a difficult task.

The problem now is that neither the school nor the community, separately, is geared to promote the unique interests, the special needs, and diverse capacities of all young people. Unfortunately, neither are they geared administratively to combine the total resources of community and school. Surely the working world and the civic world can also be more of an educational world.

For the school to identify itself with the world of work is not to lower its quality but rather to get into the main stream of life itself. In the final analysis, the full potentials of most people can be achieved only through productive work. But the world of work seems far removed from those who man the schools. Academic credits, IQ's, and the like have pushed aside and overshadowed the great productive resurgence that characterizes our times.

We should realize, of course, that our scientific and inter-related world is different from that of yesterday, but we should also remember that some of the dropouts of yesterday would never have achieved greatness, as some have, by remaining in school. For a few, the same may be true today.

The dropout should not be branded as a rebel against that which adults tend to call the sound preparation for life. Diversity, which is a precious national asset, often finds expression in a decision to quit school. It cannot and will not be preserved by incarceration in any environment that thwarts rather than assists. Right now the climate is such that school administrators should play constructive roles in helping stop the trend to brand every child or youth as an outcast and failure who is discontented with the academic world and school routine. Let us save, not just hold, our youth.

All this means a revamping of the program, a change in pupil personnel handling, and teamwork with the total community. It will take time, commitment, imagination, cooperation, money, and a willingness to use unorthodox methods and content inside and outside the school. Indeed, it must be an educational program by and for the total community.

F.E.E.

Another bit of writing which I thoroughly enjoyed was done as we prepared for the annual presentation of awards for distinctive and exemplary services at the AASA convention. I had something to do with starting this custom and assumed the responsibility of writing all the citations. While writing them, I more than ever came to believe my English professor's words—"Conciseness is the essence of good prose, but difficult to achieve." One citation which I enjoyed writing read:

> Thomas Jefferson, more than any other man, convinced the new nation that education is essential for a free people. Horace Mann, more than any other man, convinced the expanding nation that public education, supported by all and open to all, must be established if the nation is to achieve its destiny. A century later, with the people frightened, the nation threatened, free institutions held in doubt, and the public schools under severe criticism, James Bryant Conant, more than any man, by his logic, his keen analysis, patriotic sacrifice, and courageous vision rekindled the nation's flame of faith in free men's basic human values and rebuilt confidence in the public schools of America.

I feel compelled to say that I think Dr. Conant did a disservice to education later by expressing strong opinions, largely unsubstantiated, about the professional preparation needed by school superintendents.

CHAPTER XI

The Executive Committee frequently asked me to take vacations. I took few days off, but did relax for periods of two or three weeks during the summer by directing advanced university seminars in school administration for selected school administrators. These seminars went from 9 A.M. until 3:30 P.M. five days a week, for periods of two or three weeks. About half the issues and phenomena discussed were internal, such as staffing policies, negotiations, or processes for achieving sound innovations, and about half were exterior but relevant phenomena such as the civil rights movement, population change and migration, and emerging social, political, and economic phenomena. It was my privilege to introduce the Advanced Seminar in School Administration at Harvard University and to do similar seminars at the University of Oregon and the University of Wyoming.

Although I published a considerable number of articles in professional journals during my stay in Connecticut, the flow became a stronger current after going to Washington. At the urgent request of the leadership preparing the program for the White House Conference of Children and Youth in 1960, I gave a talk which was published in the proceedings. Its title was "Education for the Year 2000." Possibly the most comprehensive publication in which I participated with the help of Shirley Cooper and William Ellena was *Vignettes on the Theory and Practice of School Administration,* published by MacMillan.

Although I enjoyed all aspects of the job of executive secretary, I continued to believe, as I did when I accepted the position, that few positions in American education wielded greater influence or had greater potential for leadership. The importance of this position was on my conscience much of the time. As I grew older, I worried that I might have the poor judgment to hold the position of executive secretary beyond my peak of competence. Consequently, I quietly told the Board in late 1962 that they should start looking for a successor. They insisted that I remain at least until I was seventy years of age, but I refused. Possibly the letter I published in *The School Administrator* best described my feelings in the matter. It reads as follows:

I have never felt better; I know of no physical infirmity; I am exceedingly happy with this work, and every day is exhilarating to me. Furthermore, I like and respect the new as well as the retiring officers. No man was ever blessed with a more loyal, devoted, and efficient staff.

However, because I am devoted to the Association, because I know its opportunities and obligations, and because I know the statistics of man's physical and mental deterioration with age, I dare not take the risk of self-humiliation or the risk of failing the Association at a crucial period by allowing myself to continue long as your executive secretary. A new executive secretary would have a distinct advantage if he launched and carried through the Association's new five-year program.

I therefore submit my resignation to take effect as soon as my successor is appointed and is available for duty. Every man of you is my friend and is admired by me. Thousands of our members are in the same category. To cease this particular relationship is a terrific strain on my heartstrings.

Furthermore, I feel a great indebtedness to you and to your associates who first invited me to accept the honor of being your executive secretary. My deepest thanks are extended to all of you and to the administrators in every state of the Union who have been so kind and gracious to me.

I do wish to report that I have no intention of just sitting at home until my days run out. I have two writing projects to do. Furthermore, my interest will continue in trying to help improve public education and the university programs of preservice and inservice education of school administrators.

On September 16, 1963, I said a quiet farewell to my wonderful associates on the staff and boarded a flight to Philadelphia. The leaving gave me an emotional tug. In Philadelphia, I took a taxi to our new home in Pitman, New Jersey. The stay was short, since the next day we packed, and, by late afternoon, we were again in a taxi going back to Philadelphia Airport, armed with passports and visas for our scheduled assignment with the U.S. Department of State.

Even though some repetition is involved, I wish at this point to attempt to describe and characterize public education as I observed it between 1945 and 1965.

World War II and Its Aftermath—1940-1950

The forties had barely arrived when World War II began. The nation gave top priority to winning the war. Public schools were neglected. Budgets were inadequate. School buildings were allowed to decay. Staffs, both men and women, joined the services. Dropouts of older youth were encouraged and blessings given them as they joined the labor force or took up arms.

Colleges, in large measure, became preparatory schools for filling the ranks of officers in the Marine Corps, the Navy, the Air Force, and the Army. High quality teaching and learning were found most frequently in the schools of the military. The armed services took on a major educational project. Hundreds and hundreds of special schools designed to stimulate morale and develop special skills and general competence were established by the Department of Defense. The motivation of the students and instructors was at a maximum, and teachers who joined the service were urged to teach. Since speed in preparation for battle was pressing, all new methods and materials were seized upon. Audiovisual materials, not readily available in the public and private schools, were provided and used. With few professional inhibitions and with new media of instruction readily provided, teachers in the armed services schools breached their bonds and tried out many new innovative practices.

Meanwhile the elderly and the infirm manned the public schools from 1941 to 1946. Advances in curriculum were made, however. Health and physical education, citizenship, and science became of greater concern and made some headway. The Education Policies Commission of AASA and NEA brought forth a policy bulletin which urged the nation to give more attention to science and to prepare for a world rapidly growing more technological.

Because the federal government operated so many vocational programs to stimulate the technical and occupational competence of those entering defense industries, vocational education took on more respectability. Also, vocational programs operated by local districts as well as by states received federal funds which acted as significant stimulants.

With the war's end came the most significant step by the federal government that had ever been taken. The GI Bill of Educational Rights made scholarship and maintenance funds available to all service men and women. Colleges, professional schools, universities, and community colleges had a brand new clientele. Thousands and thousands of young people who had served in the military now found college within reach. Although they were older than the normal college student and in many cases married, they flocked to the new and undreamed-of opportunity. New data and new assumptions relative to the college student soon found their way into the American mind. These more mature young people returning from service proved that maturity, purpose, and drive made a positive difference. Thousands with mediocre records in secondary schools did superior work in college, and the federal government footed the bill.

For GI's not eligible for or not desiring higher education, on-the-job opportunities were made available and paid for by congressional appropriations and were supervised by state education agencies. Consequently, a sort of schooling-apprenticeship program made entrance to hundreds of occupations accessible. Indeed, the GI Bill of Educational Rights became the most signal giant step that had been taken by Congress since the first Morrel Act.

Late in 1945, a few months after the signing of peace in Tokyo, the organized profession exhibited a leadership unknown before that time. As stated earlier, it was at a meeting in Chautauqua, New York, that the National Education Association put forth the clarion call to unite, rebuild, and set standards for teachers. National commissions such as the National Commission on Teacher Education and Professional Standards were established. The teaching profession, at its lowest ebb of all time, decided to lift itself by its own efforts. This Commission determined that higher education institutions preparing teachers must develop strong programs and set higher standards of admission. This was a major proposal since charlatan colleges of every hue and color claimed the right to prepare teachers. The first advance was made when colleges of education in major universities agreed to join with teachers colleges, state colleges, and liberal arts colleges, to seriously attacking the problem of training teachers, and formed the American Association of Colleges for Teacher Education.

The next step was to establish a plan for enforcing standards. Many universities were opposed to any accreditation procedures. But, in time, logic and professional judgment won and the National Council for Accreditation of Teacher Education was formed. It had the official backing of the National Education Association, the Council of Chief State School Officers, the American Association of Colleges for Teacher Education, the AASA, and the National School Boards Association.

Simultaneously, the AASA, with a huge grant from the Kellogg Foundation, started a research and development program to determine and develop a suitable program for the proper education of school administrators, especially superintendents of schools.

The public, too, arose to meet the problem of rebuilding the schools, led by Roy Larsen and nationally recognized laymen of the Citizens Committee for the Public Schools. This national committee was instrumental in arousing citizen support for public schools. Many states developed programs that involved the public at all local levels. Consequently, school boards enlisted the support of thousands of local citizens committees in the study of public school problems and support. These citizens committees did magnificent work until some attempted to take over the legal prerogatives of the school board and the legally selected administrators.

But all was not support. Critics, especially from the academic community, made bitter attacks on the low standards of schools as well as on the teaching methods used. Books like *Why Johnny Can't Read* appeared. Teachers were placed on the defensive while critics ranted and raved and wrote hundreds of articles criticizing teachers and programs. Life adjustment curricula and what some mistakenly thought was a John Dewey philosophy came in for rabid attack. Interestingly, the life adjustment program had a relevancy which the critics, fifteen years later, were demanding and blasting the schools for not having.

School buildings were constructed by the scores, and because most states made appropriations to assist local communities, state departments tended to develop school building codes and set the standards, some too rigid. This often resulted in uniformity of design but also ensured the addition of new features such as libraries (even in elementary schools), laboratories, auditoriums, shops, commercial departments, playgrounds, learning resource centers, movable walls, and electrical outlets for the new electronic gadgetry that was on the horizon. Although the school buildings of this era accommodated the expanding curriculum, they tended to lack flexibility in construction, and, to the discomfort of teachers and pupils, contained exterior walls of glass which made light control as well as heat control almost impossible.

Since there was demand for higher teaching qualifications by teachers themselves, healthy curriculum reconstruction was begun. Like the First World War, the Second World War started a revolution to make the whole curriculum more comprehensive and more adequate for a new scientific and industrial mobile world. For the first time since the second decade of the century, cooperation between academic scholars in the universities and practicing educators in the elementary and secondary schools began. Due, in the main, to the efforts of the national and state commissions on teacher education and professional standards, the professors of pedagogy and child psychology joined hands with scholars in other fields to reconstruct the teacher education programs in the colleges and universities. For the first time professors in teachers colleges and those in liberal arts colleges came to know and respect each other. The term "Interdisciplinary Effort" became a byword with those preparing school administrators.

The late forties also were the period of many surveys. Local boards and state legislatures believed that survey teams and outside experts could make studies and subsequent recommendations that would be valuable blueprints. When such surveys involved local citizens and staff members, good often resulted. When done independently by outside specialists, with no involvement of staff and community, the reports often merely took up space on the superintendent's shelf.

Sputnik and the Fifties—1950-1960

Possibly nothing shocked the pride of America so much during the century as did the earth-orbiting satellite sent up by the Russian scientists; and nothing focused attention on America's schools as did this feat. Wounded pride and outright fear became a national mental state. There had to be a scapegoat, so again the critics praised Russian education and scorned the efforts of the American schools. It was said that American teachers knew nothing but method and that they lacked scholarship, especially in mathematics and science. The schools, it was charged, had no rigid standards like European schools. Everybody passed, and too many stayed in school too long, to the neglect of the talented. Never mind the dropouts, the average pupils—in fact, they should be flunked out, saving more teacher time for the bright child. That "save the best and shoot the rest" would be the best policy was sincerely believed by many.

National magazines and television for the first time took up the hue and cry, and local school authorities heard public demands that threatened to bypass the judgment of professional staffs and school boards. The academically talented were put in special small classes, and another type of social segregation began. The foundations rushed in to give merit scholarships, as did many legislatures. Teachers assigned to "bright" classes and those whose scholars made high examination marks had greatest prestige. A high school was judged not by its comprehensive curriculum that attempted to serve all pupils but by the number of merit scholars it produced. There seemed to be a turning away from the time-honored American policy of providing universal education. Subjects such as social studies, industrial arts, homemaking, and the arts gave way to the older academic disciplines. Naturally, test makers in these fields had a field day. Extracurricular activities suffered as they, too, were considered frills. Those who participated in them tended to be anti-intellectual anyway, said the critics. Teaching was successful if the students could gorge themselves on academic facts and could then regurgitate the same data on tests and standardized examinations. Test instruments too often determined what was to be taught.

But the day of "things" in eduation was almost upon the schools. Gadgetry, instruments, machines—many electronic devices—were being produced, and there were salesmen, too. Audiovisual, mechanical, and language laboratories were introduced, and because of a strong industrial lobby, state legislatures and Congress made appropriations to aid in their purchase.

The "heat and the fury" reached into the White House. The President in a speech at Oklahoma City unveiled a massive educational aid program to be proposed to Congress. He, like many others, believed the national security depended on strengthening certain subjects—disciplines believed to be most important to the general welfare.

Soon Congress was passing the massive aid program called the National Defense Education Act. Its chief provisions called for federal financial aid to strengthen science, mathematics, and modern language. A part of the Act also set aside massive sums to purchase equipment and to promote the development and use of educational television.

Although Congress has exercised control over secondary education before, when singling out vocational education to be strengthened by federal funds, the National Defense Education Act was a headlong rush by federal authorities to determine what was weak, what was important, and what should have favored treatment in the schools. Because the funds were on a matching basis, two things happened: since a dollar of local funds was spent for the subject singled out for assistance in the Act, such as mathematics, the local school board recognized the business advantage of buying more mathematics services and less art, music, or industrial arts. Here was a serious venture in federal control through the bribery of the dollar. The Act was unfair because the matching of funds requirement gave large sums to the school district with ample revenues while the poor districts suffered for lack of funds to match the federal dollar. Some districts, to gain federal grants, starved the curriculum areas of English, history, art, and music. But science programs, mathematics instruction, and modern language efforts, aided by these funds, improved rapidly. Likewise, the utilization of instructional aids, particularly those of an electronic character, was greatly enhanced. Many parents' nights were highlighted by demonstrations of overhead projectors, tape recorders, moving pictures, slides, and language laboratories as proud teachers discussed their virtues.

It was during the excitement following Sputnik that Congress established another federal agency to administer special aspects of education. The agency was called the National Science Foundation and was given more autonomy and more freedom from partisan domination than the U.S. Office of Education had.

Another development of great potential at the national level was an appropriation to the U.S. Office of Education for the support of research in education. Money was allotted on the approval of a committee appointed by the U.S. Commissioner of Education. This committee carefully reviewed all proposals and approved only those deemed to be valuable to education and scientifically structured so as to give valid research findings.

As the gross national income rose rapidly following World War II, so did the federal revenues automatically rise due to the nature of the federal income tax. Naturally, new federally supported agencies were established and old ones grew fat. Such agencies as the Civil Aeronautics Commission, the Space Agency, the Atomic Energy Commission, the military establishments, and the like needed research, promotion, and other assistance, so they turned to education. Most of their efforts in the public schools were promotional and educational in nature, with little dangling money grants. The universities and colleges were offered huge financial inducements to do programming and research. Several university budgets were dominated by contractual items. Naturally, instruction was affected. Some university presidents complained, saying the university had become the handmaiden of government and had lost its independence and been deflected from its true purpose.

Soon after World War II, foundations emerged with a strong force affecting public education. Millions and millions of dollars escaped taxes by being placed in tax-exempt foundations. Headed, for the most part, by men with little or no experience in public education as pupils or as practitioners, some of the major foundations began to do things to the public schools. These men took on the cloaks of authorities and offered themselves, their programs, and their money to change education in manners conceived by them to be good. Some of them made pronouncements; they gave endorsements to certain educators; they frowned on others; they willingly headed "study" commissions; they made overtures to politicians at state and national level. Indeed, there was evidence of premeditated planning to change the face of public education by influencing personnel and by offering funds for projects close to their own concepts. Indeed, their money was given not for carefully designed experimentation but for the promotion of programs and methods believed by them to be valid. Their full weight did not come to be realized until the following decade. But there can be little doubt that foundations, together with young turks from a few academic institutions, determined to become the new establishment. This new power structure seized upon television and the popular press to give itself visibility. Soon the politicians were affected, as were many education writers and editors. Since education was in the headlines as fundamental to national defense, it became newsworthy and major newspapers appointed education writers and education editors.

Innovation Becomes the Watchword—1960-1970

Although the fifties, affected by Sputnik and with eyes on the talented, departed from the traditional concept of an educational opportunity for everybody, by 1960 the swing was back to universal education. By then the space race was more equal and other social problems called for solution. And again the schools were called upon to solve them. Mobility and economic change brought many underprivileged people scurrying to the cities, most of whom previously had gone unnoticed. At the same time, the Supreme Court decision requiring integration of whites and blacks poured into the cities, the white streamed to the suburbs. The schools in the neighborhoods which were now becoming ghettos were, of course, inadequate for the different type of community and different clientele with different aspirations. A hue and cry arose that the leadership, the teachers, and the schools were poor, even wretched. It might be argued that the schools, the administrators, the curriculum, and the facilities were not far different from those that served the poor a decade earlier. Surely, ghettos were occupied by the Irish, the Italians, and Jews, and the Polish immigrants who had swarmed to America between 1920 and 1940. But the aspirations of the poor of the sixties, their cultural heritage, and their family patterns differed drastically from those of earlier times, and the educational pattern and the teaching methods—though seemingly satisfactory to the immigrant child of an earlier period—did not fit the needs of the Negro or the Puerto Rican. In this sense, the city schools were poor. Wealth and experienced leadership were now in the suburbs, and local city taxes were increasingly inadequate. Furthermore, state aids to education, normally determined by rural legislators, discriminated against city district school boards.

By 1960 the demand for skilled, well educated workmen and the general use of power machinery made unskilled labor obsolete in almost every field. Women, too, were coming into their own. Almost all doors to all occupations previously closed to them were swinging partially open. The education of women took on almost the same characteristics as that of men. With such shifts in status and values, the family took on a drastic change, as did enrollments. Knowledge of birth control gave an added freedom to women and changed behavior patterns and values. Sex education pushed itself into the controversial front of the curriculum.

The early part of the decade brought the most complex and comprehensive legislation ever passed by Congress. It was designed to give almost all education interests, public and private, a bite of the pie. The major bill, with all its trailers and subunits, was difficult to understand and, for the most part, carried entirely too much U.S. Office of Education control. It was called the Elementary and Secondary Education Act. Its first title or major section was designed to help the poor, whether in the city or country. The funds were allocated to districts in proportion to the number of poor families with children.

Most appropriation bills, with few exceptions, permitted money to be allocated only after local, district, state, or regional authorities developed and submitted projects for approval in Washington. The characteristic which Office of Education evaluators considered most important was the degree to which the project appeared to be innovative or exemplary. Project writers soon learned that a proposal under some titles would get the nod of the approving authority only if the description of the project made it appear to be a new approach. Indeed, project writers were necessarily added to local staffs. Many superintendents insisted that the money spent in getting and administering a federal grant was greater than the amount of the grant. Naturally, too, the U.S. Office of Education grew like Topsy as a result of this grantsmanship philosophy. The new power structure referred to earlier seemed to believe that anything new in education would be better than any patterns of the past. So the funds both from foundations and from the Office of Education were allotted, in the main, to promote change, with little effort to judge the validity of the new projects. Even though the total allotments from Washington amounted to only 8 percent of the money spent for public education, an inordinate amount of time and money was spent to get that 8 percent. No one in the new establishment seemed to believe that had the moneys been given as general aid, the authorities at the local level would have introduced new and imaginative programs designed more carefully to meet their emerging and unique local needs. None in the new power structure seemed to know the history of America, which clearly reveals that no system in the world had, over the years, done so much experimentation and developed so many approaches to teaching and learning as had America. For 100 years, daring and creative teachers and administrators at the local level had demonstrated over and over that the decentralized system stimulates and permits innovation and creativity. But even Congress, which should have known better, now moved in the direction of controlling education by Washington dictation.

During the sixties, no open sesame was so useful for getting notoriety, publicity, and federal and foundation grants as the words "innovative" and "exemplary." The new establishment or at least those on the staffs of some large foundations, many education writers, and a block in the executive branch of the federal government, taking note of what science and technology had done to revolutionize industry, transportation, and communications, sounded the alarm for change in education and for the adoption of methods used by industry and the Department of Defense. Often innovations were introduced for the wrong reason: (1) Funds were made available to introduce a new method, new materials, or a newly manufactured electronic device, or to achieve some goal that an outside force desired. (2) Some proponent had written a treatise promoting the innovation. (3) Highly advertised materials or equipment, if bought, would give an image of a progressive system. (4) An administrator or teacher made change for the sake of change and for publicity. (5) Since money was available if proposals suited the fancy of men in Washington, local project writers, often without assistance from the staff members who would execute the proposals, turned out projects that had minimum returns.

But sources outside a school system put pressure on administrators to get on the bandwagon. He who did not submit "exemplary" or "innovative" projects to the U.S. Office of Education or to a foundation for funding was branded as obsolescent and against progress.

Even though a school system had struggled for years to be modern in every respect, repeating the effective and proved materials and methods and curricula was not the thing to do. Progressive and professionally proved approaches could get little or no money to continue and strengthen creative and imaginative programs already in existence To be exemplary, a program must be "new" or disguised to seem of recent origin.

Another related segment of the new establishment was a group of graduates from a great university hell-bent to influence the federal government's philosophy and operations in education. This combine, coming at a time of great upheavals in the social and economic structure, seemed determined to discredit all leadership in education save its own. It refused to accept the fact that great experimentation and great innovative practices had penetrated public education since World War I. Since it was not accountable for efficiency and/or careful budgetary operations, per capita costs soared for many pet projects. If the excessively high costs per pupil for some federally funded projects and for others operated by foundation dollars were generally known, faith in the federal government and in foundations would be greatly depreciated.

True, many problems had become too complex and too broad in geographic scope to be solved by a purely autonomous and decentralized arrangement. Many educational problems, as well as political, social and economic ones such as pollution, transportation, and communications, simply cannot be solved at the local level. A national economy that made the old tax structure completely inadequate and obsolete, in a highly mobile and interdependent nation, called for an educational structure that accepted the team relationship between local, state, and national levels in its design. However, the roles of each and the emerging structure has not crystallized as of 1970. Little effort has been made by educational leadership at any level to develop cooperatively an acceptable new structure or to define roles and relationships. The chief effort has, in fact, been made by Congress and the executive branch which, stepping in rather blindly, have allowed Title III projects to spill over district and county lines and have given regional laboratories quasi-legal power.

One thing gradually became clear to those who thought soundly: roles and responsibilities could not remain in the old pattern. More and more decisions would be made at the state and federal level. Evidence supporting this belief appeared as study commission after study commission advocated strengthening the leadership at state and federal levels. Paradoxically, on the one hand, these study groups and organizations insisted that the local and state boards remain nonpartisan along their professional staffs, and, on the other hand, they recommended no board at the federal level and a partisan political administrator in the President's Cabinet.

As a result of the growing activities of the federal government in matters pertaining to education, a new council of state governments was formed. It seemed to supersede the Council of Chief State School Officers or possibly to supplement it. Many states elected to participate in the new commission, and some governors and chief state school officers were active. A strong central staff was appointed, and serious studies on relationships were instituted. So there was, on the one hand, pressure to centralize, and, on the other, a determined effort to keep local autonomy. On one side, the interrelated and interdependent larger community—even larger than the individual state—presents unassailable evidence to prove that much greater centralization is essential, particularly as related to financing, national interests, and many large areas of the curriculum such as vocational education and special services. On the other side, it seems clear that education in many respects is intermingled with family and local aspirations and special needs, thus demanding teacher-patron cooperative planning, managing, and evaluation. These two views are not incompatible, but the administrators of the future will have changed roles. For years some rather large units have given the neighborhood (building) administrator much responsibility and autonomy as related to the educational goals and outputs of his unit. As a principal in Kansas City during the twenties, I was expected to develop teacher teams to work closely with parents and neighborhood institutions. Each school prided itself in being on the threshold of the future and in tune with neighborhood aspirations and expectations. At the same time, they sought to achieve city-wide goals that seemed to be common to all schools throughout the city. Of course, the key to success in each building was a program involving parents in study, in planning, and in programming.

Reflecting the world revolution for human rights and the permissive spirit of the times, demonstrations, confrontations, strikes, and militant takeovers climaxed during the sixties. Teachers organizations flexed their muscles and swept the whole educational community into submission as negotiations and bargaining became the accepted practice. Teachers threw to the winds their former quiet demeanor and took on a militancy rivaling that of the United Mine Workers or the United Auto Workers. Foreseeing the growing storm, the Executive Committee of AASA asked me to prepare a statement defining roles and relationships of school boards, administrators, and teachers on welfare matters. After much discussion and some additions and deletions, the Executive Committee adopted a policy statement known as Roles, Responsibilities and Relationships. This proposal caused considerable controversy among superintendents, boards, and teachers. But the movement for organized action by teachers continued with acceleration.

During the sixties, the militancy of teacher leaders threatened to destroy the spirit of kinship and cooperative interdependence of teachers and administrators of all types. The bargaining confrontations between boards and teacher agents often placed the administrator, principal, and superintendent in new roles. The old model of the administrator as an active member of a professional team, compatible with all his associates, was altered. In some instances, he gave up his traditional role as defender of his professional associates and seeker of the school environment most suitable for teaching efficiency and became an opponent on the other side of the bargaining table. Simultaneously, a new kind of leadership arose to supplant the legally established administrator. He was the "union" agent who became the teachers' defendant and the administrator of the multitudinous aspects of the negotiated contract.

It is my judgment that this gap between administrator and teacher can be closed. Possibly, the negotiations of the future will be carried on at the state level. Many signs point in that direction. In any event, I feel that the gap must be closed and a new framework of interrelationships established. In the first place, I am convinced that hard-nosed bargaining does not imply a calloused profession or one that has lost sight of the educational welfare of children. Neither does it suggest that teachers who organize are less professional in spirit or competence. Furthermore, bargaining does not demand that the superintendent become the opponent of his staff. Once they achieve professional status in salary and working conditions, teachers will become still more competent and more devoted. They will ask for more cooperation, more teamwork, more assistance from the administrator. Thus the teachers, themselves, will take measures to close the gap.

In the meantime, administrators will remove themselves from the fray of welfare bargaining. Some other kind of negotiator on welfare matters will arise. However, he must find ways to join with staff in determining his role, which must be compatible with the complex roles of teachers. If teachers and other specialists are encouraged to participate in designing the leadership needed in the administrator, the combined creativity thus harnessed will evolve an administrative complex of new but exciting proportions. But the image of the administrator as the lone pilot of the ship will completely disappear.

The National Education Association and state teachers associations, stimulated by rivalry with the American Federation of Teachers, took strong and determined stands. Membership was at stake. Furthermore, few limits were placed on what was negotiable. During this decade the pattern of just who would represent the board of education at the negotiation table was indefinite. Clearly, the board was not a satisfactory body to act for itself and the public, and the superintendent, in most cases, was unwilling to sacrifice his role as educational leader to be a bargainer for either the board or the staff. Such superintendents insisted they should not be the "man" of either but the adviser and leader of both. In some cases, expert negotiators were employed by both teachers and school board. In some, the superintendent was the board's representative; in others, the board as a whole attempted to sit as bargainers; and, in still others, a personnel or business officer was assigned to the task.

Work stoppages, strikes, defiance of law and defiance of court injunctions were not uncommon. One state teachers association led a statewide strike, and others approved statewide holidays in protest. Since local budgets are more and more dependent on funds from the state legislature and the Congress, the district board has less and less knowledge of what funds it has with which to bargain. The finger of the future, therefore, seems to point to bargaining at the state or possibly even the federal level.

When the evidence is examined on negotiation results, it seems clear that the teachers have gained through united organization efforts many of the things good superintendents have fought for unsuccessfully for many years.

While the teachers during the sixties became more militant for their interests, so did the students. Unprecedented takeovers of university and college facilities occurred from coast to coast. Many of the most prestigious institutions felt the wrath of organized student groups. Some blamed the generation gap, but the causes were many and complex. Possibly the most volatile and militant students were the Negroes, angry over their history of oppression and the continued evidences of discrimination. Pride in black culture and black origins tended to make for segregation in reverse, and separatism was demanded by blacks on some campuses. The militancy became so extreme in several universities that buildings were stormed and occupied and property destroyed. Demands, not requests, were the pattern. In some instances, faculty members stood firm with the administration for law and order, but more often they were dormant, with faculty minorities actively supporting the students.

The secondary schools did not escape the movement, and student marches and strikes harassed some high schools. The pattern of protest and the area of student concern seemed to follow the same design as in the colleges and universities. In the cities, gangs with similar ethnic foundations stormed through subways, darkened streets, parks, and sometimes the school building attacking those of unlike origins. Many high schools were forced to employ private police forces to maintain discipline.

The sixties proved to be a great period for introducing new organizational structures, new methods, and new curricula such as the new math, the new science, an extension of the modern languages program, but it also gradually became a period of "shake down" and evaluation. Validation of assumptions and hurriedly adopted changes came to be in good taste by the late sixties. Research and experimentation results were becoming available on many so-called "exemplary" projects, and sound, stable, intelligent administrators were taking stock. Some "exemplary" activities were proving to be not "exemplary" at all. Others stood the test. But by the late sixties public school leaders dared to face the innovators and raise reasonable questions without fear of being called reactionaries and outmoded, unimaginative old fogeys. But headline hunters among education writers and university professors, as well as a few administrators heavily subsidized by foundation funds and U.S. Office of Education grants, continued to scream the failure and obsolescence of education.

During this period the American Association of School Administrators shifted its position in the National Education Association from department status to associated organization. Thus the autonomous, though cooperative, status of the associations became clearly defined.

In this decade the junior or two-year community college was the educational institution with the most phenomenal expansion and enrollment increase. This institution, which had its beginnings much earlier in the century, seemed to thrive on the new human rights movement. Because it catered to local community needs, attempted to serve every individual above age eighteen, and charged minimal tuition, if any, its popularity can easily be understood. It accepted the academically talented and gave them a curriculum suitable to their aspirations, but it even more eagerly sought youth and adults who had vocational or specialized interests. Adults who desired refresher occupational courses were catered to, as were those desiring to extend their cultural backgrounds. It operated both during the day and in the evening. People could enroll full time or part time. Opportunity to drop in as well as drop out became standard policy. In most states it was, in fact, an extension of the free school system upward and outward, with a flexibility and freedom to change seldom present in older types of institutions.

As indicated earlier, the federal government gave support to preschool or nursery education during the Depression. As good times returned economically and as federal funds diminished, these programs died out, leaving only a stronger support for public kindergartens. But with attempts to give help to the economically and culturally deprived during the sixties, early childhood education was again sponsored and aided by Washington. Head Start programs for deprived children of age three to five were initiated, particularly in the cities, and won the support of most child psychologists and many educational leaders.

With technology in the ascendency, the computers or data processing machines were introduced in many school districts and regional service centers. They served as great reservoirs of information and could retrieve data quickly for immediate use. They had to be properly fed or programmed, however, and this called for new approaches to planning by teachers and administrators, as well as technicians to process the operations. They also led to more careful projections and analysis which, in many instances, resulted in a new approach in administration called "systems analysis."

Technology, coupled with the profit motive in the free enterprise system, brought still another movement: many inventions designed to serve as aids to teaching and learning came on the market. At the same time a few people, mostly in the federal government, began to promote the idea of buying educational services through contracts from private agencies. So there grew educational-industrial complexes which sought to compete in the education world. They were most successful in the areas controlled and supported by those administering vocational education and where special projects were financed by federal grants. This phenomenon will need the thoughtful and persistent attention of public school leaders. Possibly, it may serve as a valuable supplementary aid to the public schools; possibly, it may prove to be a competitor of no mean proportions; and possibly, it will contribute to the destruction of the public school system. The high-powered advertising, the financial backing, and the enthusiastic support of a few politicians, businessmen, and theorists will tend to sweep it into practice before it can be properly evaluated and tested.

Related to this movement and stimulated by federal agencies and nonpublic schools there arose a philosophy called the voucher system. This system was designed to have public tax money used to pay for any education in any institution chosen by a parent. The arguments sound plausible, but the practical applications are exceedingly difficult to achieve, and the results, I believe, will be disastrous to public education. No proposal needs more intensive study by all school leaders, and by the public as well.

As has been suggested, the teacher of 1960-1970 utilized many teaching aids of a material character. Teacher aides in the person of paraprofessionals also were becoming popular in some school systems. Since aides in the kindergartens needed widely different skills from those in high school physics, physical education, English composition, and other specialities, their preparation became a matter of debate.

The school administrator who succeeded during the twenty-five years following World War II was the one who kept his balance and health in the midst of tremendous revolutionary upheavals. He recognized and attempted to cope with the phenomena that whirled about, but he didn't disregard the heritage more than one hundred years of public education had given him. He knew that change was inevitable but that he still had options. Above all else he played on the same team with his teachers and principals. He usually called the signals on major system-wide projects, but he did so only after having a huddle to get advice from the staff. In football language, he was willing to run interference, block, tackle, and throw the pass. He fully realized that he could fumble.

Part Four

CHAPTER XII

Retirement Years

On September 17, 1963, about 7 p.m., the team selected to make the study of American-sponsored overseas schools assembled at the international airport in New York. I had been designated as chairman. My associates were Mr. B. Melvin Cole and Dr. Eugene Youngert. In addition to the three study committee members, there were our three wives and an expediter from the Department of State. From time to time, too, during much of the trip a recently appointed member of the Department of State, Mr. Ernest N. Mannino, observed the schools, but made no effort to influence the study group. He proved to be a delightful traveling companion.

The American-sponsored overseas schools are privately controlled by boards at the local level and are designed to serve children of American parents working overseas. Thanks to including pupils and teachers of other nationalities and thanks to the foreign culture that surrounds them, these schools have a decided international flavor. The constitution of the East Asia Regional Council describes them as follows:

> American Overseas Schools are elementary and secondary schools abroad which are independent, nonprofit organizations governed by local school boards consisting of American and other nationals which offer an American type education for Americans, host country, and third country students.

If the schools meet certain standards, they are given financial assisistance by the U.S. Department of State.

These schools had their beginnings many years ago. Among the first were those established by missionaries. Soon American industry penetrated other countries and American employees working overseas demanded education for their children. After World War II, American influence suddenly became worldwide. Furthermore, the collapse of the colonial empires of Great Britain, France, and other European powers gave leeway for the establishment of many new independent countries. Almost overnight American diplomatic service expanded to scores of new countries. America's military strength and defense posture, likewise, became worldwide in scope. Thus, diplomatic activities and military bases took Americans to all corners of the globe. While only a handful of American-type schools existed before 1945, since that time they have multiplied rapidly. It is important to note, however, that the Department of Defense schools serve, in the main, only children of Defense personnel, whereas the American-sponsored schools have a strong interest in serving other nationals in a cross-cultural program, operate by local control, and have different sources of revenue.

The survey team was charged with the responsibility to appraise the general quality of the schools in the Middle East and South Asia, to note their strengths and weaknesses, and to make recommendations for their improvement. Our assignment called for visiting three schools in Greece, two in Cyprus, one in Israel, one in Jordan, one in Lebanon, two in Egypt (United Arab Republic), one in Yemen, two in Saudi Arabia, one in Syria, one in Iraq, four in Turkey, five in Afghanistan, three in Iran, three in West Pakistan, one in Nepal, four in India, one in East Pakistan, and two in Ceylon. We visited all thirty-eight schools in eighteen countries in less than three months, so sight-seeing was kept to a minimum, except for the three wives. Since specific data on each school would be needed when final appraisals were made, the necessity of compiling notes and impressions every day was obvious from the beginning. As we waited in airports and during long flights, our continuous bookkeeping and summarizing went on apace. In order to conserve energy and best utilize team talents, each of us assumed specific responsibilities. One evaluated the elementary school program, one the secondary, and one the administration, school board, overall policy, buildings, and budgeting.

After all the schools had been visited, we took two days in Calcutta, India, to discuss our findings, reach conclusions, agree on recommendations, and plan the overall design of the report. As chairman, I agreed to write the report after reaching home and submit it to them for alteration and approval. The report, entitled "American Dependents' Schools—Middle East and South Asia," was published in 1964. It characterized the schools under 17 headings and listed 18 issues and problems "badly in need of solution." There were 17 conclusions and recommendations, followed by a listing of twelve specific services that should be rendered by some federal agency.

The survey team, rather than arguing for one type of federal leadership needed for the dependents' schools, presented seven concrete designs which gave federal authorities options. When the report was printed, the survey team discussed it in detail with top officials in the Department of State. Soon the team members were gratified to note that action was taken to establish an Office of Overseas Schools within the State Department, charged with the responsibility of improving the programs in dependents' schools overseas. The Department of State official who had accompanied us was selected as the first director of this Office.

Late in the spring of 1964, the director of the Office called me to Washington and requested that I serve as senior consultant on call. I was flattered to accept, and soon we were planning a conference which would provide dialogue on the problems and needs of American-sponsored overseas schools.

In the fall of 1964, by contract with the Department of State, I, along with one associate, Dr. Samuel Lambert, was commissioned to go to sub-Sahara Africa to investigate the whole problem of how best to provide secondary education to American dependents in that area of the world. The trip took us down the west coast of Africa from Lisbon and across central Africa with extended stops in Liberia, Nigeria, the Congo, and Uganda. On the east coast, our stops were Kenya, Tanganyika, the Sudan, and Ethiopia. Since the geographical areas were huge and American dependents relatively few, much thought was given to the feasibility of very small high schools, as opposed to regional boarding schools. The possibility of transporting high school children from central Africa to Europe or the United States was thoroughly analyzed. In fact, the team stopped in Germany and Switzerland to visit boarding high schools open to Americans there. Upon reaching the Paris airport we took a few hours to design the report and to allocate writing responsibilities. As a result of our professional and personal compatibility, the writing was soon completed and agreement reached on final copy for the printer. When published, the study carried the title "A Study of American-Sponsored Secondary Education in Sub-Sahara Africa." It did not recommend boarding regional high schools for Africa, but set forth guidelines for organizing schools of minimum size. It analyzed, in some depth, the meaning of an international school and suggested increases in federal allowances for tuition and travel allowances for students of high school age who were forced to go long distances.

In the spring of 1965, the director of the Office of Overseas Schools presented to me a proposed plan to improve the quality of education in the American-sponsored overseas schools and at the same time extend the intercultural horizons of pupils, teachers, and parents in America. He believed that if an overseas dependents' school were paired as a team with a superior stateside system, both would profit exceedingly. Such a team, he suggested, would prove stimulating to everybody involved. I agreed that the idea was sound. He then said that, with the advice of others, about a dozen good systems had been identified in the United States—some East, some West, some North, some South. He then asked if I would try to sell them on the idea. I agreed to try, and within twenty-four hours, my itinerary and time schedule were complete. Within another twenty-four hours superintendents in all schools identified by him had talked to me over the telephone and agreed to have staffs and school boards available for discussion of the project on the days specified by my timetable. Everywhere I went the idea was carefully analyzed and discussed. It was gratifying that all except one of the school systems interviewed became part of the initial pairings. The pairings were as follows:

1. Roanoke, Virginia—Madrid, Spain
2. Pittsford, N.Y.—International School, Belgrade
3. Little Rock, Arkansas—La Paz, Bolivia
4. Austin, Texas—Cairo American School
5. Portland, Ore.—American School in Japan, Tokyo
6. Tacoma, Wash.—American International School, Lagos, Nigeria
7. St. Paul, Minn.—Anglo-American School, Stockholm
8. Webster Groves, Mo.—American School of Lima, Peru
9. Glens Falls, N.Y.—American Co-op School, Tunis
10. Lexington, Mass.—Warsaw Elementary School

Within four years, almost half a hundred stateside school systems were exchanging teachers, specialists, materials, and ideas with their overseas counterparts and, in turn, receiving inspiration, cultural insights, and help from abroad. In many instances, too, community organizations as well as colleges and universities became involved. By this process, the somewhat isolated overseas schools were brought into the mainstream of the many innovative developments in the United States, while the stateside schools profited by unusual contacts with specialists such as language teachers and with the cultural values of another people. These contacts were greatly multiplied after the American Association for International Education was organized at a meeting of paired school representatives, with encouragement from the Office of Overseas Schools and other associated friends. Since I was "unemployed," I agreed to act as the executive secretary without pay. Soon the officers, members of the Office of Overseas Schools, and I were in the midst of writing a constitution and bylaws, as well as an application to the Internal Revenue Service for tax-exempt status. With the help of a legal expert on the Baltimore County Board of Education, articles of incorporation were prepared and filed. About this time, a small but helpful windfall became our lot. The

Strong Foundation gave us a grant of $10,000 which was used for travel expenses of the officers of AAIE and for developing convention programs.

Since the Office of Overseas Schools did not wish to spoonfeed the AAIE directly and since the association needed full-time leadership as well as financial assistance, a proposal was made to the American Association of School Administrators. If the association would make certain budgetary contributions and establish a secretariat for international education with responsibilities for guiding AAIE, the Office of Overseas Schools would enter into contractual arrangements with them to help finance the office. Eventually the arrangements were consummated and the new associate secretary of AASA, Dr. John Wilcox, also became the secretary of AAIE. At the same time, the officers and executive committee became the advisory board on international education to the American Association of School Administrators. I was relieved of the secretaryship which I had willingly tried to carry for many months. Incidentally, no sooner had I resigned as secretary of AAIE than I was appointed as a regular member of the board.

In the fall of 1966 I received a request from the head of U.S. AID—Afghanistan to make a one-man review and evaluation of the work in primary teacher education in Afghanistan which had been conducted by a team of specialists from Teachers College, Columbia University. The study would be an on-the-spot examination during March, April, and May. Since the Columbia University Teachers College Project had run over a period of thirteen years, and since the teacher education activities were scattered over much of the area of Afghanistan, I again found myself faced with a pressing time schedule.

Mrs. Engleman and I were warmly received by the AID officials and their families in Kabul. It was gratifying, too, to be met by old friends from Yale, Harvard, Columbia, Indiana University, and Southern Illinois University. Some were with AID and some with university contract teams. The welcome from Columbia Teachers College officials was particularly warm, and their frank and full cooperation as I sought data to make the assessment was professionally gratifying. Without all cards on the table and without mutual respect, a valid report would have been impossible. An Afghan "counterpart," Mohammed Ayuub, introduced me to many Afghan education and government officials and secured much data for me. As I traveled long and lonely roads, he was my constant companion. His friendship has been lasting. Fortunately, periodic detailed reports had been filed by the Teachers College staff. These reams of descriptive materials were of inestimable value to me. Afghanistan is a fantastic and beautiful country, its people proud and personable. They were anxious to make giant strides in education.

Between 1963 and 1967, their headlong rush from a primitive society to a modern one showed great success. In 1963, for example, there was hardly a foot of hard-surfaced road; by 1967, well-engineered concrete roads stretched in all directions. No three months of my life have been so filled with excitement and wonder as were those three in Afghanistan.

During the three months' period of the teacher education study, much of my time was spent in Kabul. However, since new teacher education institutions were operating in Herat, Jellabad, Kandehar, Kerat, and Mazar-i-Shariff, I also spent considerable time in the far reaches of Afghanistan. Furthermore, middle-type schools that served as feeders for the teacher education institutions were scattered widely, and I visited many of them also. Usually, we traveled by high wheeled conveyances and carried our own food, water, and blankets. Occasionally, the Afghan officials in the outlying provinces served as our hosts.

The report was completed by late May. The title as published by AID is "An Evaluation of Primary Teacher Education in Afghanistan 1964-1967."

Soon another writing job was requested by the Office of Overseas Schools. The Secretary of AASA and the Director of O/OS agreed to publish jointly a descriptive booklet telling the story of the American-sponsored overseas schools. They asked me to prepare the preliminary copy. I wish to point out, however, that the additions and editing done by the staffs in those two offices changed greatly, for the better, the quantity and quality of my first draft. This publication is known by the name "The Mission Called O/OS."

In the summer of 1968 a request was made to AASA by the Office of Overseas Schools that their contract be amended to include a second study of dependents' schools. This would include most of the schools seen in 1963, and selected schools in Europe and Asia as well. Since I had been chief of the first study, it was agreed that I would head a team of two to take the "Second Look." Accordingly, on October 25, my wife and I took off for Vienna, where we joined my teammate, Dr. Edward Rushton. Our study included selected schools in Austria, Germany, Yugoslavia, Greece, Cyprus, Israel, Lebanon, West Pakistan, Afghanistan, Iran, India, Thailand, Hong Kong, and Japan. In addition, my associate and I spoke at regional educational conferences in Vienna, Frankfurt, Teheran, and Tokyo. Again, we found the schedule too tight, with inadequate time in some places and a travel-work pace that tested the physical stamina of all. At intervals during flights my teammate and I compared notes and resolved differences.

Once back home, he sent me a written statement and I then produced the brochure "A Second Look—American Sponsored Schools." We attempted to describe specific progress that had been made in the five-year period. The report also assessed the degree to which the recommendations of the first report had been achieved. The overall conclusion was that commendable progress had been made. The report included short vignettes describing exemplary activities observed from Athens to Kyoto. We attempted to delineate a broader program of services which should emanate from the Office of Overseas Schools and to identify weaknesses that should be remedied. It was gratifying to receive so many congratulatory letters from heads of overseas schools, from patrons of the schools, and from ambassadors.

Few professional projects had given me more satisfaction than did these two round-the-world efforts to appraise the programs in American dependents' schools. It was gratifying, too, that the findings of the reports were made the focal point of the annual meeting of AAIE at Atlantic City in February 1970.

It seems appropriate to include a few observations made while studying these overseas schools. The overseas staffs, whether of the regular diplomatic corps, the U.S. Agency for International Development, or the U.S. Information Service, impressed me as well-trained, intelligent, and culturally sophisticated. Above all else, most of these Americans were tolerant and appreciative of other cultures. They were hospitable, thoughtful and attentive to duty. Many of them were living in areas where local government was weak, unstable, and unable to provide safety. The lot of a foreign service officer in many parts of the world is not an easy one. Yet, I found them uncomplaining and attempting to give a fair and humble image of America.

Very striking, too, was the observation that wherever there were clustered a handful of American children, even in the most primitive of environments, the parents were committed to establishing an American-type school curriculum with an intercultural goal. Host-country nationals, as well as children of other diverse nationalities, were always welcome. It was not uncommon to find a school with pupils from as many as a dozen countries. In all instances, the resources of the American community were marshalled to provide the best possible education. Of course, the U.S. Department of State gives aid and the regional education officers from the Office of Overseas Schools provide leadership, but financing of these schools in many instances is inadequate, and the short tenure of teachers, administrators, and board members is a continuing weakness.

As I write these lines I am faced with another decision. A request is before me from the director of AID (Kabul, Afghanistan) to make another one-man study there in the fall of 1970. The request is that I evaluate the effort to build a strong College of Education at the University of Kabul and while there serve as a consultant to the heads of overseas schools of the Middle East and South Asia attending a week's conference during Thanksgiving week. The establishment and development of the College of Education has been done under the leadership of specialists from Teachers College, Columbia University.

As Mrs. Engleman and I ponder the assignment, we seem at this moment to be edging toward acceptance. At the age of seventy-five, the fun of action and new adventure has a strong pull.

My retirement years have not been filled entirely with work with overseas schools and their welfare, nor with consultation duties with the U.S. Department of State. Speaking engagements, major survey studies, and consultations with local school systems have taken considerable time. For example, I have made addresses to gatherings of school people in Hawaii, Maine, New Hampshire, Illinois, North Dakota, New Mexico, the District of Columbia, New Jersey, New York, Maryland, Missouri, and Pennsylvania.

At intervals I have consulted local and county officials in New Jersey, Virginia, and Pennsylvania as they wrote projects for federal funding and have advised and counseled them when the projects were underway. During these years, I had many opportunities to observe the forces trying to reconstruct public education in preconceived designs. My last thrill came in May, 1970, at the University of Connecticut. For three days I met in seminars with faculty and students. I was also cited by the University and made the first Henry Barnard Fellow with much fanfare.

Since retirement, Mrs. Engleman and I have reserved most of our summers for enjoying our cottage on Pushaw Lake, Old Town, Maine, but all my time has not been given to fishing, swimming, and loafing. The University of Maine has honored me by assigning me concurrent seminars in Personnel Management and the Role and Competencies of the Superintendent of Schools. These seminars meet for full five-hour day sessions on Tuesday, Wednesday, and Thursday. They are attended for the most part by young administrators from New England and Canada who are reaching for new horizons. The seminar topics for the superintendency are grouped in two broad areas. During the mornings, major contemporary issues and problems of a social, political, economic, or scientific character are discussed after position papers are presented. Such problems as population growth, character and mobility; scientific change and technology; economic affluence and value change; communications and transportation; the human rights revolution; and the one man, one vote concept are analyzed and the implications for education noted. Always specific actions to relate education to these problems are proposed. During the afternoon, internal issues and problems are attacked in much the same manner. Among the topics examined are negotiations and teacher militancy; community expansion and the changing role of the school board; the emerging education team of local, state and federal authorities; school system evaluation; the unrest of youth; and the analysis of experimental designs such as team teaching, the instructional media center, the middle school, and new approaches to inservice education for staff.

As has been true with all my professional undertakings, the greatest thrill comes from trying to think in broadened dimensions when participating in a search for new knowledge, a reaching for broader understanding about education. If education is to prepare people for coping with change, it, too, must be reaching for the new. Only while teaching have I experienced the groping for tomorrow at its best. Incidentally, at every stage of my life in administration, I succeeded in keeping my hand in teaching. As a secondary school principal, I taught English, physics, and geometry; as a superintendent, I substituted in the high school and taught demonstration classes for elementary school teachers. While city elementary school principal, because of my desire to teach, I called a substitute only when more than one teacher was ill on a given day. I acted as substitute teacher from kindergarten through grade seven. Also during that time, I taught extension classes at the City Teachers College and in the junior college evening program. While associate director of the junior college, I taught English, and during my presidency of the Teachers College, I taught on Saturdays at Yale University. After going to the state department of education in Hartford, I continued graduate seminar teaching in the late afternoon at Yale. While at AASA, most of my formal teaching was abandoned, although I took short assignments during the summers at the University of Oregon, Columbia Teachers College, Harvard, and the University of Wyoming. Of course, directing some of the High Horizon Seminars sponsored by AASA constituted a form of teaching for me. Also, some people would brand my talks to many groups across the land as a form of teaching. I call that a lower form of the teaching art—lecturing is more preaching than teaching.

One of the greatest recent additions to the tools of learning is television. If used properly, it could be the biggest inservice aid to teacher development. Unfortunately, many who use it to demonstrate master teaching select great actor teachers—those who can hold great groups in the palms of their hands, those who lecture at the front of the stage while the learner listens. Seldom selected for demonstration are teachers who are close observers of the learner as he seeks to understand or those who set up an environment that challenges the diversity of talents and interests and releases creativity. Even with the resurgence of emphasis on having each child "do his own thing," even when some schools set goals of "reaching" every child, the old emphasis on lecture and reading holds sway, particularly in high school and college. In most cases, the programmed materials and the teaching machine place the emphasis on mechanical stimulus response and on the pace of learning. Interaction between people often has low priority in the teacher-learning process in many so-called innovative methods of teaching. It seems to me that education involves so much beyond the speedy mastery of fact or skill. The individual guidance given by the teacher—the interaction of the teacher and the learner—cannot safely be overlooked in the name of innovation. In fact, good guidance is good teaching. The limited resources of the school guidance officer should never be allowed to be a substitute for the personal and educational guidance that is at the heart of good teaching. When teachers so conceive their job, the gap between teacher and student is lessened. If maximum concern by the teacher for always respecting individual personality is coupled with complete awareness of how much students may differ one from the other, the gap can be closed to a tiny crack.

But the teacher and administrator, too, are limited by what the times demand. Public opinion is fickle, often dominated by a temporary phenomenon or a social crisis. Between the years 1950 and 1960, the changing tides of public opinion, coupled with several power structures pertinent in those days, gave direction to the course of education.

But during my retirement years, the priorities in education changed again. A prominent educator wrote a report giving facts about the plight of youth in the city, calling their status "social dynamite." Youth delinquency and crime rose sharply. It was no longer safe to be on the city streets, particularly at night. America became conscious of a terrible social and economic problem. Young people, ignorant young people, neglected young people, forced out of school, had become a menace to society. And they, together with their parents, had become angry. Black militancy became a disconcerting phenomenon.

Soon another group of critics, and sometimes the same old critics, took up the cry, "The schools have failed again. Look at the dropouts. City schools are a blackboard jungle." The federal government and the courts insisted that all children, and from an earlier age, must be accommodated in the public schools. Integration in schools, never mind the community, must be achieved. Indeed, the philosophy in which all educators of the thirties were well grounded reappeared. Poverty was a problem that the schools could cure. Vocational education again became recognized as a respectable undertaking; childhood education, which had first become common during the depression years, was centered in "Head Start"; and, most encouraging to the professionally trained administrators, a special emphasis for educating all children returned. Humanitarian goals reappeared. The feelings, the emotions, the expectations or lack of them, group dynamics, health, sex education, even life adjustment, and a host of other interpersonal activities were again given emphasis, and the "new establishment," not knowing America's educational history, thought these things were unique and new and accused those in charge of the schools of disregarding them. School administrators and teachers, they said, refuse to see the needs and refuse to change.

Teachers often became confused as society quickly changed its emphasis, and the federal agencies, not trusting local leadership to understand education's most pressing needs, set up a grant-in-aid program to rectify the ills Washington believed to exist.

At any rate, a much more balanced concept of what universal education involved became reestablished.

CHAPTER XIII

Some Issues and Problems with Which the School Administrator of the 1970's Is Faced

The problems and issues facing today's school administrator, like his opportunities and responsibilities, are many. Without trying to discuss them all, I shall try to identify those which appear to me to be most important.

1. An accommodation must be made to an ever enlarging and complex community. With the old, small, almost autonomous self-supporting neighborhood destroyed by a technological, interdependent state and national community, the school administrator must turn his attention to helping the people and his staff face the problem and work toward new and larger organizational structures, new relationships, and new controls. At the same time, he must strive for more parent participation in school governance.

    The school administrator is the key figure in moving a school system toward high quality education. Possibly no one plays the role of change agent so much as he. He can cause complacency by inaction and by catering to the past, or his sensitivity to the need for change can be the key to progress. But, often overlooked, there is the danger of pushing a staff beyond its beliefs and its competencies. Nothing sets a school back as much as driving it so far into the vanguard as to give the staff insecurity, doubt, and even fear. No new program can long succeed except as the teachers are committed to its goals and have the understandings and skills essential to its operation. Thus, any change which involves a shift in philosophy, in content, and in method must be an evolution, not a revolution. In other words, don't put a teacher out of land sight and without her accustomed oars when she has not yet learned to read the stars or start the outboard motor.

    During the "Second Look" study, I found a school completely demoralized and in rebellion. The cause was an imported expediter of change. The superintendent and school board, wishing to be out in front, contracted for an administrator to come and introduce a somewhat revolutionary project which involved much cooperation, shifting teaching roles, giving up many professional prerogatives, and radically changing personal goals and philosophy.

Rather than involving the staff in a study of the new system to give them understandings and new commitments, the program was introduced by edict. Soon the administrator knew his school was falling apart, but he had not realized that his "change agent's" tactics had completely demoralized the staff. He knew most of his teachers came from many countries with many independent judgments of the teachers' role, but he did not realize that this meant deliberations in making change. He knew that most of his teachers were threatening to resign, but removing his "change agent" had not entered his mind.

Long before the superintendent came to me with his problem, I sensed both the problem and the solution. The project had to be abandoned and the "change maker" relieved of his duties. Furthermore, I made the superintendent realize that any further innovations had been blurred and that any major shift in program would first require teacher involvement and acceptance.

As I thought of this superintendent's plight on the next long flight, I recalled many others who, hurrying to be exemplary and innovative, had made the same mistake. Unfortunately, some hurriedly gained the reputation for innovations, and teachers dashed to other better positions before the roof fell in.

2. The school administrator has a new relationship with the teaching staff. As teachers grow more closely organized and make more demands, it becomes increasingly difficult for the administrator to have person-to-person relationships. Dealing with an organization rather than with individuals requires a new quality of administration. Teachers probably will demand to have their own man—the union agent—who will be given many responsibilities previously belonging to the administrator. The problem of the dual roles developing between the union representative and the administrator is a thorny one. I predict that the role of the school administrator will drastically shift as it relates to personnel management. However, if the board finds a negotiator other than the superintendent, and if teachers achieve reasonable salary and working conditions, they may insist that the superintendent again be a part of their team. This issue should occupy the best minds in the entire profession—school board, administrators, teachers, and secretaries

of teachers organizations. Undoubtedly, the place of teachers or their elected representatives will be spelled out in the negotiated contract of the future, as will limitations on the activities and powers of the administrator. It is past time for some person or agency to negotiate an appropriate role, together with rights, privileges and responsibilities, for the superintendent.

3. The industrial education complexes within the private sector and with a profit motive are a new phenomenon which leaders of public education face. How best to evaluate and use the professional services and technological soft- and hardware becomes a serious responsibility of the superintendent. He must decide what should be bought, contracted, or rejected.

4. Never before has there been so much pressure to provide at public expense multiple choices of school attendance. The matter of church-state separation is presented as an outworn philosophy by those advocating change in the long-standing public policy on the matter of use of tax funds to support church-controlled schools. The voucher plan proposal, if legally adopted, will make a shambles of public education. School administrators now need to show to the public the full deteriorating effects on all education and the possible loss of religious freedom if the long-established policy is changed. On the other hand, every effort should be made to perfect the plan of shared time for pupils desiring some aspects of their education in a church environment.

5. The rapidly expanding community suggests the need for immediate restudy of the whole structure and control of public education. Obviously, new and intimate team relationships must quickly evolve between the local district, the county, the state, and the federal government. Clearly, much of the old autonomy of operation and control of the local district is obsolete. However, a role must be found for the neighborhood. As the major aspects of control shift to the larger community, there is urgent need for even more participation in school affairs by the parents. Ways should be sought at once to get public participation locally, while much of the research and programming will be done by a team of local, state, and federal levels.

6. Related to the above problem is the more immediate demand that the financial support be shifted greatly, if not entirely, to the state and federal revenue-producing agencies. This practical matter should be faced and supported by administrators.

7. Accountability is in the air, and the problem is pressing. However, the urge to fix responsibility for outcomes can lead to haste in

ting minimum and easily measured pupil achievements. Ed-
...ion is a multipurpose enterprise. It is oriented to values,
...ative developments, complex understandings, and attitudes,
...well as skills and knowledge. Accountability in these areas and
...or the great diversity of human beings involved is a most complex
matter, and administrators should resist oversimplified or unsound
assessments.
8. Cybernetics has become a must in the education and preparation of school administrators. The next decade demands that the superintendent understand the uses and misuses to which the computer and allied electronic and technical devices can be applied in education. Furthermore, he should lead the whole professional staff to understand, evaluate, and use those devices related to their roles. Coupled with the computer is the systems approach, which has potential for aiding administration and teaching.
9. The successful administrator shuns the very appearance of obsolescence. It is urgent that he hurriedly but calmly lead the professional staff to become acquainted with the successful innovations that have been introduced to education recently and that he set a climate for experimentation that will produce many more. Particularly, it is important that the curriculum be relevant to the changing needs of all pupils.
10. The administrator, with the help of other officials at all levels, including university professors, should develop plans, policies, and programs for coping with the controls and influences inherent in many money grants from individuals, business enterprises, foundations, and agencies of the federal government. Those who make grants now sometimes do so to achieve goals of questionable value to public education. Dangling money with strings attached may be an insidious influence. Such monies should never be looked upon as a substitute for public taxation.
11. School administrators should develop new ways of involving citizens in matters pertaining to the schools. Although most decisions of major importance will be made by officials at the state and federal levels, citizen participation continues to be essential. As the town meeting type of action dwindles, how can the average citizen make himself heard? If democracy is to survive, ways and means must be developed for citizen action in the larger community. Likewise, renewing parent-teacher dialogue and exchange of information seems urgent.
12. The changing role of youth in decision making will challenge the

leadership of education in days ahead. Students have more and more maturity, and their spirit and resources can be utilized for strengthening both program and policy. Student unrest must be taken seriously. Tomorrow's administrator dares not overlook these potentials as he strives for changed relationships.

13. Education has outgrown the confines of the school walls and the limits of childhood and youth. The superintendent is now faced with the necessity of making it a total community problem. No longer can he, the board, or the public overlook a concern for a favorable total community environment. The matter is urgent, desperately so.
14. Even though some critics find little to praise in the schools of 1970, there has never been a greater outpouring in faith in education as the one institution that can do most to cure man's social, political, and economic problems. The President of the United States, the Congress, the Supreme Court, and the public generally insist that poverty, intolerance, racism, unemployment, inequality, injustice, and war itself can be eliminated by education. Even though the power of education is exaggerated, the faith of a people can be seized upon by school leaders. This confidence, if really accepted, may be the very leverage which will lift public education to the heights envisioned by its founders. But, simultaneously, multiple differences exist among this people as to what the program and structure of the school should be. As more and more people insist on a role in school governance, the administrator more than at any previous time in history faces groups with uncompromising convictions of a conflicting nature.
15. Unquestionably, the most difficult and significant contemporary problem in which the schools can play a prominent role is the elimination of racism, the lessening of cultural intolerance of all kinds. Every energy to conquer racism by rational means is imperative. The first and foremost area is the black-white problem. Once it is mastered, education may be successful in getting intercultural understanding on a world basis.
16. Securing the best and most suitable education for each child demands flexibility. Flexible scheduling is a complex undertaking, so much so, in fact, that the computer is being called upon to do the job. Certainly, anyone who has studied the diversity in competences, needs, skills, interests, emotions, and aspirations of a student group must recognize the need for flexibility in job undertaking, time allotments, and availability of learning and teaching resources, but the computer must be used with discretion. The

differences that exist among individuals in any given group shift frequently. The individual changes rapidly and irregularly from day to day. Nothing can become more rigid than a computer, and this fact must be known by those who use it to obtain flexibility. So, as innovation is sought, the professional educator must be ever alert to what education he is seeking, for what child, and at what stage of his development.

Next comes the analysis of the complex processes by which the educational goals for each child can be reached. As an acquaintance of mine has said,

> How shall we differentiate among staff responsibilities and resources which goals are best achieved by individual effort, in large groups, in small groups? When can the learning resource center, the individual cubicle, the outside of school resource, the laboratory or solitude for creative expression best be used and by whom? When are individual conferences with teachers needed, when with another pupil? If the program is to be ungraded, how is it evaluated and by what standards? If time modules are to be fed into the computer, who determines the minutes for each subject or skill? How long should the school day, week, or year be? What subjects can be programmed and which are unsuitable?

Some Hypotheses

Recently I reviewed some of the notions found in my diary notes and speeches. Although I am not now in complete harmony with some of the generalizations which served as my guide in earlier years, I repeat them here to prove that my actions usually rested on principles believed, at the time, to be valid. Rightly or wrongly, I tried to base my decisions and actions on what I considered to be sound hypotheses. Consequently, I probably failed to compromise sometimes when flexibility might have brought wiser and more compatible solutions.

As I have tried to seek greater truth, as I have striven to question the contemporary, as I have somehow hoped to be heretical, I probably have often been blocked by my previously accepted values and concepts. My false idols have been reluctant to fall. Perhaps I was like one of the chiefs in the following story told to me by an Australian friend. Among the Australian aborigines there is a custom of exchanging gifts on certain feast days. On one occasion a prominent chief gave another a newly designed boomerang. It was faster than any other weapon, more accurate, and more deadly. However, the receiver of the gift tried unsuccessfully for ten days to throw his old one away.

My intellectual arrangement of things and my emotional fixes were almost always in a state of insecurity. But somehow intellectual insecurity can come to be lived with, and imbalance becomes balance.

1. Education is greatly enhanced when school authorities join hands with other community resources.
2. There is no substitute for firsthand experience.
3. Immediate learner evaluation and obvious proof of achievement are strong stimulants to further learning.
4. When goals in the mind of the learner are clear and, to him, achievable, learning likely goes forward; obscurity frustrates.
5. When learners in a group are compatible and searching for the same ends, each stimulates the other.
6. Nothing improves inservice growth more than when a staff group becomes involved in planning, executing, and evaluating an experimental type of instructional enterprise.
7. The superintendent who does not prepare in detail the agenda for each school board meeting, together with documentation and recommendations, is headed for trouble.
8. One of the surest ways for a school administrator to be abreast of the times is to become involved in the studies of his professional organization.
9. Greater diversity and greater creativity in experimentation result when autonomy in classroom and in local school district prevails.
10. America's greatest contribution to the world is the free-tuition public school system.
11. I came more and more to believe Theodore Roosevelt when he said, "If you teachers do not do your work well, this generation will not outlast the span of a single generation."
12. Teachers badly need tested skills, techniques, and a knowledge of how children learn, as well as broad and specialized academic understanding and knowledge.
13. One of American education's greatest weaknesses is postponement of formal education until age five or six.
14. The first and foremost characteristic of a good teacher education institution is that it has a carefully constructed selection program for those who plan to be teachers. This selection process should take place not earlier than the junior year in multipurpose colleges.
15. Education limited to school environment is likely to be ineffective. The total environment must be the concern of the school administrator.
16. School boards should have budget items which support many types of inservice growth. But teachers should be encouraged to determine the areas of competence in need of being strengthened.
17. Teacher education institutions should have funds and staff which

are devoted to experimentation and research, as well as laboratory schools for demonstrating the findings.
18. Student teachers should have supervised experiences with children, not only in a classroom environment but also with community organizations such as the YMCA, the Boy Scouts, recreation departments, community houses, welfare agencies, etc.
19. As the community expands, the role of the state department of education takes on added proportions.
20. As America's economic, political, social, cultural, and scientific phenomena become more interrelated and interdependent, thus making local school districts less able to solve many educational problems, the role of the state becomes much greater.
21. A board of education devoted to America and to the public schools and independent of special interests and partisan politics is the first essential in state or local school operations.
22. It seems clear that as stronger and more coordinated interrelationship in education develops between the local district, the state, and the federal government, the state department of education must be strengthened and must become the key figure in the team.
23. If the state department of education is strong and free of special interest pressures, local school boards tend to be likewise.
24. No aspect of education is more important than adult education. The greatest danger facing the nation politically and industrially is adult obsolescence.
25. Strongly committed, honest, and intelligent school board members are the most important ingredients for ensuring good public schools.
26. As tax revenues for schools shift from local to state and federal, the power and control of the local school board become less and less, unless the authorities at higher levels legally delegate responsibilities.
27. As teachers organize and provide their own agent to negotiate all sorts of matters pertaining to the operation and services of a school, the role of their organizational agent and the role of school administrators and supervisors will tend to merge or clash.
28. One of the most important questions to negotiate is the role and responsibilities of principals and superintendents.
29. The more complex the organizational structure and the more diverse the professional specialization become, the more difficult it will be to have sound negotiation procedures.
30. There is no greater inducement to learn than knowing that survival is at stake.

31. Most knowledge and almost all skills become obsolete quickly; thus, continuous education is a necessity.
32. Imprecise learning is wasteful and often downright dangerous.
33. Little past learning can function in a situation approaching the unique, except the will to improvise.
34. Learning is expedited when it is urgent and relevant.
35. Many types of learning are enhanced when more than one sense is employed. To make the most of sight and hearing, skill in the utilization of both should be developed.
36. When learning goals can be specifically described, the learner becomes the evaluator of his efforts and the teacher can be readily held accountable.
37. Shared time by church-operated schools and the public schools is sound and is much more to be sought than direct tax support for the nonpublic school.
38. Developing a respect for others and being sensitive to others' values and aspirations are top priority goals for the school administrator.
39. Knowing the way to encourage high morale in professional associates and students is a necessary competence in a school administrator.
40. Timing is of signal importance when making a recommendation for action by a board.
41. Without frankness and concern for justice and fairness, a superintendent will eventually fail.
42. A sense of humor and the humility to laugh at oneself are administrative musts.
43. Preventing role conflict, including his own, is a master quality of the administrator.
44. The elimination of cultural prejudice and racism in any form is a continuous goal.
45. When angry, resist decision and action.
46. Nearly all parents sincerely desire the best from and for their children. Parent-teacher contacts are important.
47. To discourage public participation in the affairs of the school is to hazard their success.
48. To legally require negotiations at the local level and financially tie the hands of a board or to prohibit the right of teachers to withhold services is to make a shambles of bargaining.
49. School boards, too, should have a set of propositions for which to negotiate.
50. Listen more attentively to the critics than to those who praise.

51. The teacher's classroom is his "castle," but the superintendent's hope is that he willingly will lower the drawbridge at the approach of an associate.
52. The commitments of teachers to the service of children are like those of the administrator.

CHAPTER XIV

And Now Tomorrow

We hear it said in 1970 that school administration is dead. But my analysis of the emerging educational scene indicates that such statements are sheer nonsense. I don't believe that if the administrator, particularly the superintendent, does not understand emerging social, economic, cultural, political, and scientific phenomena and their relevance to education he will become obsolete as a leader and die like the dinosaur and for the same reason.

My navy experience opened my eyes relative to the rapidity of change. Upon my return to the state commissionership of education in 1945, I gave many speeches to laymen, to teachers, to administrators. They often opened with the words: "If Marshal and King, if Eisenhower and Nimitz had not quickly abandoned the tactics and strategies of World War I, we would have lost World War II in twelve months. Educators should take a leaf from their book."

Twenty-five years later the acceleration of change increases and educators must somehow find ways to cope with it. The superintendent during this next quarter century who neglects the findings of research; who permits himself to be unrelated to the work and problems of his teaching associates in the classroom; who continues the old role of the lone man on the quarter-deck; and who does not see the new relationships with federal, state, and even international agencies will go the way of the dodo bird. If he does not carve out a considerably altered role, the teachers and others connected with education will be forced to *create* their own leader as a substitute for him. In other words he must cut away many old moorings and steer by a different compass course and with the assistance of an altered team. In any case, there must be continued administrative leadership, so that a new design of administration with a crosshatch of relationships and communications of a comprehensive character will emerge. Surely, too, the complex, professional services will demand role definitions more clearly stated than ever before.

He who believes the school administrator is dead needs to review the history of America. No nobler political design was ever created than that done by the founders of this country. And the amazing thing about that design is the built-in scheme for altering and improving it. Its very nature gives it both flexibility and stability. Thus it has functioned, and I believe will continue to function, as a living, growing invention of man. Unlike political structures with no plan for self-renewal and development and hence doomed to obsolescence and death—and with death, the destruction of whole civilizations—the United States continues as a viable, growing, changing political institution. But I am convinced that a genius equal to that of our nation's founders arose with the leadership of Horace Mann, Henry Barnard and others sixty years later. As Jacksonian Democracy opened the door for universal citizenship participation, ignorance threatened to destroy the principle of self-governance. But the tuition-free public schools arose to give to universal suffrage the underpinnings it needed along with the keys to personal fulfillment of every man. Careful examination of America's progress—scientifically, politically, culturally, and economically—shows a direct parallel to the expansion and character of education. Democracy and public education are the warp and woof of our cultural heritage. Each depends upon the other. As the nation has required statesmen, education has depended on school administrators of vision.

But both grow wider in services and more complex in structure and the end is not yet.

Rather than needing less administration in the future, education will need more.

In my view, the more complex our society becomes, the more people reach for self-fulfillment; the more extensive our knowledge, the more our education will be expanded and extended.

Thus the task of humane management of organization, of coordination, of cooperation and of leadership will be imperative. Only the educational statesman dares to become an administrator tomorrow. Our excursions into outer space are puny efforts compared to the institution designed to develop the full potentials of every person and to provide the know-how for successful completion of such excursions.

Although the future clearly suggests many tasks for the school administrator, none seems to be of such urgency as that of stimulating teachers to change the image many parents and pupils have of them. The rapid shift in the cultural make up of enrollments, particularly in the inner cities, together with the findings of research and the shortage of funds, has left many teachers without the understandings, the emotional responses and the technical skills they need. All this—together with confrontations, work stoppages, and hard nose bargaining practices—has shifted the old image of the teacher as the great humanitarian seeking in every way to promote the emotional and intellectual welfare of every child to that of a cold, impersonal, and even inept and unfriendly despot. This gap between the teacher and those he should serve is a serious threat not only to the teacher's professional status but to public education. Nothing fosters disruptive schemes such as the voucher system so many special interests now promote as much as does the fading image of the public school teacher. A sensitiveness to this danger must be induced by the school administrator and teacher leaders. Hurriedly, the total profession should set about putting its own house in order. An immediate self-appraisal is needed and a hurried effort made to achieve devoted commitments by all in a profession to superior service to all children and to the competencies for professional success at all levels, in all fields and for all tough situations. If the spirit for self-improvement among teachers and administrators, so abundant in the late forties, can be aroused, the public schools will retain their old goals and purposes and the public confidence in the teachers again will be restored. And thus, those who selfishly would discredit those working in the public schools would be frustrated.

In close priority to the matter of improving professional competency of teachers is a determined effort by administrators and other leaders to receive a larger share of the money pouring into the federal treasury. Unless the superintendents stop fighting their friends and allies—the local police, fire, welfare, and street departments—over the small, local tax dollar and square off to get a big hunk of the big dollar from Washington, the future seems a bit black. It would make much more sense to go where the money really is. Indeed, an education lobby in Washington superior to that of the military-industrial complex should emerge, and soon. Many of the educational problems of the local community, particularly the inner city, will never be solved by local revenues.

Tomorrow, too, administrators face an increasingly difficult task of guiding and working with a public that is increasingly diverse in cultural values, in aspirations, in prejudices, and often beset by fears. No community any more is isolated from beliefs held by unlike cultures. Because of radio, television, and a dramatic press, every home sees, hears, and reads of people the world over in ideological, religious, political, economic, and cultural conflicts. Thus one set of values held by one family may seem threatened by what others do and propose. No home, no community, can close its gates to the diversity that is man. And now, more than at any other time, American democracy and freedom is exercised. The right to protest and to participate in social institutions, together with time on their hands, is now a reality. Administrators have long sought citizen participation in school matters but now as they come in angry, diverse, and militant groups, ways must be found to bring about a modest and workable unity. This is a task of no mean proportions which must be faced by the superintendents.

There are many straws in the wind that suggest many other important emerging issues and problems. But by only a continuous scrutiny of the changing times can the administrator identify the problems that demand his priorities and, as stated earlier, as public education grows in scope and complexity, wise and professionally trained administrators will be needed more than ever.

Just as the superintendent, more than any man, was the chief factor in gaining excellence in the past, so will he be in the future. However, his competencies will be altered and his role made compatible with more sophisticated and independent associates, more demanding parents, and more restless, inquiring and independent learners.